D1731825

LAW, IDEOLOGY AND PUNISHMENT

Law and Philosophy Library

VOLUME 12

The titles published in this series are listed at the end of this volume.

ALAN W. NORRIE

School of Law, University of Warwick, Coventry, U.K.

LAW, IDEOLOGY AND PUNISHMENT

*⌊Retrieval⌋and Critique of the
Liberal Ideal of Criminal Justice*

⌊⌋ e hva: Wiedergewinnung ; Neubelebung

KLUWER ACADEMIC PUBLISHERS

DORDRECHT / BOSTON / LONDON

Library of Congress Cataloging-in-Publication Data

Norrie, Alan W. (Alan William), 1953-
    Law, ideology, and punishment : historical critique of the liberal
ideal of criminal justice / by Alan W. Norrie.
        p.   cm. -- (Law and philosophy library ; v. 12)
    Includes bibliographical references (p.) and index.
    ISBN 0-7923-1013-6 (HB : printed on acid free paper)
    1. Punishment. 2. Criminal justice, Administration of. 3. Kant,
Immanuel, 1724-1804.   I. Title. II. Series.
K5103.N67 1990
340'.1--dc20   90-48892

ISBN 0-7923-1013-6

Published by Kluwer Academic Publishers,
P.O. Box 17, 3300 AA Dordrecht, The Netherlands.

Kluwer Academic Publishers incorporates
the publishing programmes of
D. Reidel, Martinus Nijhoff, Dr W. Junk and MTP Press.

Sold and distributed in the U.S.A. and Canada
by Kluwer Academic Publishers,
101 Philip Drive, Norwell, MA 02061, U.S.A.

In all other countries, sold and distributed
by Kluwer Academic Publishers Group,
P.O. Box 322, 3300 AH Dordrecht, The Netherlands.

Printed on acid-free paper

Printed in the Netherlands

for my father, Tom,
and in memory of my mother, Gertrude

TABLE OF CONTENTS

PREFACE

This book is about 'Kantianism' in both a narrow and a broad sense. In the former, it is about the tracing of the development of the retributive philosophy of punishment into and beyond its classical phase in the work of a number of philosophers, one of the most prominent of whom is Kant. In the latter, it is an exploration of the many instantiations of the 'Kantian' ideas of individual guilt, responsibility and justice within the substantive criminal law. On their face, such discussions may owe more or less explicitly to Kant, but, in their basic intellectual structure, they share a recognisably common commitment to certain ideas emerging from the liberal Enlightenment and embodied within a theory of criminal justice and punishment which is in this broader sense 'Kantian'.

The work has its roots in the emergence in the 1970s and early 1980s in the United States and Britain of the 'justice model' of penal reform, a development that was as interesting in terms of the sociology of philosophical knowledge as it was in its own right. Only a few years earlier, I had been taught in undergraduate criminology (which appeared at the time to be the only discipline to have anything interesting to say about crime and punishment) that 'classical criminology' (that is, Beccaria and the other Enlightenment reformers, who had been colonised as a 'school' within criminology) had died a major death in the 19th century, from which there was no hope of resuscitation. It was part of the prehistory of valid knowledge. Yet within a few years, classicism was back on the agenda with, literally, a 'vengeance'. Intellectually, how could this be? There were clear political reasons why classicism was making a comeback, but are ideas entirely recyclable, so that tomorrow's thoughts are dictated not at all by intellectual enquiry, but entirely by social circumstance? Clearly, there is a social dimension to all knowledge, but can society so easily overturn its convictions about ideas that had only a few years earlier seemed discredited?

One way of asking this question less reductively was to examine the ideas of criminal justice internally, for themselves. How was it that the

Kantian structure of ideas had developed in the Enlightenment; why was it that those ideas had eventually fallen into disrepute, so that philosophers, just as much as criminologists, no longer held to them? How did the lost tribes of 'Kantianism' themselves justify the return to these old ideas; more particularly, how did they get around the old philosophical problems that had previously loomed so large and led to disenchantment? These questions do not admit of answers with a purely sociological content, for they force us to take seriously the process of idea formation as an intellectual practice within an existing intellectual tradition. That tradition is itself emergent from and related to a historical context, but not reductively so. It must be traced out within the broader social context, as part, indeed, of a *dialogue* with it.

Having been spurred initially into these questions by inquiring into the return of the 'justice model', it became clear to me that the field of enquiry opened up by these investigations was actually much broader than I had originally supposed. 'Kantianism' was not only an intellectual source of penal reform, but also a fundamental premise of legal thinking in general. The same structure of problems that could be identified within the philosophical theory of punishment could also be identified within the criminal law itself, admittedly in more prosaic forms. This book is therefore both about the intellectual history and present of a philosophical set of ideas and a commentary on the fundamental presuppositions of the law. Why do these two sets of ideas cohere? My answer is that the fundamental connection lies in the deep structure of juridical categories in modern market societies, which structure lies at the heart of both philosophical thought and legal practice. To move from the philosophy of punishment to the categories of the criminal law is to move from one level of a discourse to another level of the same discourse. Once one analyses the basic features of modern Western legal thinking, and particularly the contradictions within that thinking, one has the key both to the internal philosophical development of the philosophy of punishment and to the central intellectual problems of the criminal law. Thus at its deepest level this book is a work of legal theory, but in the process, it is an attempt to synthesise the problems of law and philosophy in the area of crime and punishment. (In any case, intellectual labels which are the product of modern institutional divisions mean little in a situation where the aim is to recreate the intrinsic connections between 'law' and 'philosophy').

The analysis presented here developed out of the European interest in the late 1970s in legal form analysis, and particularly out of the reading of theorists who were 'rediscovered' in this period such as E.B. Pashukanis and Franz Neumann. North American scholars will recognise similarities and differences with the work of writers in the Critical Legal Studies movement. Because of the amorphous nature of that movement, generalisations as to its basic character are difficult. However, drawing upon Mark Kelman's recent account, it is perhaps not unfair to describe the strength of CLS as residing in its negative, critical approach to legal phenomena rather than in its ability to locate both itself and law more broadly and positively within social theory and history.[1] CLS is at its best when it is tearing legal doctrine to pieces rather than constructing an analysis that situates and contextualises that activity in a wider setting. For example, Kennedy's work on Blackstone[2] was more effective in its recognition of contradiction than in its situation of contradiction historically; likewise, Unger's essay on CLS[3] was better at attacking orthodoxy than in spelling out a programme that could get beyond it. Kelman's own work on criminal law, which is most relevant to this book, is similarly immersed in the attack on doctrine to the exclusion of questions as to *why* the characteristic forms of law and state created to deal with social control in Western society should have emerged as they did.[4] It is, I think, significant that when the 'Guide' to CLS came to be written, it should have taken the form of an account of the various critical impacts that CLS has had on mainstream thought, rather than deal with the relationship between CLS and critical theory more broadly,[5] for that has been where the strength of the movement has lain. It is relevant to note that one of the main weaknesses of CLS has been its treatment of history, where it has promoted its own illusory abstractions, different though these are from mainstream thought.[6] It is also significant, if Kelman's book is a reliable 'guide', that CLS makes little reference to central, European critical legal thinkers such as Foucault, Neumann and Pashukanis, who all sought to ground their

---

[1] M. Kelman, *A Guide To Critical Legal Studies* (Cambridge, Mass., 1987). Cf. J. Stick, 'Charting the Development of Critical Legal Studies' (1988) *Columbia Law Review* 88, p.407.

[2] D. Kennedy, 'The Structure of Blackstone's Commentaries' (1979) *Buffalo Law Review* 28, p.205

[3] R. Unger, 'The Critical Legal Studies Movement' (1983) *Harvard Law Review* 96, p.561.

[4] M. Kelman, 'Interpretive Construction in the Substantive Criminal Law' (1981) *Stanford Law Review* 33, p.591.

[5] M. Kelman, *op.cit.*, pp.9-10.

[6] *Ibid.*, pp.234-241.

critiques of the contradictions of law squarely in real historical developments.[7]

With particular regard to criminal law and justice, I am not aware of any critical work in North America, or indeed anywhere else, which seeks to tackle the historical roots of the Western approach to punishment in a systematic way. Kelman has identified persistent contradictions in the law, but these are addressed in a modern legal-theoretical context rather than an historical one.[8] This means that the philosophical high ground within criminal law theory, the classical Enlightenment account of crime and punishment, remains the terrain of those whose work can be seen as a defence and legitimation of legal practice. Classical theory, because it has not been subjected to a fundamental critique, remains a resource for those who wish to rationalise the existing legal forms. 'Kantianism', in both a broad and a narrow sense, is alive and well in the modern theory of criminal responsibility and legal punishment. This work is an attempt to challenge it by reaching back to Enlightenment thought and charting the historical location of, and dislocations caused by, the deep contradictions within its ideology. In so doing, however, I try to avoid the rather overbroad and ahistorical approach to 'fundamental contradiction' employed by Kennedy by setting the law's theory in the context of the emergent historical ideologies of a society based upon market exchange, and I hope that this grounds my analysis more solidly.

The book began life as a doctoral thesis, and due to the time lags in transferring from thesis production to publication, the arguments in it were mainly developed a few years ago. This has the advantage of time in which to polish the ideas, but the disadvantage of allowing doubts, or at least broader questions, to creep into one's mind. I still hold to the critical analysis presented here, but am now aware of some of the further questions that it generates. One of my thesis examiners was Professor Neil MacCormick of Edinburgh University, who planted the seed of a question in my mind. If it is allowed that Western legal discourse is contradictory, is that not because of the fundamental features of any society based upon rules, so that the contradictions are at the same time more widespread and less critically important than my analysis suggests? Do not all societies, including those we used to call state socialist, reflect exactly the same contradictions? The question is a disarming one, and I

---

[7] See references in Chapter I, below. It is true that Kennedy pays homage to the 'continental' tradition of social theory in his Blackstone essay (*op.cit.*, p.272) but the effect on his work is diffuse and non-specific.

[8] In both his *Stanford Law Review* piece and more recently in his *'Guide'*.

regret to say that the reader will find no answer to it in this book. At one point I thought about including a discussion of ideas of the withering away of law, of informalism and of 'popular justice' in a final chapter in an attempt to locate the tensions and contradictions within socialist societies between formalism and informalism and to explain the tenacity of legal forms that look fairly similar to those evolved in the West, but then realised that a proper answer was the work of another book that I am not yet prepared to write. Such a book would examine the emergence of legal forms of social control in societies both past and present, and in societies not based upon market relations and capitalism as much as those that are, but in which law is generated by the particular, historical relations at play. A key element in such an enquiry would be the question of *difference* between legal forms in different social contexts. In this way, one could account for the existence of legal forms in other kinds of society, maintain an essentially historical perspective on the material, and not accept the reductionist view that all societies at all times replicate the contradictions of Western legal liberalism. For the moment, however, I can only say that I recognise Neil MacCormick's question, think there is a way of answering it, but have not done so here.[9]

One further point I would like to make clear concerns the issue of gender. It is now an accepted practice for academics dealing with political philosophy either to adopt some form of gender neutrality or to positively promote the position of women through the use of both male and female pronouns, or simply the female pronoun itself. This has a particular significance in a discourse in which that mysterious abstract individual known as 'man' plays such a major role, and seems to me a perfectly sensible and proper usage for those who work within the liberal tradition in a critical way. For myself, however, having a position outside traditional liberalism, and seeing that tradition as a historical product of a particular society and period of history, I find it misleading and inaccurate to change the terms in which the philosophers wrote. When they said 'man', they meant what they said.[10] This work is not a critique of the sexism of liberal philosophy, but nor is it a cover for it. One part of my argument is that the classical liberal philosophy of punishment systematically excludes from view the social experience of crime and punishment in Western society, so I am not going to adopt a usage which presents that philosophy as not involved in an equally

---

9   For a beginning, see Norrie, 'Locating the Socialist *Rechtsstaat*: Criminal Justice and Underdevelopment in the Soviet Union' (1990) *International Journal of the Sociology of Law* 18, pp.343-359.

10 See, e.g., Z. Eisenstein, *The Radical Future of Liberal Feminism* (Boston, 1986); D. Coole, *Women in Political Theory* (Sussex, 1988).

fundamental sexual exclusion at the same time. My own preference is to use bisexual or non-sexual terminology where possible, and in the latter chapters of the book, which deal with the modern usage of legal categories, I have tried to do this. But where Hobbes, Kant or Hegel spoke of 'man', I have stuck to their usage.

A work like this, produced over a number of years as an intellectually 'formative experience', attracts many debts of gratitude. A number of people have helped me as teachers, colleagues and friends. Amongst these, I would like to mention Zen Bankowski who introduced me to the early Habermas as an undergraduate and whose lively and entertaining seminars first gave me the bug for theoretical enquiry. I would also wish to acknowledge the help I derived early on from the work of Stuart Midgely, whose regrettably unpublished doctoral thesis first showed me how legal form analysis could be applied to philosophical thought. Professor Ian Willock of Dundee University was my doctoral supervisor and Head of Department for a number of years. Under his benign and liberal leadership, I was free to pursue my ideas without pressure at a time when I needed the space to work things out for myself. It is to be regretted that more pressure is now put on young academics to produce earlier than is often good for them. I am grateful that I was allowed to dig deep and find my own way in my own time. I also owe thanks to honours students at Dundee in the early eighties, who put up with some considerably less refined versions of the ideas that are presented here, and were often sympathetic but perceptive critics of them. I owe thanks to Professor Michael Freeman of University College, London for his strong encouragement as a reader of my manuscript at an earlier stage; to Nicola Lacey at Oxford on similar grounds and for her friendly support as someone working in the same area but with a different overall perspective; to David Garland at Ediburgh, who offered sound advice on publication; and to Neil MacCormick, whom I have already mentioned, for his consistent support and kindness over a number of years. In addition, many people have read either bits or the whole of the manuscript and made helpful comments over a long period of time. The list includes Jim McManus and Bob Ferguson in Dundee, and a number of people at Warwick including Robert Fine, Sol Picciotto, and Anne Barron (now, sadly, left). Joe McCahery was a great support during the final stage, particularly in helping me to locate some of the more recent North American debates. Peter Langford proof read and commented on the whole manuscript.

The book has been prepared with camera ready copy using the computer facilities available at Warwick Law School and in Warwick

University. This proved a more difficult task than was initially anticipated, and would not have been possible at all without the hard work of Wiebina Heesterman in particular, with additional help from Andy Clark and Sammy Adelman. Above all, I owe an enormous debt to Carol Chapman who formatted and reformatted the manuscript until it was coming out of her ears, but always with the greatest of patience.

Chapter VII of the work appeared in an earlier, shorter version as 'Freewill, Determinism and Criminal Justice', in (1983) *Legal Studies* 3, pp.60-73 and is reproduced by permission of the Society of Public Teachers of Law.

Lastly, I would like to thank my wife Gwen for helping with the index when it seemed likely to be the final straw that would break the camel's back. Far above that, however, I would like to thank her for her love, friendship and strength over the years. Our children Richard and Stephen in their own way, and quite unwittingly, ensured that the work would eventually see the light of day. This book is a testimony to the forbearance and love of them all. They deserve better.

xx

When a science goes round in circles without managing to overcome its contradictions it is always because it is based on concepts, on a definition of its object, which have not been subjected to a sufficiently radical critique, one which is sufficiently well-informed philosophically.

L. Seve

One does not know social reality if one has seen it only from the outside and has ignored its foundations. In order to know how it is constituted, one has to know how it has constituted itself; i.e. one must have followed historically the way in which it has developed.

E. Durkheim

... philosophical thinking, if pursued far enough, turns into historical thinking, and the understanding of abstract thought ultimately resolves itself back into an awareness of the content of that thought, which is to say, of the basic historical situation in which it took place.

F. Jameson

The philosophical system appropriate to the Rechtsstaat *is that of Enlightenment.... [B]ut only because man was seen as universal man, as infinitely perfect being without individual features, ... was ... a pre-established harmony ... between state and society ... possible.*

F. Neumann

CHAPTER I

LAW, IDEOLOGY AND PUNISHMENT

Wieder gewinnung

1. INTRODUCTION: CRITIQUE AND RETRIEVAL OF THE
LIBERAL IDEAL OF CRIMINAL PUNISHMENT

Many years ago, Maine wrote that 'All theories on the subject of Punishment have more or less broken down; and we are at sea as to first principles.'[1]   What causes a theory to break down?   Why should a society be all at sea as to the basic principles of a central and morally crucial institution?   How did this situation come about?   Is it symptomatic at the level of ideas of some deeper ailment in the social body?   The impetus to these questions came out of the development in philosophical thinking about punishment in the late 1970s and early 1980s when it had become clear that the existing theoretical and practical consensus around punishment was no longer sustainable.   In penological thinking, the belief in rehabilitation and the benign potential in punishment had given way to cynicism and disillusion, while, paralleling this in philosophical discussion, there was an increasing rejection of both the philosophy of treatment and what came to be seen as the empty nostrums of utilitarian theory.   When utilitarianism was not being amoral in vindicating individual punishment for the greater good, it was being positively immoral in sacrificing individual justice to social well-being.   The debate about punishing the innocent had rumbled on for decades without getting anywhere.[2]

In this situation of political and philosophical malaise, there was a popular move to return to first liberal principles, and to Kant in

---

[1] *Speeches*, p.123, quoted in L. Radzinowicz and J. Turner, *The Modern Approach to Criminal Law* (London, 1945), p.48.

[2] See below, Chapter VI.

particular through the formulation of a 'justice model' with practical
implications both for the penal and criminal justice systems.[3]   Sanctuary
from authoritarian practices and philosophies was sought in the
rediscovery of the retributive principles of Enlightenment thought:
principles of justice, desert and proportionality which afforded
individuals their due respect.

Yet, this return to the liberal retributive ideal of criminal punishment
was hardly undertaken with great enthusiasm.   Proponents declared a
fundamental ambivalence to the rediscovery of Kant, or proclaimed a
cynical 'least harm' attitude as the basis for return.[4]   Fundamental
problems with the theory - that were as old as the theory itself - were
noted and dwelt upon.[5]   The return to first principles, in other words,
rather than resolving the issues, tended to confirm Maine's view that
things were decidedly awry in the theory of punishment.   The state of
malaise developed into a state of impasse in which an impending crisis
in penal practice was accompanied by a crisis in philosophical thought.
The two were interconnected: the problems confronting the penal system
were quite incompatible with the philosophical forms by which the
system sought to grasp and resolve them, and thereby to legitimate
itself.[6]

It was in this context that the quotation from Lucien Seve at the
beginning of this book,[7] referring to a quite different set of problems,
brought home to me the need to think about such a situation of impasse
in a radical, critical fashion.   The 'justice model' with its liberal, Kantian
basis had brought the historical turn of the philosophical wheel through
360 degrees, and at the end, we were no wiser than at the beginning.
Here indeed was a science going round in circles.   A radical critique of
the liberal tradition, returning to first principles but subjecting them to a
fundamental scrutiny, could, I thought, reveal what the root problems of
punishment theory were.

The critique offered in the following chapters takes the form of an
historical analysis of the development of the modern philosophy of
punishment, laying particular emphasis on the evolution in thinking
about the retributive element which dominated classical liberal

---

[3]   See below, Chapter IX.

[4]   A. Von Hirsch, *Doing Justice: The Choice of Punishment* (New York, 1976),
p.xxxiv; see below, Chapter IX.

[5]   See, for example, J.G. Murphy, *Retribution, Justice and Therapy* (Dordrecht,
1979), pp. 77-147.

[6]   A.E. Bottoms and R. Preston, *The Coming Penal Crisis* (Edinburgh, 1980).

[7]   The quotation is from *Marxism and the Theory of Human Personality* (London,
1975), p.20.

Enlightenment thought, and which remains central to any attempt today to speak of criminal punishment as entailing individual justice. Only for the few most consistent utilitarians who are prepared to sacrifice individuals to the common good with a clear conscience is the retributive element not the central question to be resolved within the liberal theory of punishment.[8]   The analysis of retributivism *is* the analysis of the liberal ideal of criminal punishment, as generations of legal and moral philosophers have borne witness in their work.   The key to the modern impasse in punishment theory lies in analysing critically the formulation of retributive thought, first, in the classic form given to it by Hobbes, Kant and Hegel,[9] and then through its period of decline and fall in the hands of the English Idealists (Green, Bradley and Bosanquet) and the twentieth century utilitarians.[10]   This latter period is, I argue, crucial in coming to terms with the nature of liberal thinking about punishment. There was a *historical logic* to the decline and fall of retributive thinking at the turn of the twentieth century that modern retributivists ignore at their peril.

The essentially *critical* nature of the argument lies in the claim I make that at the core of retributive theory, there are two central contradictions which its proponents cannot overcome, for they are constituent elements of the theory itself.   Throughout its historical development, we see successive generations of legal and moral philosophers grappling with and being defeated by these contradictions.   Ultimately the contradictions so utterly undermine the theory that it becomes transformed into its opposite: from being a defence of individual right, it becomes (in the hands of the English Idealists) a legitimation of totalitarian state power. This development, I argue, was no accident, no result of simple philosophical error and, consequently, nothing that can be put right by a 'little more' philosophical work.

Rather, the contradictions at the heart of the liberal theory of punishment are fundamentally historical premises given within the socio-legal context of a developing, then aging, capitalist social order. The philosophy of punishment is, in short, an historical ideology, an

---

[8] See below, Chapter VI.

[9] Chapters II, III and IV below. The discussion of the retributivism of Kant and Hegel requires no explanation. Hobbes is discussed as the first modern classical moral empiricist and contractarian, who, because he was first, established the basic framework within which the classical retributive philosophers, in part, by way of reaction, would write about punishment.

[10] Chapters V, VI and IX below.

element of *social* reality, which in the spirit of Durkheim,[11] must be viewed in the context of its social foundations. To put it around another way, the abstractions of philosophical thinking are understood in this work as intellectual representations, albeit of a rarefied kind, of the experience of real historical relations and processes, as Jameson expresses it.[12]   Those relations and processes are, I argue, themselves contradictory, so that their philosophical representations partake of an inherent contradictoriness.

Retrieval   If this work is one of historical critique, it is also one of retrieval. I am aware of the danger of a too narrow reduction of philosophical method to historical reality, of the risk of 'crashing the gears' of philosophical development by an oversimplistic approach to the relationship between philosophy and history.   In fact, if anything, I have gone in the opposite direction, for, as the subsequent chapters bear out, this is a work of philosophical retrieval as well as critique.

It became clear to me in thinking about the development of the theory of punishment that the level of understanding of its main arguments was in general very low, despite the obvious centrality of that development to modern concerns.   This was true both of individual philosophers and of the tradition as a whole.   Thus Hobbes's significance is hardly appreciated at all; Kant is better known for a few isolated passages than for a general theory of punishment (and knowledge of his general theory tends to be in a heavily distorted form); and Hegel is often regarded as too obscure to be taken seriously, or, the other side of the same coin, is seen as adaptable to justify any passing fad in current penal practice. Green and the other English Idealists are generally treated as no more than philosophical skeletons in the closet, to be rattled to warn the innocent away from idealism.   Yet these thinkers are at the core of the liberal tradition in the philosophy of punishment and without a clear understanding of their thought, the roots of the modern impasse cannot be diagnosed.

Furthermore without understanding the development of their thought as a whole, modern confusions and the current opacity of the classical tradition cannot be grasped.   Crucial here, once again, is the pivotal revisionism of the late 19th and early 20th centuries.   In that period, the contradictions at the heart of the classical theory were really forced to the surface, so distorting its central terms that they became

---

[11] See the prefatory quotation on p.xii, which is from 'Two Laws of Penal Evolution', *Economy and Society* (1973), p.307.

[12] *Ibid.*, quotation from *Marxism and Form* (Princeton, 1971), p.345.

unrecognisable.[13]   Yet it is from these distortions that the 20th century
debate commences.[14]   The work of critique is then also a work of
retrieval, with the latter reinforcing the value of the former.   The
classical theory of punishment accordingly is not reduced to the
underlying social reality, to which it must nonetheless be related.

At the heart of my approach is the historical importance of the
ideological form of the abstract, legal (juridical) individual.[15]   The
reason for this is, as the prefatory quote from Neumann argues,[16] that
there is a fundamental interconnection between liberal Enlightenment
philosophy and the juridical concepts of individual subjectivity and the
Rechtsstaat.   It is liberal philosophy that stresses individual liberty and
justice, the 'rights of man' within the rule of law.   This homology of
concepts is not accidental, for liberal philosophy, historically, flew the
ideological flag for the legal and constitutional reforms of the
Enlightenment.   Liberal philosophy is, one might say, legal thought by
other means: Hegel's political philosophy was quite naturally entitled the
Philosophy of Right.   But if legal thought is essentially contradictory,
and liberal philosophy is ultimately juridical in its base, then liberal
philosophy will also be contradictory.   Hence the title of this work: law,
ideology and punishment.   It is law, understood as a contradictory
ideology, which lies at the heart of our thought on punishment.   The
way to a critical understanding of the latter lies through a critique of the
forms of legal ideology.   Legal ideology lies at the core of the liberal
theory of criminal punishment.

In recent years, works by Foucault,[17] Pashukanis[18] and Neumann[19]
have all stressed the significance of legal form analysis.   In his
discussion of forms of social control emerging in the Enlightenment,

---

13 See below, Chapter V.

14 See below, Chapter VI.

15 The adjectives 'abstract', 'legal' and 'juridical' attached to the noun 'individualism'
are used interchangeably in the work, in the sense explained below in section 2 of
this Chapter.

16 From F. Neumann and O. Kircheimer, *Social Democracy and the Rule of Law*
(London, 1987), p.70.

17 M. Foucault, *Discipline and Punish* (Harmondsworth, 1977).

18 E. Pashukanis, *Law and Marxism: a General Theory* (London, 1978). See also
Selected Writings (ed. P. Beirne and R. Sharlet) (London, 1980).

19 F. Neumann, *The Rule of Law* (Leamington Spa, 1986) and (with O. Kircheimer)
Social Democracy and the Rule of Law (London, 1987).   See also the earlier
collection of his essays in *The Democratic and the Authoritarian State* (New
York, 1964), and G. Lukacs, *History and Class Consciousness* (London, 1968)
pp. 83-110.

Foucault draws a distinction between 'punishment' and 'discipline' in which the former is understood as a juridical form emerging out of the struggle of the bourgeoisie against absolutism, and as an ideal form for regulating social relations in a society of free and rational individuals. Free subjects can read and understand the law and moderate their behaviour accordingly. 'Punishment' is the ideological embodiment of Enlightenment discourse. But operating behind the facade of the juridical form, there lurks the real power base of social control in disciplinary techniques which freeze and fix an object-population in the postures of law-abidingness. 'Punishment', enlightened and liberal, but really no more than a sham in practice, is counterposed to the all-pervasive 'disciplines'.

Whatever the problems with this antithesis,[20] Foucault has rightly been acclaimed for his insistence on attending to the *forms* through which social power is mediated. Yet, Foucault does not take the analysis of the juridical form of 'punishment', which is of particular interest to us, very far. In truth, he is more interested in generating an antithesis to which he can oppose the disciplines which really concern him and which he sees as more important. Foucault notes certain contradictions in the ideology of 'punishment', for example the contradiction between an ideal, universal individualism and the reality of infinitely diverse human individuality,[21] but he does not probe very deeply into the material roots of the legal form before his thorough analysis of the emerging disciplines begins. We need to know what the contradictions of the legal form are, and whence they emerge. In one passage, Foucault proposes an answer, but hesitantly and without enthusiasm:

> It is often said that the model of a society that has individuals as its constituent elements is borrowed from the abstract juridical forms of contract and exchange. Mercantile society, according to this view, is represented as a contractual association of isolated juridical subjects. Perhaps. Indeed the political theory of the seventeenth and eighteenth centuries often seems to follow this scheme.[22]

Here is the core of the issue: the connection between liberal political theory and the 'abstract juridical forms of contract and exchange.' But Foucault can take us no further. We must turn to the work of

---

[20] See for example B. Fine, *Democracy and the Rule of Law* (London, 1984) pp.189-203, and D. Garland, Foucault's 'Discipline and Punish: An Exposition and Critique' (1987) *American Bar Foundation Research Journal*, 847.

[21] *Op.cit*, pp.98-99: 'How is one to apply fixed laws to particular individuals?'

[22] *Ibid.*, p.194.

Pashukanis and Neumann in order to explore these interconnections as the route into the liberal ideology of criminal punishment.

2. BETWEEN APPEARANCE AND REALITY: THE CONTRADICTIONS OF LEGAL IDEOLOGY

In his *General Theory of Law and Marxism*, Pashukanis developed arguments in Marx's *Capital*[23] and *Grundrisse*[24] to provide the basis of a theory of law and legal ideology emphasising the interconnection between legal and economic forms.   It has been cogently argued that in his mature work, Marx adopted a philosophical method that would today be described as one of critical realism.[25]   His distinction between science and ideology and his insistence that science penetrates to the essence of things while ideologies remain at the level of appearances, of phenomenal forms, was realist in character; while his critical method is seen in his identification of the 'extent and limits' of ideological knowledge, its contradictions, its inability to transcend a framework of analysis that proves ultimately inadequate to its object of study.   These limitations of ideology - in Marx's case generated by the discourse of political economy - were not accidental.   Rather they were historical limits which political economy could not transcend because it remained transfixed by analysis of surface appearances rather than getting to the essence of things.

Like political economy, Pashukanis argued, legal science remains locked within a discourse that takes the appearance of things to be their essence.   The starting point of jurisprudence is the double ideology of the legal subject and the *Rechtsstaat*.   The legal world is populated with

---

[23] *Capital*, Volume 1 (London 1954) pp.88-89, 172, 547.

[24] *Grundrisse* (London, 1973) pp.240-248, 281-284.

[25] This statement and what immediately follows draws upon but only gestures at an important debate within the philosophy of science and Marxism on the nature of science, ideology and Marx's method.   Main works include T. Benton, *The Rise and Fall of Structural Marxism* (London, 1984); R. Keat and J. Urry, *Social Theory as Science* (London, 1975); R. Bhaskar, *A Realist Theory of Science* (Leeds, 1975) and *The Possibility of Naturalism* (Brighton, 1979), esp. pp.83-91; and D. Sayer, *Marx's Method* (Brighton, 1979).   For a recent overview, see W. Outhwaite, *New Philosophies of Social Science* (London, 1987).

a mass of abstract individual rights-bearing subjects protected from each other and the state by principles of the rule of law. But these images of individual and state, while not entirely illusory, do mystify the real relations of individuals and the real character of the state. These mystificatory notions have their source in the sphere of exchange, that is, the character of capitalism as a market society. But capitalism is more than just a market society in which all individuals participate on equal terms under an impersonal public power. It is also a society of exploitation and inherent economic inequality, and one in which social antagonisms are to the fore. Jurisprudence, in both its liberal natural law and positivist phases, never got beyond the sphere of exchange to the underlying economic essence of relations of production which were inherently exploitative. It remained stuck at the level of superficial appearances. Between the appearance and the reality of capitalist society, between its spheres of exchange and production, there were engendered two central contradictions of legal thought.

(1)   Abstract Individualism versus Concrete Individuality

In an early essay, Marx contrasted the abstract legal and political individual of civil (liberal) society - 'the egoistic, independent individual', 'the citizen, the moral person'[26] - with the true potential of the human being to 'become a species-being in his empirical life, his individual work and his individual relations.'[27] Marx's work was at this point informed mainly by humanist thought, yet he already sensed that there were material roots to this contradiction between human life and its abstract existence in alienated forms, and that these roots were to be found in 'the materialism of civil society' which consisted of 'independent individuals... related by law.'[28]

In *Capital* and the *Grundrisse*, these material roots were further specified as pertaining to the process of the exchange of commodities, which generated a juridical relation, that is, a relationship of the mutual recognition of rights between two free and equal wills.[29] The sphere of exchange presents an image of social life conforming to liberal ideals. Within it all are free and equal, yet this freedom and equality of the

---

[26] 'On the Jewish Question' in *Early Writings* (Harmondsworth, 1975) p.232.

[27] *Ibid.*

[28] *Ibid.* p.233.

[29] *Capital, op.cit.*, pp.88-172, *Grundrisse., op.cit.*, pp.243-244.

market place stands in contradiction to the realities of social life beyond the exchange relation. It is true that each individual is free to part with his or her commodity by means of an act of his or her own free will, yet exchange is a socially and historically evolved mechanism, and the society in which exchange has come to predominate is one in which individuals have been forced and cajoled into exchange in order to survive, and regardless of their will in the matter:[30] exchange is socially determined and only a superficial abstract notion of individual freedom could obscure that fact. Juridical freedom is precisely such a notion.

It is also true that all individuals are equal in the process of exchange, since all are regarded only from the point of view of the exchange of equivalent values. The worker 'who buys commodities for 3s. appears to the seller in the same function, in the same equality - in the form of 3s. - as the king who does the same.'[31] But this equality is again purely formal, for beyond the moment of exchange, anything but equality exists between workers, capitalists and kings. The apparent realisation of freedom and equality in the market place in fact obscures the reality of social compulsion and inequality.

Thus it is that *juridical* ideas of freedom and equality, arising from the exchange relation, present an appearance in contradiction with the realities of actual human life. They are not outright falsehoods for they have a real basis in social relations, but they are one-sided and mystifying as a depiction of the real condition of social life in capitalist society. Juridical individualism involves an abstract, natural, ahistorical view of the human subject, and this 'abstraction of man in general, man as a legal subject'[32] exists in antithesis with the real lives of real human beings, caught in the all-embracing grasp of economic relations. A 'miraculous contradiction' is at play:

After he has become slavishly dependent on economic relations, which arise behind his back in the shape of the law of value, the economically active subject - now as a legal subject - acquires, in compensation as it were, a rare gift: a will, juridically constituted, which makes him absolutely free and equal to other owners of commodities like himself.[33]

---

[30] Cf. *Grundrisse, op.cit.*, pp.247-248.
[31] *Ibid.* p.246.
[32] Pashukanis, *General Theory* (*op.cit*), p.113.
[33] *Ibid.*, p.114.

(2) Individual Right versus Social Power

The ideological correlate of legal subjectivity at the level of the state is the concept of the _Rechtsstaat_ ('the state based upon/governed by the law'). The constitutional state is no mere fantasy, it has its basis in the need to guarantee the freedom and equality of market exchange. The abstract individualism of legal subjectivity is matched by 'the impersonal abstraction of State power functioning with ideal stability and continuity in time and space'.[34] Coercive state power in a market society must respect individual freedom and equality, and must accordingly be exercised under the rule of law. But the _rechtsstaatlich_ view of the state is, like the abstract individualism of legal subjectivity, based upon an appearance of the state rather than its reality. The theory of the _Rechtsstaat_ holds good in so far as the machinery of the state does actually conduct itself in accordance with the rule of law, but this is only possible to the extent that society does actually represent a market, and ignores the underlying realities of social conflict and class antagonism within capitalist societies. The state is not only the embodiment, both in legal and political theory and practice, of legal rectitude and individual right. It is also the locus of political power of the dominant class. The dark underbelly of the _rechtsstaatlich_ representation of state power as impersonal and abstract is the reality of a 'well-ordered _bourgeois_ state'[35] in which class interests dictate a _raison d'etat_ with the permanent potential to override the abstractions of individual right of the rule of law. The embodiment and safeguarding of individual right under the rule of law can never be more than conditional, for the class state has always - potentially or actually - other fish to fry.

Furthermore, the ideology of the _Rechtsstaat_ is threatened by the general historical trajectory of the capitalist economy and state. When at the end of the nineteenth century, free trade gave way to monopoly in the economic sphere, so in the legal/political sphere, the principles of individualism gave way before an emphasis on state regulation and interventionism.[36] The principles of individual right within the

---

[34] _Ibid._, p.119. Cf. Neumann, _The Rule of Law (op.cit)_, ch.14. I also use the terms 'social' and 'state' power interchangeably.

[35] _Ibid._, p.115.

[36] I represent this movement in a necessarily schematic form which ignores complexities and unevenness in historical development: see, on the developments in penal policy, the compromises identified by Garland in his _Punishment and Welfare_ (Aldershot, 1985); and, in relation to the economic analysis of 'state monopoly capitalism' which overstates the development generally, the recent essay by P. Auerbach et al, 'The Transition from Actually Existing Capitalism'

rechsstaatlich theory of law came to be undermined by a new view of the state as an interventionist power, overriding individual interests for the 'general' welfare. In law, there was a move from private to public law forms in which individual rights ceased to play so central a part. Consequently, from the turn of the century, the ideology of the *Rechtsstaat* enters into a period of decline, undermined by the developing reality of extending state power. As Pashukanis puts it:

> This practical modification of the legal fabric could not leave theory untouched. In the rosy dawn of its evolution, industrial capitalism surrounded the principle of legal subjectivity with a halo by elevating it to the level of an absolute attribute of the human personality. Nowadays people are beginning to regard this principle rather as a purely technical determinant, which is well-suited to 'distinguishing risks and liabilities' or, alternatively, they pose it simply as a speculative hypothesis lacking any material basis.[37]

3. JURIDICAL IDEOLOGY AND THE PHILOSOPHY OF PUNISHMENT

The analysis presented here of law and legal ideology starts from the connection between the legal and the exchange relation in capitalist society and reveals the way in which the 'natural' conception of 'man', the juridical individual, that is the individual who is regarded as free and equal with all other individuals, involves an historically generated and contradictory ideology. Such a view is only possible by means of an abstraction of one's concept of the individual from the concrete realities and social conditions of human life. Juridical individualism can be designated as ideology because it is inadequate to the reality of human life and obscures its true basis in fundamental social relations and individual characteristics of men and women. The free and equal

---

(1988), *New Left Review* 170, 61-78. However these cautions do not deny the basic truth of a more developed interventionist role for capitalist states in the twentieth century resulting in a weakening of classical liberal legal forms. See Neumann's work in particular, as well as more recent analyses by R. Unger, *Law in Modern Society* (New York, 1976) and E. Kamenka and A.Tay, 'Beyond Bourgeois Individualism: the Contemporary Crisis in Law and Legal Ideology' in E. Kamenka and R. Neale, *Feudalism, Capitalism and Beyond* (London, 1975).

[37] *Op.cit.*, pp.129-130.

individual is an absurd mystification of the reality of concrete human
individuality within particular social contexts.

Likewise, the idea of the *Rechtsstaat*, of an abstract, independent,
ahistorical state, while complementing the 'natural' abstract
individualism of this metaphysical 'man', fetishises the reality of a
concrete state representing particular political interests, and acting
according to *raison d'etat*. The formalistic, phenomenal form of the
Rechtsstaat has a particular tendency to be undermined by reality both
because of the fundamental political nature of the state, which emerges
particularly in time of crisis, and because of the historical trajectory of
the state towards interventionism from the late nineteenth century
onwards.

Thus, there are two fundamental ideologies derived from the nature of
law as a social form. These relate to the conception of individuals and
of the state within legal ideology. Both exist as ideal mystifying forms
of a reality they only partially and misleadingly represent. Both
therefore establish a tension between their representation of the
individual and the state and the corresponding realities. In this analysis,
it is argued that these two tensions are at the heart of certain fundamental
contradictions within the philosophy of punishment, and that their
identification is the key to an understanding of that philosophy's
twentieth century impasse.

In Chapters II - V, I chart the rise and fall of the classical retributive
theory of punishment from its beginning in the work of Hobbes to its
effective downfall in the work of the English Hegelians of the late
nineteenth and early twentieth century. In Chapter II, it is argued that
the key to an understanding of Hobbes's work is the fundamental
contradiction existing within it between his juridical individualism (his
contractarianism) and his conception of individuals as determined by
their passions, i.e. as concretely established individuals. This leads to
many contradictory formulations in his work, which at times exhibits a
retributive aspect, at others a utilitarian. Only an account of his theory
which grasps its two-sidedness around the juridical
individualism/concrete individuality contradiction can adequately
explain it.

In Chapters III and IV, it is argued that the same contradiction is the
theoretical driving force behind the retributivism of Kant and Hegel.
Both attempt to suppress it, with differing degrees of success, but in
both, at the end of the day, reality (concrete individuality) returns to
undermine juridical individualism. Also, in Chapter IV, it is argued that
Hegel's doctrine of punishment falls foul of the second contradiction

between the *Rechtsstaat* and the doctrine of *raison d'etat* in a way that fundamentally undermines the integrity of his work.

In Chapter V, the retributivism of the English Idealists is considered. Like Hegel, these writers incorporated the ideological nature of the *Rechtsstaat* within their work but in a new more complex way. Writing at the end of the nineteenth century, they sought in different ways to incorporate the reality of the interventionist state into their theories whilst attempting to cling fast to the ideology of the *Rechtsstaat*. The result was profuse contradiction, and, ultimately, a totalitarianism which was to transform the meaning of, and completely undermine the credibility of the retributive theory in the first half of the twentieth century. Retributivism, an individualistic doctrine, ironically became associated with some of the most authoritarian views ever to be expressed in the Anglo-American philosophical world, in the work of Bosanquet and, particularly, Bradley. The English Idealists ended by throwing into utter confusion not only the doctrines of the *Rechtsstaat*, but also the juridical individualism on which it was based.

In Chapter VI, it is argued that the new interventionist role of the state in the twentieth century at the same time as it threw the retributivist theory into disarray also strengthened the position of the utilitarians, who became the dominant theorists. However while for them, juridical individualism is regarded as a metaphysical nonsense, they cannot, to the extent that they wish to remain politically liberal in their thought, escape the need to incorporate individualistic doctrines within their general theory of state action. Utilitarianism is therefore caught within the second contradiction between *raison d'etat* and the *Rechtsstaat*, for it attempts to have it both ways: to justify punishment in terms of collective well-being *and* individual justice. This chapter completes the analysis of the historical development of the philosophy of punishment.

In Chapters VII and VIII, the same analysis of the two contradictions relating to the nature of the individual and the state is brought to bear on modern issues within the philosophy of punishment. In Chapter VII, the debate within legal philosophy concerning the relationship between freewill and determinism is examined. In particular, the justification of punishment on the basis of a soft determinist theory is considered. It is argued that this compromise position fails because it is a compromise between two irreconcilables: juridical individualism (freewill) and concrete individuality (determinism). The chapter then proceeds to show that this apparently abstruse philosophical debate has a real basis within the practice of law itself through an analysis of the criminal law's 'excusing conditions' and the process of mitigation of punishment.

In Chapter VIII, the consequences of the second contradiction
between the *Rechtsstaat* and *raison d'etat* are explored for a theory of
legal reasoning which attempts to see judicial reasoning as essentially
rational. Using an analysis of recent criminal law cases, it is argued that
the rationality of law is undermined by the felt need of judges to employ
arguments based upon *raison d'etat* in contradiction of legal doctrines
embodying individual right in deciding cases concerning criminal
responsibility. Thus, it is shown, in parallel with the second half of
Chapter VII, that the second contradiction at the heart of the law is also
generated within legal practice itself.

Finally, in a concluding chapter, I discuss the significance of the
analysis presented in the book for modern penal reform movements
based upon the ideal of criminal justice and consider the position of the
liberal justification of criminal punishment in Western society today.

CHAPTER II

THE BIRTH OF JURIDICAL INDIVIDUALISM: HOBBES AND THE PHILOSOPHY OF PUNISHMENT

1. INTRODUCTION

The emergence of the liberal ideal of criminal justice with its emphasis on individual responsibility is closely connected with the development of modern theories of punishment. There are three main theories - the retributive, the utilitarian and the rehabilitative - and of these, the liberal ideal is most closely linked with, indeed based upon, the retributive theory of punishment. That is why even modern legal philosophers, writing within a utilitarian tradition, find it important to return to retributive principles when they seek to explain the place of justice for individuals within the criminal law.[1] Hence it is necessary to seek the roots of this intellectual tradition in order to get to the heart of the liberal ideal. My argument in this chapter is that those roots are to be found not in the work of the classical retributivists Kant and Hegel where, one might say, the plant has already reached its full development, but in the social contract theory of Thomas Hobbes. This will come as a surprise to many for Hobbes is commonly regarded as of no great importance in the development of the theory of punishment. Furthermore, he is usually seen, where he is discussed, not as a retributivist of any colour but as a utilitarian (by implication opposed to the retributive philosophy) of secondary importance.[2]

---

[1] See in particular, H.L.A. Hart, *Punishment and Responsibility* (Oxford, 1968), ch.1, and ch.6. The connection between retributive theory and criminal justice practice is explicitly made by those developing the justice model of penal reform. See ch.IX.

[2] For example: 'Hobbes's conception contains in essence the basic principles of a utilitarian theory of punishment, principles that were later developed and

I will further claim that Hobbes's theory of punishment has much greater significance than that attributed to it so far because he laid down an intellectual structure which has been developed in various ways but not fundamentally altered by later philosophers, and that his work is central to an understanding of the later development of the philosophy of punishment in *all* its major forms: retributive, utilitarian and rehabilitative. Hobbes is the founding father of the modern theory of punishment, and hence absolutely central to any analysis of the liberal ideal of criminal punishment.

This may seem a large claim. For one thing it is generally assumed (and I would not deny it) that the principal philosophies of punishment are contradictory alternatives. How, then, can they all be contained within one philosophical system? The answer given here is that they cannot with any degree of logical consistency, and that the key to understanding Hobbes is to recognise the contradictory nature of his philosophy of punishment. Furthermore, it is argued that the fundamental contradictions within his account stem from an antithesis between his juridical individualism (his concept of the individual as an abstract, free being) and his materialism (his view of individuals as concretely determined by their characters). The key to understanding Hobbes, therefore, is to identify within his work the first contradiction of legal ideology described in the previous chapter, that between juridical (abstract) individualism and concrete individuality.

This chapter takes the following form. In the remains of this introduction, I focus on a particular problem identified in recent accounts of Hobbes's theory of punishment, which I then proceed in the next section to trace to its source in Hobbes's work. I show that logical inconsistencies in Hobbes are based on contradictions within his analysis. In section 3, I then proceed to locate these contradictions within the juridical individualism/concrete individuality antithesis, and, finally, in section 4, I show the significance of this for the subsequent development of the philosophy of punishment.

In examining Hobbes's theory of punishment, the basic question that must be asked is, from where does the sovereign derive the right to

---

elaborated by Beccaria and Bentham'. (M. Cattaneo, 'Hobbes's Theory of Punishment' in K.C. Brown (ed.) *Hobbes Studies* (Oxford, 1965) pp.275-297, at 289. Whereas retributivists are primarily concerned with punishing individuals *justly*, utilitarians are more concerned with punishing them *effectively*, in order to promote social well-being through deterrence and example. The key issue between the two theories is that effective punishment on utilitarian principles may be incompatible with just punishment on retributive principles. See ch.VI for analysis of this issue.

punish his subjects?[3] The problem is this: the sovereign's rights all come from the people who appoint him, but the people's primary purpose in creating the sovereign is their own comfort and, most particularly, the avoidance of death (a constant fear in the state of nature). Therefore it is hard for Hobbes to argue that the sovereign gains a right to punish, the exercise of which would undermine their purpose in appointing him. Now Hobbes in parts of *Leviathan* recognised this problem and conceded that the right of punishment could not be 'grounded on any concession or gift of the subjects'.[4] What happens instead, he argues, is that when making their covenant (the social contract) to appoint a sovereign, men lay down the right to punish others (which they held in the state of nature) but the sovereign does not. Thus, argues Hobbes:

the right, which the commonwealth [the sovereign - AN] hath to put a man to death for crimes ... remains from the first right of nature, which every man hath to preserve himself.[5]

People do not, then, agree to the sovereign having a right to punish; rather his right is drawn from the pre-existing state of nature and carried over into the social state. The sovereign does not have a right to punish based on the social contract. What is more, and adding to the difficulties, not only have men not consented to their punishment, they also have a right, stemming from the state of nature, to resist the sovereign's punishment. As Hobbes also acknowledges, a man 'cannot lay down the right of resisting them, that assault him by force, to take away his life'.[6]

Thus while the social contract was established to get men out of the state of nature by appointing a sovereign with the power to keep them in line through punishment, it turns out that not only does the sovereign not have a right to punish them, they have a right to resist him. The problem is a general one in relation to punishment, but particularly acute in relation to the death penalty, where sovereign and subject become no more than 'two antagonists in a state of nature, except that now one of these is much more powerful than the other'.[7]

The significance of the issues raised by this problem are acutely brought out by Gauthier in his explanation of Hobbes's doctrine of

---

3 See J. Watkins, *Hobbes's System of Ideas*, (London, 1973), p.97.
4 T. Hobbes, *Leviathan* (ed. C. MacPherson) (Harmondsworth, 1968), p.354.
5 *Ibid.*
6 Hobbes, *op.cit.*, p.192.
7 J. Watkins, *op.cit.*, p.98.

authorisation.[8]   When the people appoint the sovereign, they do not simply establish a *de facto* power able to dominate them through superior might. Rather, they authorise him to act as he sees fit so that he acts by right of the people, who are *de jure* obligated to obey him.   The social contract does not merely create the sovereign *de facto*, it creates a moral-juridical relationship between sovereign and people in which the people acknowledge the sovereign's acts as their own and are *obligated* to obey his commands because he commands as of right.[9]

If we regard Hobbes's theory from this point of view, we see very clearly the nature of the problem with his justification of punishment. From the standpoint of the sovereign's legal/moral authorisation by the people, Hobbes can argue that 'in owning all of the actions of the sovereign, the subjects therefore own the acts whereby they are punished.'[10]   In other words, punishment is justified by the authorisation doctrine.   There is one very clear passage where Hobbes makes this argument in relation to the position of a rebel against the sovereign:

Besides, if he that attempteth to depose his sovereign, be killed, or punished by him for such attempt, he is author of his own punishment, as being by the institution, author of all his sovereign shall do: and because it is injustice for a man to do

---

[8] D. Gauthier, *The Logic of Leviathan* (Oxford, 1969), ch.IV.

[9] Cf. D. Raphael, *Hobbes* (London, 1977), p.98.   In her *Hobbes and the Social Contract Tradition* (Cambridge, 1986), J. Hampton disputes Gauthier's interpretation, arguing that the moral authorisation of the sovereign is textually sanctioned by chapter 16 of *Leviathan* but not by the work as a whole.   The predominant line of Hobbes's work, she argues (pp.117-122), is that people surrender their rights as a matter of fact rather than as a matter of moral-juridical transfer, as 'authorisation' suggests.   But Hampton overlooks other examples of the moral authorisation stance elsewhere in *Leviathan*.   For example there are passages in ch.14 (p.191), ch.18 (pp.229-230, 232), and ch.21 (pp.264-265) which conform to Gauthier's account.   On p.118, Hampton quotes in favour of her reading a passage (*Leviathan*, p.227) in which Hobbes apparently equates authorisation with simply the giving up of right.   She does not note, however, that this is immediately preceded by lines in which Hobbes talks of men *conferring* 'all their power and strength upon one man' and of creating a consent that is 'a reall Unitie of them all' in which 'everyone [is] to owne, and acknowledge himself to be Author of whatsoever' the sovereign does.   This is more than simple renunciation of right.   It is the active enabling of the sovereign to act in the individual's place.   As we shall see, Hobbes's position on punishment is also much more ambiguous and ambivalent than Hampton allows (p.119) as between authorisation and surrender.

[10] Gauthier, *op.cit.*, p.146.

anything, for which he may be punished by his own authority, he is also by that title unjust.[11]

At the same time, one cannot get away from the fact that the individual's right of nature (as we have seen) is one of self-preservation so that it is hard to understand why the people would authorise their own punishment in the first place.

Gauthier suggests that in this passage Hobbes has made a mistake in linking punishment directly to the authorisation doctrine, and that later in *Leviathan* he recognises this and revises his account by deducing the right to punish not from social authorisation but from the natural state. In the revised theory, Hobbes goes back to that time:

before the institution of commonwealth [when] every man had a right to everything, and to do whatsoever he though necessary to his own preservation; subduing, hurting, or killing any man in order thereunto.[12]

Hobbes is forced to concede that it is in the right of nature that there exists:

the foundation of that right of punishing, which is exercised in every commonwealth. For the subjects did not give the sovereign that right; but only in laying down theirs, strengthened him to use his own, as he should think fit, for the preservation of them all.[13]

Thus Gauthier, despite (or rather because of) his awareness of the moral/legal nature of the doctrine of the contract, is forced like Watkins to trace the right to punish back to the state of nature. In the process, he makes us aware that Hobbes himself was ambivalent about the source of rightful punishment. Was it in the authorisation doctrine (as the discussion of the rebel suggests) or was it in the state and right of nature? Hobbes says both.

Gauthier himself attempts a solution to Hobbes's problem by modifying yet retaining the authorisation doctrine. His argument is that each individual authorises the punishment of all other individuals, *but not his own*, so that while the sovereign's punishment is never authorised by the person who is to be punished, it is always authorised by every other individual in society. But this is not a happy resolution of the problem for it means that the person who is most essential to the authorisation process, the person to be punished, does not authorise the punishment. Gauthier is forced to admit, in line with Watkins, that in

---

[11] *Ibid.*, p.147; Hobbes, *ibid.*, p.229.
[12] Gauthier, *ibid.*; Hobbes, *ibid.*, p.354.
[13] *Ibid.*; Hobbes, *ibid.*

punishment, the sovereign does not act as a representative of the person
punished, or with his authorisation, but in effect as an enemy in the state
of nature,[14] and ultimately, Gauthier concedes, the authorisation doctrine
fails for he argues that punishment is justified because the person
concerned 'has already placed himself, in effect, in the state of nature
with respect to the other members of civil society, as represented in the
person of the sovereign'.[15]

What is the nature of this tension between the state of nature and the
social state, between the doctrine of natural right and the doctrine of
authorisation in Hobbes's theory of punishment? Is it simply a question
of Hobbes failing to notice a problem, as Gauthier suggests, or does the
tension go much deeper in Hobbes's work? Before answering that
second question in the next section, I will consider one other discussion
of Hobbes which brings out a little further the nature of the ambiguity in
his work.

Speaking of his view of the death penalty, Cattaneo has observed that
Hobbes recognises both that the sovereign has the right to inflict capital
punishment and that the condemned subject has the right to resist. This
is because the law of nature denies that an individual can validly oblige
himself not to oppose violence against himself.[16]   Following Leo
Strauss's view,[17] he argues that there is in Hobbes's work 'a discrepancy
between his *theory of sovereignty* and his conception of the basic and
primary character of *the natural right to self preservation*'.[18]   This
discrepancy exists because 'each of these two conceptions claims to be
absolute, but finds an insurmountable obstacle in the similar claim of the
other'. On the one hand, the claim of nature is that no right of
punishment can be handed over to a sovereign, and that the individual
may, indeed must, resist the death penalty; on the other hand, there is the

---

[14] *Ibid.*, p.148.

[15] *Ibid.* Cf. J. Hampton, *op.cit.*, pp.174-178. Hampton argues that the people
cannot consent to their own punishment but can participate in the punishment of
others. She concludes, following the logic of this through, that the juridical idea
of binding contractual obligation is inconsistent with Hobbes's egoistic
psychology. The power to punish accordingly must be understood in terms of a
de facto accrual of power by the sovereign through the exploitation of the self-
interest of some, but by no means all, individuals. She analogises the
achievement of sovereign power with that of a Genghis Khan or Los Angeles
gang leader. I would not deny her the logic of her argument, but I do not think it
was Hobbes's logic. See the conclusion of this chapter.

[16] *Op.cit.*, p.291.

[17] L. Strauss, 'The Spirit of Hobbes's Political Philosophy' in K. Brown, *op.cit.*,
p.26.

[18] *Op.cit.*, p.293, emphasis added.

claim of the sovereign to an absolute right to punish, and to punish by death.

Cattaneo is on the right lines here, but he has not quite traced the contradiction to its root. Yes, the sovereign does have an absolute right to punish, but the really interesting point is that he derives it, along with all his other rights, from *consent of the people*: those same people who given their natural constitution would never dream of giving away such a right. The discrepancy is not just between a conception of human nature and a theory of sovereignty, for the theory of sovereignty is itself derived from a theory of human consent. Hence the discrepancy is really, fundamentally, between the equally absolute claims of a theory of human nature on the one hand, and a theory of (moral-juridical) human consent on the other.

In that discrepancy, I shall argue, there lurks *in embryo* the entire subsequent development of the retributive philosophy of punishment. For the meantime, it is necessary to establish beyond question its existence within Hobbes's work, and to explain why it should be there.

2. CONTRADICTION IN THE HOBBESIAN PHILOSOPHY OF PUNISHMENT

For Hobbes, the purpose of men joining a Commonwealth and establishing a sovereign is so that they may get

themselves out from that miserable condition of Warre, which is necessarily consequent ... to the natural Passions of men, when there is no visible Power to keep them in awe, and tye them by feare of punishment to the performance of their Covenants, and observation of [the] Lawes of Nature.[19]

This passage introduces Part II of *Leviathan*, in which Hobbes deals with the constitution of a Commonwealth. It is clearly stated that a principal aim of the social contract is to establish a system of punishment together with the individual who is to apply that system, the sovereign. From the contract 'are derived all the Rights, and Facultyes of him, or them, on

---

[19] Hobbes, *op.cit.*, p.223, emphasis added.

whom the Sovereigne Power is conferred by the consent of the people assembled'.[20]   And lest there be any doubt, this includes

the Power of ... Punishing with corporall, or pecuniary punishment, or with ignominy every subject according to the law that he hath formerly made.[21]

Further, this power is clearly *authorised* by the subject:

[since] every Subject is by this Institution Author of all the Actions, and Judgements of the Soveraigne Instituted; it followes, that whatsoever he doth it can be no Injury to any of his Subjects; nor ought he to be by any of them accused of Injustice. For he that doth any thing by authority from another, doth therein no injury to him by whose authority he acteth: But by this Institution of a Common-Wealth, every particular man is Author of all the Soveraigne doth; and consequently he that complaineth of injury from his Soveraigne, complaineth of that whereof he himselfe is Author; and therefore ought not to accuse any man but himselfe; no nor himselfe of injury; because to do injury to onesselfe, is impossible.[22]

These passages, and others besides,[23] establish beyond doubt that for Hobbes the justification of punishment is inherent within the concept of the social contract. By a contract, a man alienates rights, and by the social contract, he alienates the right of nature. That right is the right of self-preservation,[24] but it is a right and not a duty. Thus while no man may have the right to harm himself, as Gauthier argues,[25] it does not follow that a man may not give up the right to do what is conducive to his preservation. In other words, the possession of right - any right - is consistent with the ability to alienate right through a contract. There is nothing wrong in Hobbes's formulation of the right to punish in these terms - he simply follows through the implications of the legal form of a contract, i.e., the free alienation of right.

However, where a problem does emerge for Hobbes concerns the question whether in fact a man would ever transfer such a right, and we now see Hobbes change his tune. Having established the right to punish through the individual transfer of the right of nature through the social contract, he now denies that such a thing could ever have occurred:

---

[20] *Ibid.*, p.229.

[21] *Ibid.*, p.235.

[22] *Ibid.*, p.232.

[23] *Ibid.*, pp.229-230, p.264.

[24] *Ibid.*, p.189.

[25] Gauthier, *op.cit.*, p.147: 'But no man can be supposed to authorise another to punish him, or kill him. For in authorising, one man gives another the use of his right, but no man has the right to harm himself, for the right of nature is a right to do what is conducive to one's preservation'.

Whensoever a man Transferreth his Right, or Renounceth it; it is either in consideration of some Right reciprocally transferred to himselfe; or for some other good he hopeth for thereby. For it is a voluntary act; and of the voluntary acts of every man, the object is some Good to himselfe. And therefore there be some rights, which no man can be understood by any words, or other signes, to have abandoned, or transferred. As first, a man cannot lay down the right of resisting ... Wounds and Chayns, and Imprisonment; ... because there is no benefit consequent to such patience ... And ... the motive, and end for which this renouncing, and transferring of Right is introduced, is nothing else but the security of a mans person, in his life, and in the means of so preserving life, as not to be weary of it.[26]

Thus Hobbes is now as clear in practice that a man would never grant a right of punishment as he was in principle that such a right-grant was the basis of the sovereign's power. Any man who purports to transfer such a right, he insists, 'is not to be understood as if he meant it, or that it was his will; but that he was ignorant of how such words and actions were to be interpreted'.[27]   Yet it must be recalled that a central aim of the Commonwealth was to 'tye [men] by fear of punishment' and that to establish it was a dictate of reason.[28]   Now we are told that only those without reason would agree to what previously had been said to be a product of man's reason.

   Given this contradiction, we can now return to the passage in which Hobbes amends his theory of punishment and see its significance in context.   Having established the existence of the contract, the Commonwealth, and the sovereign, and having retreated on the right to punish, Hobbes proceeds to discuss the question of the nature of punishments and rewards towards the end of the second part of *Leviathan*.   Before so doing, however, he pauses to reformulate the right to punish and to re-enquire 'by what door' it came in.   Hobbes now argues that

the Subjects did not give the Sovereign that; but only in laying down theirs, strengthened him to use his own, as he should think fit, for the preservation of them all: so that it was not given, but left to him, and to him only...[29]

Hobbes, in other words, reverts to the sovereign's right of nature, preserved and aggrandised by the renunciation of the same right by all his subjects.   But this shift from the authorisation doctrine to the natural right doctrine is impossible given the general logic of his argument: it either leads to the conclusion that the individual does grant the sovereign

---

26 *Ibid.*, p.192. See also p.199.
27 *Ibid.*
28 *Ibid.*, ch.14.
29 *Ibid.*, p.354.

the right to punish - regardless of Hobbes's claim to the contrary, or to the imminent collapse of, and the implicit denial of the possibility of, the social state and the institution of punishment. Let us examine these two options in turn.

First, in appointing a Sovereign, the people make a conscious and rational choice to establish a ruler with supreme power over them. In laying down their right to punish, thereby aggrandising the sovereign's natural right, they may not explicitly grant the sovereign the right of punishment, but they must implicitly or tacitly do so. Laying down one's right while appointing a sovereign who does not lay down his entails at least the implicit approval on the people's part of the sovereign's retention of his right. As Hobbes himself says, right is laid aside '*either* by simply Renouncing it; or by Transferring it to another'.[30] The people do not need to explicitly transfer their right to the sovereign. If he retains his natural right and (we assume) the people know this, then they implicitly recognise the sovereign's right of punishment in the Commonwealth. The transfer of right in this situation may be 'under the table', but a transfer of right, no matter the verbal intricacies, it remains.

Second, on the other hand, if the sovereign retains a natural right to punish, and the individual does not consent to that right, it follows that the institution of the Commonwealth is a self-defeating proposition. The aim of the Commonwealth and the sovereign is to establish a state of society where before there had been a state of nature, which was one of war. Integral to the maintenance of society and the avoidance of nature (war) is the institution of punishment. But if the exercise of punishment is based upon an unconceded right of nature, then every threat or act of punishment is itself a reversion to the state of nature. Every such threat or act is a potential or actual act of war. Thus while the sovereign is supposed to protect men from the state of nature, the sovereign's primary tool for achieving this is itself a weapon of war and a logical conduit back into the natural state. The sovereign is a double agent on Hobbes's logic here.[31]

Thus Hobbes's solution to the problem of the right of punishment is no solution at all. For either the revised justification becomes implicated in the general conceptual structure of the social contract, in which case the people do give the sovereign a right to punish ('under the table') or it completely undermines the entire concept of society, bringing it in line with the concept of man as a natural warring being. The whole structure

---

[30] *Ibid.*, p.191, emphasis added.

[31] This is essentially the conclusion to which Gauthier is forced. See above, text at fn.14.

of *Leviathan* is shaken if the sovereign's right of punishment is natural and not social, for the state of nature has never really been transcended. Thus, Hobbes's revised justification of punishment cannot resolve the contradiction that exists between his contractual justification of punishment and his naturalistic conception of men, between what in principle ought to happen and what in practice never would, between his doctrines of human consent and human nature. Having established the inherent nature of this contradiction within his work, we must now enquire as to why it should exist.

3. HOBBES'S JURIDICAL INDIVIDUALISM

The contradiction between a juridical conception of the social contract and a naturalistic description of man's being is fundamental to the Hobbesian philosophy. Strauss has described it as 'the classic example of the typically modern combination of political idealism with a materialistic and atheistic view of the whole.'[32] A brief excursion into what this means in terms of Hobbes's views on natural law will help us to understand the significance of his social contract doctrine, which concerns us here.

Hobbes lived at the beginning of the modern scientific era, an era which was to be dominated by the discovery of physical laws of cause and effect, and hence by a new intellectual method of enquiry. He was much impressed by the successes of this new natural scientific method and by the legitimacy the method was able to claim because of its success. Hobbes wished to procure some of this legitimacy for political philosophy, and therefore sought to introduce the methodology of natural science with its identification of laws of cause and effect (laws of nature) into his own account of the foundation of society: he described a material, causal process whereby men were forced to agree the contract because of their passions. At the same time, however, he wanted to retain alongside the causal necessity of the contract a notion of its moral necessity, that is, an older philosophical notion of natural law as being what 'ought to happen'. Strauss explains this by comparing and contrasting Hobbes with Machiavelli. Like Machiavelli, he saw that 'the correct way of answering the question of the right order of society

---

[32] L. Strauss, *Natural Right and History* (Chicago, 1953), p.170.

consists in taking one's bearings by how men actually do live,' but he did not accept Machiavelli's logical conclusion that the only virtue was *political* virtue. To that he added the quest for *moral* virtue in an attempt to restore 'the moral principles of politics, i.e. of natural law, on the plane of Machiavelli's 'realism'.'[33]

Habermas, developing a similar interpretation of Hobbes's work, reveals the problematic way in which Hobbes attempts to have it both ways by conjoining natural and moral necessity.   He portrays the creation of social order and the nature of human behaviour as

the material of science. The engineers of the correct order can disregard the categories of ethical social intercourse and confine themselves to the construction of conditions under which human beings, just like objects within nature, will necessarily behave in a calculable manner.[34]

This material of science becomes the basis for natural laws, interpreted physically, as laws of nature. But Hobbes then proceeds to transmute these physical laws of nature into *Leges Naturales,* laws of nature in a moral sense:

Hobbes projects absolute Natural Law onto a relationship among men interpreted in the Machiavellian manner; this produces the appearance that the lawfulness of the state of nature has been formulated normatively. But ... his analysis of the natural state of the human species prior to all sociation is not ethical at all; it is purely physicalistic.[35]

(*laun*)

There is duplicity in this 'cinematic dissolve'[36] from physical natural law to moral natural law in that the former cannot provide an adequate foundation for the latter. Physical laws of nature give rise not to moral commands but to prudential directives, to 'hypothetical' rather than 'categorical' imperatives.[37]   While Hobbes without doubt elaborates the laws of nature as *Leges Naturales* in the moral sense, describing them as the 'true Morall Philosophie' and speaking of them as binding 'in foro interno'[38] he ultimately concedes that these moral natural laws are only improperly so called 'for they are but Conclusions, or theoremes

---

33 *Ibid.*, p.179.

34 J. Habermas, *Theory and Practice* (London, 1974), p.43.

35 *Ibid.*, p.65; and see generally, pp.62-67.

36 *Ibid.*

37 C.B. MacPherson, *Political Theory of Possessive Individualism*, pp.72-74.
     Against MacPherson, my argument is that Hobbes did intend to postulate a moral and not merely prudential theory of obligation.

38 *Ibid.*, pp.215, 216.

concerning what conduceth to the conservation and defence of [men].'[39] Hobbes's naturalism and scientific realism provide an inadequate foundation for his moral philosophy. At best, he describes what actually happens, not what ought to happen.

If we now return from this excursion into the different meanings of natural law in Hobbes's philosophy to his justification of punishment, we see that, albeit in different terms, precisely the same problem exists there. In *Leviathan*, the weight of the moral argument is borne on not one but two foundations: the *Leges Naturales* and the social contract. The two in fact complement each other. Whereas the *Leges Naturales* direct the individual to the necessity of a Commonwealth and sovereign as an objective rational necessity, the social contract binds the individual subjectively in that adherence to the Commonwealth and submission to the sovereign become his own free act. The transfer of right in the contract is the subjective complement of the objective laws of man's nature. The individual is morally and legally bound by his free act:

And when a man hath...abandoned, or granted away his Right; then is he said to be OBLIGED, or BOUND, not to hinder those to whom such Right is granted, or abandoned, from the benefit of it: and that he ought, and it is his DUTY, not to make voyd that voluntary act of his own: and that such hindrance is INJUSTICE, and INJURY, as being Sine Jure; the right being before renounced, or transferred....it is called Injustice, and Injury, voluntarily to undo that which from the beginning he had voluntarily done.[40]

It is in this other part of Hobbes's moral doctrine that we locate the right to punish for that right is a product (on the juridical side of his philosophy) of the transfer of right in the contract. The problem, however, is that just as the moral *Leges Naturales* are undermined by their foundation in scientifically described physical natural laws, so is the just transfer of right as a voluntary individual act undermined by man's nature as a physical being. We can see this if we investigate Hobbes's claim that in transferring right, man obliges himself through his own voluntary act. Let us take the three main components of this position and analyse them more closely.

(1) The transfer of right is a voluntary act.

But what does it mean to act voluntarily? To act voluntarily is to act freely but for Hobbes, man is governed by the causal necessity of his

---

[39] *Ibid.*, pp.216-217.
[40] *Ibid.*, p.191.

nature. Thus the object of every voluntary act is some good to the
individual, and it is fear that drives him into the Commonwealth. Can he
be both driven into the contract by fear and said to act freely? Can his
contractual act truly be said to be a voluntary one in such circumstances?
Hobbes's answer is to state that although the strongest passion is fear,
nonetheless,

> Feare and Liberty are consistent; as when a man throeth his goods into the Sea for
> feare the ship should sink, he doth it nevertheless very willingly, and may refuse to
> do it if he will: It is therefore the action of one that was free....[41]

Philosophically, he explains this argument as follows:

> Liberty and Necessity are Consistent: As in the water, that hath not only Liberty,
> but a necessity of descending by the Channel: so likewise in the Actions which men
> voluntarily doe...[42]

While such a conception of freedom is intelligible, it is clearly not the
material from which moral obligation can be derived. It is essentially a
'soft determinist' position in which freedom is defined as an absence of
external impediments.[43]   It concerns not whether an action was freely
chosen but whether an action, determined by circumstances beyond
individual choice, meets with external hindrance. 'Water descending by
a channel' can clearly only be free in the latter, and not the former sense,
for it would be nonsense to suggest that water could 'choose' to follow its
law of nature, the law of gravity. Moral freedom on the other hand, as
Kenny argues, entails the power to do otherwise than one does.[44]
Objects governed by nature do not enjoy such a power, and are therefore
not attributable with moral freedom. If Hobbes's concept of humankind
aligns people with other objects of nature in their subservience to natural
forces, then he cannot at the same time attribute them with the
moral-juridical freedom of choice which makes consent to the contract
their 'own' act.

---

[41] Ibid., p.262.

[42] *Ibid.*, p.263.

[43] *Ibid.*, pp.189, 262. Cf. P. Edwards, 'Hard and Soft Determinism' in S. Hook,
       Determinism and Freedom in the Age of Modern Science (New York, 1961). See
       also below, ch.VII.

[44] A. Kenny, *Freewill and Responsibility* (London, 1978), p.26.

(2) A transfer of right is possible.

Hobbes defines the Right of Nature which man alienates/transfers in the social contract as the

Liberty each man hath, to use his own power, as he will himself, for the preservation of his own Nature.[45]

There seems nothing wrong with the idea that a man may alienate/transfer his own liberty until we discover that 'liberty' is defined as an 'absence of externall Impediments'.[46]   What does it mean to say that the individual alienates/transfers his 'absence of externall Impediments'?   By definition, the absence of such externalities (or indeed their presence) is something over which the individual has no control. Their alienation by the individual is an impossibility. If man's liberty consists in finding 'no stop, in doing what he has the will, desire, or inclination to do',[47] how can he transfer such an external negative to another?

The problem here once again stems from Hobbes's concept of man. If men are governed by their natures, their liberty cannot be defined by reference to any internal principle of freedom of actions, for their actions are determined by their natures. Liberty can only be defined as the absence of forces and controls external to the force that is the individual's own natural motion. But precisely because such forces are external to the individual he cannot alienate them for they are forces beyond him, acting upon him. The Right of Nature defined in these terms is not really a right at all, it is a description of a factual state, and no more.

(3) The voluntary transfer of right is just.

It is unjust to hinder those to whom a right has been granted so that the individual is obliged or bound not to do so. But is this true of the transfer of right in the social contract? Hobbes also argued that in the state of nature there can be no justice or injustice 'while men are in the naturall condition of Warre' so that

---

[45] *Ibid.*, p.189.
[46] *Ibid.*
[47] *Ibid.*, p.262.

übereinkommen

before the names of Just and Unjust can have place, there must be some coercive Power, to compel men equally to the performance of their Covenants.... Therefore where there is no Common-wealth, there nothing is Unjust.[48]

But this means that for the social contract and the creation of the Commonwealth, the sovereign and his rights, the argument is circular. The Commonwealth (a sovereign and his rights) is just because of the agreement to establish a Commonwealth but the agreement so to establish them is just because of the establishment of the Commonwealth. More simply: the Commonwealth is just because of the social contract while the social contract is just because of the existence of the Commonwealth. Hobbes cannot logically have it both ways.

Again the roots of this problem are to be found in the conflict between the individual as a free moral/juridical being and as a determined natural being. While the former can commit himself as he wills and honour his commitments regardless of whether he is in the state of nature or society, the latter is determined never to respect his commitments unless it is convenient and therefore requires an external power to enforce them.

Thus, to sum up, just as Hobbes interprets the concept of a natural law both physically and normatively, so he attempts to have it both ways with his concept of man as both a natural and juridical being. Men are both determined objects and free subjects. But if they are determined by their nature, they are not free morally to oblige themselves by their voluntary acts; nor is it possible for them to establish the rights of the sovereign on the basis of an adequately defined Right of Nature; nor is it possible for them to be obliged by the inherent justness of the transfer of such a right. The juridical form of the social contract is in complete contradiction with the natural content of the personalities of the contracting parties. Accordingly, the problems that we identified in the last section concerning the philosophy of punishment can now be seen to be one aspect of a fundamental contradiction within Hobbes's work between his conception of men as free contractual beings and his conception of them as actually determined by their natures, i.e. the juridical individualism/concrete individuality antithesis outlined in Chapter I.

I now wish to turn to the significance of this analysis for Hobbes's philosophy of punishment in the context of that philosophy's subsequent development.

---

[48] *Ibid.*, p.202.

4. HOBBES AND THE HISTORICAL DEVELOPMENT OF THE PHILOSOPHY OF PUNISHMENT

I have already referred to Cattaneo's view of Hobbes's theory of punishment, and it is worth considering it more fully. Cattaneo argues that of the three classical theories of punishment, the retributive, the corrective and the preventive, Hobbes rejects the first and accepts the other two:

He rejects the theory of retribution as an expression of one of the baser feelings, that of vainglory as the fruit of a desire for revenge... [H]e accepts the theory of correction and the theory of prevention - the former because 'correction of the offender' is one of the purposes of punishment; and (especially) the latter, since the principle end of punishment is 'that the will of men may thereby the better be disposed to obedience', i.e. to prevent crime.[49]

This account of Hobbes as anything but a retributivist rests upon a highly tendentious account of the nature of the retributive theory. It is true that Hobbes rejects revenge as a justification of punishment as a base emotion, but the classical retributivists did not found their theories upon revenge either. On the contrary, the formulations of Kant and Hegel are quite similar to that of Hobbes. Compare Hobbes's view:

by this Institution of a Common-wealth, every particular man is Author of all the Soveraigne doth; and consequently he that complaineth of injury from his Soveraigne, complaineth of that whereof he himself is Author....[50]

With Kant's:

To say, 'I will to be punished if I murder someone', can mean nothing more than, I submit myself along with everyone else to those laws which, if there are any criminals among the people, will naturally include penal laws.[51]

And Hegel's:

The injury [the penalty] which falls on the criminal is ... a right established within the criminal himself, i.e. in his objectively embodied will, in his action. The reason

---

[49] *Op.cit.*, pp.288-289.
[50] *Op.cit.*, p. 232.

for this is that ... by doing it the criminal has laid down a law which he has explicitly recognised in his action and under which he should be brought as under his right.[52]

It is because of Hobbes's contractualist framework that his work exhibits a retributivist tendency. At the root of the social contract lies the classical retributivist idea of the individual qualifying for punishment through his prior legislative act. For Hobbes the legislative act is one of agreement guided by reason, whereas for Kant and Hegel the actual existence of an agreement is unnecessary given man's nature as a rational being.[53] In all three cases, however, the individual establishes a law for himself, and his punishment for crime is his 'own act' returning to him. Hobbes, then, deserves the credit for establishing, through the social contract, the basis for the modern retributivist justification of punishment. The terms of the theory were to be developed by later writers such as Kant and Hegel but not essentially transformed. The idea of the individual's consent to the social contract is the historical foundation stone of modern retributivism.

Having established this point, however, we must not ignore the rest of Cattaneo's judgment, that Hobbes is a forerunner of the utilitarian school. The aim of punishment for Hobbes is so that 'the will of men may thereby the better be disposed to obedience',[54] and lies in the 'possibility of disposing the Delinquent, or (by his example) other men, to obey the Lawes....'[55] Nor are these comments logically aberrant. In keeping with the materialist side of his philosophy, Hobbes's discussion of punishment as a practice of the sovereign quite recognisably, and naturally, follows a very modern utilitarian logic. Thus in discussing the punishment of the innocent, Hobbes argues that all such punishments are against the Law of Nature which

forbiddeth all men, in their Revenges, to look to any things but some future good: For there can arrive no good to the Common-Wealth, by punishing the Innocent.[56]

But if punishment is concerned with the deterrence of all men and not just the criminal, as Hobbes recognises, then it does not follow that no

---

[51] I. Kant, *The Metaphysical Elements of Justice* (transl. J. Ladd) (Indianapolis,1965), p.105.

[52] G. Hegel, *The Philosophy of Right* (transl. T. Knox) (Oxford, 1952), p.70.

[53] The precise nature of Kant's theory of punishment, and the extent to which he based it upon the social contract is considered in the next chapter.

[54] *Op.cit.*, p.353.

[55] *Ibid.*, p.355.

[56] *Ibid.*, p.359-360.

good will follow the punishment of an innocent.   It is in principle possible that some would. This is exactly the 'spectacular *non sequitur*' of which Hart has accused Bentham in recent times.[57]

Whether aware of this problem or not, Hobbes proceeds in a manner reminiscent of many modern utilitarians, to qualify his position by the addition of distinct non-utilitarian principles - of gratitude[58] and equity. The principle of equity is close to Hart's concept of 'retribution in distribution'[59] for it commands 'an equal distribution of Justice; which in Punishing the Innocent is not observed.'[60]   Given the blanket utilitarian power of the Hobbesian sovereign to 'do whatever he shall think necessary to be done' and to 'use the strength and means of them all, as he shall think expedient',[61] only additional and discrepant principles of individual justice could check his power.

Thus Hobbes's position is a genuine hybrid, and the reason why his theory should appear now as retributive, now as utilitarian lies in his contradictory conception of human individuality.   On the one hand, Hobbes sees man as a free individual able to establish and consent to the institution of punishment. As a free juridical being, the individual can form the conceptual basis for a retributive theory of punishment. On the other hand, Hobbes portrays man as an individual determined by the passions. Consequently, from this point of view, it is natural to portray law in terms of its ability to determine behaviour by sanctions, as a utilitarian institution.   Historically, Hobbes straddles the later great divide in the philosophy of punishment. On the one hand, his theory is the forerunner of the German Idealist school of Kant and Hegel for whom the rational individual constituted the moral basis of political power. On the other hand, his theory foreshadows the utilitarianism of British philosophers such as Hume and Bentham who, while cracking open the contractual shell of the Hobbesian philosophy, extracted from it the kernel of his scientific materialism and naturalism.[62]   This is Hobbes's great historical significance: that he was the founding father of not one, but two of the great theories of punishment.

Finally, no mention has been made of the third theory of punishment, the theory of rehabilitation. Now that theory is a child of the late 19th

---

[57] H.L.A. Hart, *Punishment and Responsibility* (Oxford, 1968) p.19.

[58] *Op.cit.*, p.360.

[59] Hart, *op.cit.*, ch.1, and see below, ch.VI.

[60] *Op.cit.*, p.360

[61] *Ibid.*, pp.232-233, p.228.

[62] D. Hume, 'Of the Original Contract' in *Essays Literary, Moral and Political* (London, 1898).

and early 20th centuries, so it is implausible to suggest that Hobbes might have founded it as well. I will not attempt to do so here, although it is worth considering one passage in *Leviathan* both for its rehabilitative logic and in order to reflect upon Hobbes's individualism.

The passage I have in mind is one where Hobbes considers a potential objection to his account of the contract, that the common people lack the reason to become citizens by consent to a sovereign. Given that the social contract is presented by Hobbes as an agreement by all the people, one might expect him simply to reject this objection out of hand. But instead, he argues that the common people can become reasonable through education:

> [T]he Common Peoples minds, unless they be tainted with dependence on the Potent, or scribbled over with opinions of their Doctors, are like clean paper, fit to receive whatsoever by Publique Authority shall be imprinted in them... [S]hall not men be able, by their teaching, and preaching protected by the Law, to make that received which is so consonant to Reason, that any unprejudicated man, needs no more to learn it, than to hear it? I conclude therefore, that in the instruction of the people in the Essential Rights (which are the Naturall, and Fundamentall Lawes) of Sovereignty, there is no difficulty....[63]

Hobbes argues that the common people can grasp the principles of reason which justify sovereignty by means of teaching by the public authority (that is, the sovereign power). This means that the common people only become rational after the creation of sovereignty, and are therefore considered in this passage to be lacking in the reason that *leads to* the creation of the social contract and the Commonwealth. They lack the reason, in other words, required for a rational consent to the contract; their reason is not 'spontaneous' or self-established, it is taught to them by the public authority.

Hobbes is not discussing punishment - far less rehabilitation - in this passage. Nonetheless his nod in the direction of the pedagogic function of the state as a means of educating the common people into the responsibilities of citizenship prefigures the kinds of shift in social thought which led to movements such as those of the criminological positivists and rehabilitationists two centuries later. They too considered that the criminal classes could not be seen as spontaneously rational individuals capable of voluntary, unmediated assumption of the responsibilities of citizenship.

The connection between Hobbes and the rehabilitationists flows from the logic of their positions. The rehabilitative doctrine, like the view that individuals are determined by their natures, stands in opposition to any

---

[63] *Ibid.*, pp.378-379.

theory based upon juridical individualism. The need for rehabilitation implies that individuals are concretely determined by their social, biological or physiological characters, and that the freewill model of man is therefore an abstraction.[64] Hobbes's model of the individual consenting to the social contract is also based on such an abstraction. In his case, it is predominantly an abstraction from what he regards as man's nature as a passion-riven creature. But it is also an abstraction from social reality: the reality of a society divided between aristocracy and middle class, and also between these two and the mass of common people at the bottom of the social pile.[65] For Hobbes - as for the rehabilitationists - the gap between abstract juridical individualism and the reality of the common people is too great to ignore, but the admission that they are not inherently capable of being party to the social contract is a grave one for the logic of his theory.

5. CONCLUSION

We have seen that there is an essential contradiction in Hobbes's work between his scientific materialism and his juridical individualism, which derives from his establishment of the social contract upon the basis of his conception of man as a creature determined by his natural passions. There is a contradiction here between form and content, between the 'juridical superstructure' of his theory and its 'material base'.

In arguing this, I have explicitly sought to steer a middle course between the two interpretations of Hobbes's work that seek to render it in a consistent fashion. Jean Hampton is the latest author to attempt to impose an overall logic on his work, in her case by stressing its materialist side. The price of this however, is to see the objective moral side of his work as aberrant, mistaken, or, as Hampton puts it, as a 'cheat'.[66] Nor does such an approach allow one to ask seriously how

---

[64] See, for example, E. Ferri, *The Positive School of Criminology* (Chicago, 1901), for whom crime had natural and social causes 'which lie outside of that mathematical point called the free will of the criminal.' (p.81). See also below, ch.V.

[65] Cf. C.B. MacPherson, *op.cit.*, ch.2.

[66] *Op.cit.*, p.205.

other writers like Taylor and Warrender,[67] could read Hobbes in such a different moralistic fashion. Hampton's problem is to know what to do with the core of the moral-juridical element in Hobbes: the social contract. She is forced, because she follows the logic of his materialism, to reject it entirely. The social contract argument works, she says, only on the basis that it is misnamed, and misleadingly so.[68]

One can respect the internal logic of Hampton's account, but her rejection of the social contract throws into question its accuracy as a representation of Hobbes's argument. The result of denying the relevance of the contract is that Hampton can analogise sovereign power with gang leaders and other historically unpleasant power-brokers. This surely was not Hobbes's intention. There is enough in Hobbes alongside the materialist psychology to indicate that the kind of middle line of Strauss and Habermas, stressing the contradictory nature of his theory, more accurately captures its spirit. At the beginning of modern-classical Enlightenment thought, Hobbes sought to marry a materialist theory of human conduct with an ethical theory of the relationship between the individual and the state. It was through the moral-juridical doctrine of the social contract and the 'play' on the old idea of natural law that he did so. The two aspects of his theory were however in conflict with each other.

In terms of his theory of punishment, the contradiction between the 'juridical superstructure' and the 'material base' of the theory emerges in that on the one hand the social contract founds a right to punish, while on the other, man's nature dictates that no such right could be given. In the 'revised' version of his theory, this ambiguity is 'resolved' by allowing the sovereign the right to punish and the subject the right to resist. Yet this revision as we have seen either leads to a reversion to the state of nature, or is inadequate to escape the view that the individual has nonetheless consented to his punishment.

We have also explored the connections between his philosophical positions and the three main positions within the modern theory of punishment. As a theorist of juridical individualism, Hobbes is a retributivist, and therefore is able to justify punishing individuals because of their own prior commitment undertaken by free acts. The spectre that haunts this philosophy is the view that individuals are determined by their nature. Such a view is more consistent with a utilitarian theory of punishment, in which the state is regarded from the

---

[67] A.E. Taylor, 'The Ethical Doctrine of Hobbes' in K. Brown (ed.) *Hobbes Studies* (Oxford, 1965); H. Warrender, *The Political Philosophy of Hobbes* (Oxford, 1957).

[68] *Op.cit.*, p.279.

standpoint of its functions (to deter, to maintain good order by imposing fear and threatening pain). The problem is that to see the State and punishment in this light is to deny that individuals are the sorts of persons who could freely consent to the appointment of a sovereign.

This spectre haunting Hobbes's individualism assumes distinctly modern garb in his brief discussion of what was in the nineteenth century to become known as the 'social question': the problem of how to achieve individual consent to social order among the lower classes. Here, his view is, as indicated, more consistent with a rehabilitative standpoint on punishment. The significant point for us is that once again, his abstract individualism is undercut, this time by a somewhat rudimentary sociological determinism (in the shape of social education).

It was suggested in Chapter I that the modern ideal of criminal punishment is based upon the idea of treating individuals justly, with respect for their autonomy and responsibility. The retributive theory of punishment seeks to do this by establishing a conception of free individuals who permit the state to punish them when they do wrong. Hobbes, at the beginning of modern bourgeois society, adopted such a retributive standpoint through his conception of the individual, the social contract and the sovereign. But in the initial conception, there was a fundamental flaw, his view of persons as free individuals was undermined by his other view, that people are determined by their natures, or (potentially) by society. This is the flaw that we identified in Chapter I as the contradiction between abstract individualism and concrete individuality. The juridical element at the heart of the Hobbesian theory of punishment is at war with what he understood to be the natural springs of human behaviour. In Chapter I, I argued that the key to juridical ideology was its basis in the prevalence of market relations. It is then not surprising that at the beginning of market society, Hobbes should have represented the legitimacy of the state power to punish in the figure of a universal social contract.[69]

That flaw had the most serious implications for the logic of his theory of punishment, as we have seen. In leaving Hobbes now, and proceeding to the classical retributive thories of criminal justice, we may ask, was the flaw in his account of retributive justice no more than an infantile philosophical disorder to be discarded with maturity, or was it the mark of the fully grown person, persisting into full philosophical

---

[69] This argument supplements MacPherson's account of Hobbes's 'possessive individualism' (*op.cit.*, fn.37) as based upon the egoism of market relations. Those relations also gave rise, in a thoroughly contradictory fashion, to an abstract, disinterested moral-juridical individualism. The core of *Leviathan* is made up of the antithesis of these two ideological images of humankind.

adulthood?   Will   the   contradictions   between   abstract   juridical
individualism and concrete natural or social individuality be resolved by
later philosophers, or will they continue to dog the ideal of criminal
justice, and with what cost?   (*verfolgen*)

CHAPTER III

PURIFYING JURIDICAL INDIVIDUALISM:
KANTIAN RETRIBUTIVISM

1. INTRODUCTION

In analysing the Hobbesian philosophy of punishment, we observed a clash between a naturalistic account of man's nature as a passion-dominated creature and an ideal juridical account of political obligation which 'liberated' man from his natural self. But in Hobbes, man's material nature continues to contradict his other ideal juridical self, for the liberation is only superficial. The result is a philosophical eclecticism in which opposing views of man persistently cut across each other. The process of idealisation and abstraction necessary to create legal and political obligation via a social contract does not expunge man's natural being, and so must face it at every turn. In Hobbes, the *form* of the justification of punishment is locked in conflict with the *content* of human nature. My argument in this chapter will be that the process of idealisation and abstraction begun by Hobbes and at the root of his proto-retributivism is maintained and developed by Kant in a more sophisticated fashion. With regard to the philosophy of punishment, this means that the retributive element in the Kantian theory assumes a predominant role. At the same time, however, because the idealisation process remains one of abstraction from man's material nature (which does not go away), utilitarian concepts retain a role in Kant's overall conception, but not his justification[1], of punishment. I shall also argue

---

[1] Both Kant and Hegel recognised that punishment could have effects upon individual and collective behaviour which were useful, but which were nothing to do with the justification of punishment. They could therefore recognise the need for an understanding of how punishment worked in practice, even although they themselves were concerned with the different question of its justification. This

that because the fundamental dichotomy between the ideal/abstract and the material/natural is not transcended by Kant, only more effectively suppressed, it does not go away. On the contrary, it ultimately returns to haunt his retributive justification of punishment. At root the problem remains one of contradiction between abstract individualism and the perceived realities of material human nature.

Any interpretation of Kant's philosophy must take into account two fundamental features of his position. First, it must recognise his insistence that criminal desert is a moral absolute, sufficient in itself to justify punishment in general as well as the distribution of punishment among individuals. For Kant, punishment is only justified because the individual has committed a crime. Even although punishment may have good consequences, these have nothing to do with the *justification* of punishment:

Judicial punishment can never be used merely as a means to promote some other good for the criminal himself or for civil society, but instead it must in all cases be imposed on him only on the ground that he has committed a crime; for a human being can never be manipulated merely as a means to the purposes of someone else.... He must first be found to be deserving of punishment before any consideration is given to the utility of this punishment for himself or for his fellow citizens.[2]

Thus punishment may have value from a utilitarian point of view, but guilt is both the necessary and sufficient justification for its award in all cases. There is no starker illustration of this principle than Kant's example of the dissolving island society. If such a society were on the point of breaking up and dispersing around the world, the execution of the last murderer would still be a moral necessity 'so that everyone will receive what his actions are worth and so that the bloodguilt thereof will not be fixed on the people because they failed to insist on carrying out the punishment.'[3]

The second principal element in Kant's position concerns the equal distribution of punishment according to the *jus talionis*. It is interesting

---

is the significance of the famous passage (below, at fn.2) in which Kant does not reject utilitarian effects of punishment but insists that punishment must first be deserved in the individual case. In what follows, I have used the modern translation by John Ladd: I. Kant, *The Metaphysical Elements of Justice* (New York, 1965). The implications of George Fletcher's recent criticisms of the Ladd translation ((1987) *Columbia Law Review* 87, p.429) are not clear. Because of this and given that it remains the most accessible rendition, I have stuck with Ladd. In general, I refer to the work hereafter by its initials.

[2] *Op.cit.*, p.100.
[3] *Ibid.*, p.102.

to note here the way in which Kant has developed retributivism from the position taken by Hobbes.   For him, the amount of punishment was established by means of a separate principle of equity.   For Kant, the same principle (described as the 'principle of equality..., of not treating one side more favourably than the other'[4]) is an inherent principle of the retributive philosophy of punishment itself.   The concept of 'just deserts' already presupposes a just amount of punishment since 'Only the Law of retribution (*jus talionis*) can determine exactly the kind and degree of punishment.'[5]   Precisely why this should be the case remains to be seen, but it is worth noting that at least one modern writer, Aune (who is in general correct in identifying the source of Kant's retributivism if not its true significance), finds the philosophical rationale for the *jus talionis* to be 'highly uncertain and conjectural'.[6]

Turning to the modern commentators, there is a disagreement as to how one is to locate Kant's retributivism within his general moral theory. None would deny that it must be seen within that overall context. Murphy, for example, argues that the right to punish cannot be seen as a 'moral primitive' but must on the contrary be regarded 'as a kind of theorem' within his moral system.[7]   But disagreement exists as to whether that theorem is to be understood within a doctrine of hypothetical contract or within Kant's discussion of justice and coercion in the *M.E.J.*   Murphy and Williams both agree that the hypothetical social contract is the basis for Kant's retributivism.   Thus Murphy suggests that Kant 'offers a theory of punishment that is based on his general view that political obligation is to be analysed, quasi-contractually, in terms of reciprocity.'[8]   Williams writes in similar vein that the 'possibility of coercion is built in to the social contract', which is

---

4   *Ibid.*, p.101.

5   *Ibid.*

6   B. Aune, *Kant's Theory of Morals* (Princeton, 1979), p.169.

7   J. Murphy, *Retribution Justice and Therapy* (Dordrecht, 1979), p.100.

8   *Ibid.*   In 'Does Kant Have a Theory of Punishment?' (1987) *Columbia Law Review* 87, p.509, Murphy partially recants his interpretation of Kant in the Rawlsian manner, stating that it does not properly square with the texts (p.523). But when he seeks to explain Kant's position, he falls back on it (pp.521, 528-529), while acknowledging its failure to generate anything other than a hypothetical, not categorical, imperative (p.521).   Not surprisingly, given this ambivalence, Murphy now doubts whether Kant had a theory of punishment. Murphy is right to identify the contradictions he does in Kant, but these should be the starting point for understanding the theory, not a reason for discarding it. For the important differences between Rawls and Kant, see A. Levine, 'Rawls' Kantianism', *Social Theory and Practice* (1974) 3, pp.47-63.

a 'moral fiction' underlying the constitution of civil society.[9]   While it is true that Kant regards the social contract as an 'Idea of reason'[10] and that he discusses punishment in one place in terms of the submission of individuals as co-legislators in the penal law to that law,[11] it is also true that there is little other support in his work for this interpretation. Aune is correct to describe it as largely conjectural.   Furthermore, and more importantly, it is a dubious interpretation on philosophical grounds. Murphy suggests that the Kantian theory is to be understood in terms of costs and benefits.   The cost of enjoying the benefit of a legal system is that the individual must obey the law.   The individual expects this of others, so it is only fair that he should himself comply.   The person who does not obey the law gains an unfair advantage, accordingly criminal punishment redresses the imbalance in gains and losses by ensuring that there is no profit in wrongdoing.   Punishment is connected with a balance between costs and benefits, ensuring that they are evenly shared out in the community.[12] But talk of costs and benefits immediately suggests a connection with utilitarianism, and as we have seen, all discussions of the 'theory of happiness'[13] are rigorously disconnected by Kant from the justification of punishment.   Murphy's response to this objection is that it is not costs and benefits *per se* which are relevant, but their *balance*, which must be fair and just.[14]   Certainly a discussion of the justice of punishment is completely in line with Kant's thinking, but Murphy has attached that concept to a utilitarian analysis of costs and benefits.   He has not sought a *moral* basis for Kant's discussion of fairness or justice in punishment, so that either his discussion is tied to an essentially utilitarian schema, or, if he detaches justice and fairness from the cost-benefit conception, he is left with the kind of moral primitive he himself wished to avoid.

    There is also a second philosophical ground for rejecting the quasi-contractual interpretation.   The *Metaphysical Elements of Justice* constitute Part I of the *Metaphysics of Morals* and must be read in the light of the overall work.   Similarly, within the *M.E.J.*, there is a

---

[9]   H. Williams, *Kant's Political Philosophy* (Oxford, 1983), p.97.

[10] Kant, *op.cit.*, p.80 and see Translator's Introduction, p.xxvii.

[11] *Ibid.*, p.105.

[12] *Op.cit.*, p.83. See also R. Plant, 'Justice, Punishment and the State' in A. Bottoms and R. Preston, *The Coming Penal Crisis* (Edinburgh, 1980) for a similar position.

[13] Kant, *Op.cit.*, p.100. Murphy now implicitly concedes as much in his acknowledgement that the Rawlsian influenced interpretation generates only a hypothetical imperative to punish (above, fn.8)

[14] *Op.cit.*, p.84.

distinction which Kant draws between the 'pure' and the 'applied' elements in his philosophy of right. The concept of justice, for example, 'is a pure concept which at the same time also takes practice (i.e. the application of the concept to particular cases presented in experience) into consideration.'[15]   Kant's views on the right to punish are located within an overall discussion of the nature of the sovereign's rights within public law.   Punishment, accordingly, is not a pure concept, but is one in which 'the application of the concept to particular cases presented in experience' is considered. Accordingly it is necessary to examine Kant's philosophy of punishment within the overall context of the philosophy of right, and also, within the general context of the *Metaphysics of Morals* (in particular, the *Introduction* to the overall work).   The quasi-contractual interpretation has regard to neither of those broader contexts for the simple reason that the hypothetical contract plays very little part in them. If however we take seriously this overall context, we will see that there is in both the Introduction to the *Metaphysics of Morals* and the Introduction to the *M.E.J.* a very obvious (if not necessarily very clear) line of argument which establishes a right to punish quite separately from the idea of the social contract.

This brings me to the second interpretation of the nature of the Kantian system within which the right to punish is to be placed.   Aune argues that punishment is to be understood in accordance with the doctrine, expressed in the Introduction to the *M.E.J.*, that 'justice is united with the authorisation to use coercion.'[16]   In a succinct but complex passage, Kant argues as follows: justice concerns the compatibility of the freedom of one individual with other individuals according to universal laws. Coercion is defined as the hindrance of the freedom of an individual. He who coerces the will of another individual who is acting justly, i.e. compatibly with freedom according to universal laws, acts unjustly. State coercion is the hindrance of the freedom of an individual who has hindered the freedom of another individual unjustly. By a double negation, the hindrance of the hindrance of freedom, state coercion restores a balance of freedom and is therefore just. We shall

---

[15] *Op.cit.* p.3.

[16] *Ibid.*, p.35. Murphy mentions the doctrine of just coercion (*op.cit.*, p.97) only three pages before he argues for the quasi-contractual analysis, but does not attempt to link the two, presumably because of the Rawlsian influence. More puzzlingly, Williams correctly notes in his discussion of justice that 'the initial lawless act suspends the individual's freedom' and the punishment is allowed 'because it counteracts the hindrance of an effect'(*op.cit.*, p.70). Yet he does not carry this insight over into his discussion of punishment itself, two chapters later.

return to an explanation of this difficult argument in the next section, but
here is Kant's own statement of the justification of coercion:

> Any opposition that counteracts the hindrance of an effect promotes that effect and
> is consistent with it. Now, everything that is unjust is a hindrance to freedom
> according to universal laws. Coercion, however, is a hindrance or opposition to
> freedom. Consequently, if a certain use of freedom is itself a hindrance according
> to universal laws (that is, is unjust), then the use of coercion to counteract it,
> *inasmuch as it is the prevention of a hindrance to freedom,* is consistent with
> freedom according to universal laws; in other words, this use of coercion is just. It
> follows by the law of contradiction that justice [a right] is united with the
> authorisation to use coercion against anyone who violates justice [or a right].[17]

Nein!   I agree with Aune that this is the crucial passage for understanding
Kant's philosophy of punishment, but I cannot agree with his
interpretation of it.   Aune focusses on the qualifier (that I have
emphasised) that coercion is justified 'inasmuch as it is the prevention of
a hindrance of freedom', and points out that punishment typically cannot
prevent the hindrance of freedom that is crime because it normally
follows the crime in temporal sequence. It is rarely that punishment can
intervene during a crime, and it is impossible to prevent a crime that has
already occurred.   Thus interpreted, Kant's philosophy is severely
deficient as a justification of punishment.

   I do not agree that Kant is to be understood in the way that Aune
suggests. In effect, Aune is treating his philosophy as a covert form of
utilitarianism since he sees punishment as being a means of practically
preventing actual crimes.   That this is so becomes apparent when we
consider Aune's 'solution' to Kant's 'deficiency'. He suggests that while
punishment cannot prevent the crime for which it is given, it can
indirectly prevent other crimes by deterring future offenders.   Being
punished for a criminal offence has, he argues, a coercive effect on the
wills of citizens.   It inhibits the unjust acts they might otherwise
perform.   Punishments do not inhibit the crimes for which they are
given, but they do 'hinder, interfere with, or more exactly, deter potential
offences'.[18]

   Precisely how one squares such a utilitarian interpretation with Kant's
absolute refusal to consider the practical effects of punishment prior to
the establishment of guilt as punishment's necessary and sufficient
condition is hard to see.   In the island society example, how could
Nicht ganz   punishment deter potential future offences when there are to be no
erlaubt.   potential offenders available to commit them?

---

[17] *Ibid.*, pp.35-36 emphasis added.
[18] Aune, *op.cit.* p.164.

Thus, while Aune is correct to focus upon Kant's discussion of justified coercion, we must give that doctrine an interpretation that is compatible with the absolute retributivism displayed in his discussion of punishment. Finally, I have already noted that, for Aune, the *jus talionis* doctrine's connection to the justification of coercion is obscure, and so it will be necessary to examine the interrelationship between the two positions.

2. THE METAPHYSICAL BASIS OF PUNISHMENT

The essence of Kant's justification of coercion is this[19]: if a certain use of freedom is contrary to freedom according to universal laws, then coercion as a hindrance of freedom is justified in so far as it counteracts the initial use (abuse) of freedom. The key to understanding Kant's metaphysical justification of coercion is an understanding of the two concepts of freedom which are implicit in this position. On the one hand there is a 'certain use of freedom', on the other, there is 'freedom according to universal laws'. The two concepts of freedom contained in these standpoints underlie Kant's conceptions of the will, law, justice and coercion which are all parts of the philosophical progression which eventually leads to the justification of punishment.

(1)   Two Concepts of Will and Freedom   (schwach)

In the Introduction to the *Metaphysics of Morals*, Kant distinguishes between will which is morally legislative and will which is naturally determined. The latter he terms *Willkur* (will), the former *der Wille* (Will). *Willkur* relates to the 'faculty of desiring in accordance with concepts...of doing or forbearing as one likes' combined with 'the consciousness of the capacity of its action to produce its object'[20] The faculty of desiring in turn is concerned with the pursuit of material, practical pleasures which determine will to action. *Der Wille* on the

---

[19] I paraphrase the passage quoted above at fn.17.
[20] *Op.cit.*, p.12.

other hand is self-determining because it has as its 'internal ground of determination' not practical pleasure but practical reason: the reason of the subject himself as a rational being.[21]   Because *Willkur* is determined by natural causes, it cannot be morally free, whereas *der Wille* can be free both *negatively* in so far as the rational will divorces itself from external causes and *positively* in so far as it subjects itself to the moral law:

A will that can be determined by pure reason is called free will. A will that is determined only by inclination (sensible impulse, *stimulus*) would be animal will (*arbitrium brutum*). Human will, on the other hand, is the kind of will that is affected but not determined by impulses. Accordingly, in itself (apart from an acquired facility with reason), it is not pure; but it can nevertheless be determined to actions by pure Will. Freedom of will is just the aforementioned independence from determination by sensible impulses; this is the negative concept of freedom. The positive concept of freedom is that of the capacity of pure reason to be of itself practical. Now, this is possible only through the subjection of the maxim of every action to the condition of its fitness to be a universal law.[22]

To be positively free is to follow the commands of the rational universal law, the categorical imperative, which is expressed by Kant in the *M.E.J.* in the following form: 'act according to a maxim that can at the same time be valid as a universal law.'[23] The morally free will is the will that follows this imperative; the morally unfree will is subject to imperatives derived from its nature of a hypothetical and only conditional variety.[24]

Now this seems a fairly clear position to adopt. *Der Wille* and *Willkur* are contrasted in black-and-white terms so that the former, the free will is understood to exist by means of an opposition to the unfree causally determined *Willkur*. *Willkur* cannot be free because it is subject to 'determination by causes in the sensible world' and is therefore 'infallibly determined in accordance with the laws of nature'.[25]   Yet it is important to note that Kant does not always stick to these positions for there is, he says, both a sense in which *der Wille* cannot be said to be

---

[21] These positions are developed by Kant in chapter 3 of his *Groundwork of the Metaphysics of Morals*. I have used H. Paton's translation: *The Moral Law* (London, 1948), and also referred to his *The Categorical Imperative* (London, 1953), chs. XX, XXVI, along with L. Beck, *A Commentary on Kant's Critique of Practical Reason* (Chicago, 1960) ch.XI. I have also found helpful S. Korner, *Kant* (Harmondsworth, 1955), ch.7; R. Walker, *Kant* (London 1978), ch.X; and H. Williams, *op.cit.*, ch.3.

[22] *M.E.J.*, p.13.

[23] *Op.cit.*, p.26.

[24] *Ibid.*, pp.22-23.

[25] *The Moral Law*, p.115.

free and in which *Willkur* can be said to be free.[26]   We must be clear as to what he means by this, for, particularly, the question of the sense in which *Willkur* can be said to be free is important for our purposes.

But first, *der Wille*.   While *der Wille* is the morally free will, there is a sense in which it cannot be said to be free at all.   It cannot be said to be free in that as a rational will, it must be absolutely compelling for rational beings.   It relates not to a free choice of actions but 'immediately to legislation for the maxims of action (and is therefore practical reason itself).'[27]   It is rather confusing for Kant to make this point, but we can understand what he means not as a contradiction of his earlier statements on the freedom of *der Wille* but rather as a different way of looking at the matter.   From the point of view of the moral necessity of the rational law for a rational being *der Wille* is compelled and compelling.   But from the point of view of a contrast between *der Wille* and *Willkur*, only *der Wille* is free for it is unaffected by extraneous determinations.   As Beck puts it, it remains 'free in that its decree follows from its own nature',[28] regardless of whether that nature is compelling or not.   *Der Wille* is autonomous, and in that lies its freedom.

Second, in what sense can *Willkur* be said to be free if it is determined by natural causes?   *Willkur* is not morally free but it can be taken to be free in a 'psychological' or 'comparative' way. By this, Kant means the sort of liberty of spontaneity recognised by Hobbes and Hume to direct one's actions according to one's desires, regardless of the source of those desires.[29]   From a moral point of view, such freedom is insignificant, and this is part of Kant's disagreement with moral philosophers who adopt an empiricist approach to their subject.[30]   But,

---

[26] E.g., *M.E.J.*, p.27: 'Laws proceed from the Will; maxims, from the will. In man, the will is free. The Will, which relates to nothing but the law, cannot be called either free or unfree....   Only will can, therefore, be called free.'

[27] *M.E.J.*, p.27.

[28] *Op.cit.*, p.180.

[29] Paton, *op.cit.*, p.210; Beck, *op.cit.*, p.190. For a concise definition of the two conceptions of freedom - liberty of spontaneity and liberty of indifference - see A.Kenny, *Freewill and Responsibility,* (London, 1978), pp.25-26.

[30] Beck, *op.cit.*, p.190. Kant's position on the nature of *Willkur* is slightly more complex than that suggested in the quote above from the *M.E.J.* for he discussed it elsewhere under the title of *arbitrium liberum* in addition to *arbitrium brutum.* By the former Kant meant the ability of men to rise above immediate sensible impulses in order to comprehend their long-term interests. Such a position was also recognised by Hume and did not entail any shift away from the deterministic conception of *Willkur* since *arbitrium liberum* still falls 'under the head of 'natural necessity" (Paton, *op.cit.*, p.210).

nonetheless, there is a non-moral sense in which one can say that an individual's acts within the mechanism of nature are free.

This sense in which *Willkur* can be said to be free is important for Kant's discussion of law and justice (which he regards as a juridical concept), for all juridical concepts are concerned not with individuals as morally free beings but with individuals in their relations with other individuals within the sensible, phenomenal world. Justice, for example, is concerned with 'the external and... practical relationship of one person to another in which their actions can in fact exert an influence on each other (directly or indirectly)'.[31]   It concerns 'only the form of the relationship between the wills insofar as they are regarded as free'[32] and freedom in this sense means 'independence from the constraints of another's will'.[33]   So it is important that law regulates the behaviour of free individuals in the sense of their exercising *Willkur*, i.e. psychological or comparative, not moral, freedom.

To sum up, Kant provides us with two concepts of will, and two concepts of freedom. On the one hand, *Willkur* is unfree in a moral sense but may be regarded as possessing a sort of freedom which is compatible with natural necessity.   *Willkur* possesses liberty of spontaneity. The freedom of the individual in this sense 'is still only the freedom of a well-run machine like a clock'[34] but this is the kind of freedom available to men in the sensible, phenomenal world.   It is the freedom of the man whom Kant calls *homo phaenomenon*.[35]

Der Wille on the other hand is self-governing and possesses freedom of indifference, i.e., it is 'a power to produce effects without being determined - or caused - to do so by anything other than itself'.[36]   In the sensible world man is determined, in the rational (intelligible) world, man - *homo noumenon* - is free.   It should be noted that these latter concepts of will and freedom are obtained *by negation of* the concept of *Willkur* and its freedom. *Der Wille* is only free because it has detached itself from the sensible world, and consequently the two kinds of freedom are in their concepts mutually contradictory.   One cannot be free to choose rational actions if one is at the same time free in the sense of being able to follow one's determined choices.

---

[31] *M.E.J.*, p.34.
[32] *Ibid.*
[33] *Ibid.*, p.43.
[34] Beck, *op.cit.*, p.196.
[35] *M.E.J.*, p.105.
[36] Paton, *op.cit.*, p.209.

(2)   Law and Justice

It is in fact an over-simplification to say that law is only concerned with the regulation of interests in the sensible world, for Kant regards law as being in a sense at the intersection of man's rationality and his nature.[37] As regards man's nature, we have already seen that justice concerns the external relations between individuals, not their internal moral relation. For this reason, juridical concepts do not appeal to an internal moral duty in order to secure obedience, but seek simply to achieve external behavioural conformity to the law regardless of the internal perspective of the individual. They rest satisfied with securing the legality of men's actions, recognising that an immoral man may still act within the law. Because of this, juridical laws employ sanctions ('external incentives'[38]) to secure obedience. These affect man's material nature by encouraging good and deterring bad behaviour:

As regards juridical legislation it is easily seen that the incentive here, being different from the Idea of duty, must be derived from the pathological grounds determining will, that is, from inclinations and disinclinations and, among these, specifically from disinclinations, since it is supposed to be the kind of legislation that constrains, not an allurement that invites.[39]

But juridical legislation, as well as being directed at men in the sensible world, is at the same time morally legitimate because such legislation stems from moral laws. Juridical laws are *also* a sub-group of moral laws, only differing from ethical duties in terms of the way in which they secure obedience. The difference between the juridical and the ethical is one of *form* not substance. Thus, Kant can write that insofar as moral laws 'are directed to mere external actions and their legality, they are called juridical'[40]; and even where juridical laws cover matters which are

[37] I disagree with George Fletcher's argument that Kant's moral and legal theory are distinct and non-intersectional ('Law and Morality: a Kantian Perspective' (1987) *Columbia Law Review* 87, 533). They are different, but should be seen as interconnected elements in a single philosophical project. Fletcher's approach cannot explain Kant's theory of punishment which, he recognises, embraces both the juridical element and the categorical imperative (*ibid.*, pp.551-2). Kant's theory can only be understood in the context of the dualisms at the heart of his discussions of freedom, law and morality. In that light, the interconnection between legal punishment and moral command is understandable, even if the end product is a contradictory theory.

[38] See discussion in *M.E.J.*, pp.18-20.

[39] *Ibid.*, p.19. Here we see clearly the scope for utilitarian considerations, in Kant's general conception of law and punishments.

[40] *Ibid.*, p.13.

not already legislated for by the moral law, Kant stipulates the requirement of a mediating moral link through the moral title of the sovereign:

it is possible to conceive of an external legislation which contains only positive laws..., [but] it would have to be preceded by a natural (i.e. moral - A.N.] law providing the ground of the authority of the legislator (that is, his authorisation to obligate others through his mere will).[41]

In summary, while juridical laws have their effect on men through their nature as sentient beings subject to external causes, their metaphysical justification is derived from the moral law which is a law of man's reason and freedom.   Juridical laws affect *Willkur* but stem from *der Wille*.

This basic position is applied by Kant to the juridical concept of justice. We have already seen that justice concerns the external relations of freedom between individuals, and it is defined in such a way as to render compatible the individual freedom of each with all others. But onto this standard liberal conception of justice Kant imposes the moral formula that individual freedoms must also be compatible in accordance with universal law:

Justice is therefore the aggregate of those conditions under which the will of one person can be conjoined with the will of another *in accordance with a universal law of freedom*.[42]

Justice concerns the freedom of phenomenal men, but is incorporated within Kantian metaphysics by means of a modified formulation of the categorical imperative:

Every action is just [right] that in itself or in its maxim is such that the freedom of the will can coexist together with the freedom of everyone in accordance with a universal law.[43]

(3)   Coercion and Punishment

It is from this definition of justice that the passage that we quoted at the end of the last section concerning coercion is derived, for, as Kant says,

---

[41] *Ibid.*, p.26.
[42] *Ibid.*, p.34, emphasis added.
[43] *Ibid.*, p.35.

justice is united with the authorisation to use coercion. Kant's reasoning is that, given his definition of justice (above), an unjust act is one which opposes or hinders any act which is compatible with universal freedom. Such an unjust act is itself incompatible with universal freedom since it is a hindrance of freedom according to universal laws. Now, coercion is in general a hindrance of the freedom of the individual who is coerced, so in so far as one hindrance of freedom can counteract another hindrance of freedom, the coercion which follows an unjust act is consistent with freedom according to universal laws. Coercion is in general unjust because it is a hindrance of freedom, but *state* coercion following on an unjust hindrance of freedom is just, for it is a hindrance of a hindrance of freedom, which is consistent with universal freedom.

The discussion returns us now to Aune's objection to the qualifier that coercion is just 'inasmuch as it is the prevention of a hindrance of freedom'. What on earth does Kant mean? Clearly, if he means that punishment can actually *prevent* the crime for which it is given, his justification is inadequate. The answer to this question must bear in mind the dualistic nature of his position.

Coercion must be seen in both its aspects: as a concrete negation of phenomenal freedom *and* as a metaphysical affirmation of moral freedom. While coercion cannot prevent individual abuses of the law which have already occurred in the sensible world, it can quite readily be understood to operate at a metaphysical level as an ideal 'hindrance of a hindrance'. While *the operation* of coercion in the natural world in accordance with justice requires 'no determining grounds of the will besides those that are purely external',[44] it remains, on the metaphysical plane, 'compatible with the freedom of everyone in accordance with universal laws.'[45] For this reason, the prosaic, material fact of coercion can at the same time be rationally exhibited as 'a pure a priori intuition'[46] under the 'law of contradiction',[47] that is, the 'law of equality of action and reaction'.[48] If we understand punishment to be justified in this way, then the qualifier raised by Kant and objected to by Aune ceases to be an obstacle. For coercion may hinder a hindrance of freedom in a

---

[44] *Ibid.*, p.36.
[45] *Ibid.*, p.37.
[46] *Ibid.*
[47] *Ibid.*, p.36.
[48] *Ibid.*, p.37.

metaphysical sense regardless of the impossibility of its doing any such thing in a practical, phenomenal sense.[49]

To elucidate this argument, it may be helpful to anticipate the discussion of Hegel in the next chapter. In Hegel's retributivism, the 'hindrance of the hindrance' becomes the 'negation of the negation'[50] in which punishment 'annuls'[51] crime. Now in relation to this doctrine, it would be a grave mistake to think that these ideas were to be regarded as anything other than rational constructions of a social reality or that one could conceive of 'annulment' in any literal or practical sense.[52] Certainly there is no indication that Hegel thought in such terms, indeed quite the contrary. Thus Kant's retributivism should and can be seen as a forerunner of Hegel's and his justification of coercion should be read as an abstract and ideal justification even although, as a juridical concept, its *application* is directed to man in his external phenomenal existence. Coercion, like law and justice, is aimed at *Willkur*, but is justified by *der Wille*.

We may now conclude this section by considering the way in which Kant's discussion of coercion in the Introduction of the *M.E.J.* ties in with his better known discussion of punishment in the section on Public Law.   He begins by stating, apparently in the manner of legal positivism, that the right to punish 'is the right that the magistrate has to inflict pain on a subject in consequence of his having committed a crime'.[53]   But he then adds that the commission of a crime deserves punishment because of the criminal's 'innate personality [that is, his right as a person]'.[54]   Now for Kant the only innate right of personality is derived from the concept of justice and is accordingly defined as the

---

[49] Ladd's translation may be misleading here since 'inasmuch as it is the prevention of a hinderance to freedom' perhaps suggests a more practical than metaphysical meaning. The original German reads: '*als Verhinderung eines Hindernesses der Freiheit*'. Als is normally translated as 'as' and Verhinderung can mean 'hindrance', 'obstacle' or 'impediment' in addition to the more practical 'prevention'. Thus the passage can be rendered more metaphysically as 'as being the hindering of a hindrance of freedom'. This is the translation given by W. Hastie in *The Philosophy of Law* (Edinburgh, 1887), p.47. The German is from volume 6 of Kant's *Werke* (Konigliche Preussische Akademie edition) p.231.

[50] G. Hegel, *The Philosophy of Right* (transl. T.M.Knox) (Oxford, 1952), p.246.

[51] *Ibid.*, p.67

[52] Not that this has stopped 20th century 'ordinary language' philosophers from wrenching Hegel's meaning from its context. See, e.g. A. Quinton, 'On Punishment' in H. Acton, *The Philosophy of Punishment* (London, 1969). See chapter IV below.

[53] *M.E.J.*, p.99.

[54] *Ibid.*, p.100

right to individual freedom 'insofar as it is compatible with the freedom of everyone else in accordance with a universal law.'[55]   Thus the right of innate moral personality is derived from the concept of justice and justice is logically united with the right of coercion.   Therefore the right of innate moral personality implies the right to a just punishment.

This position is elaborated and confirmed when Kant discusses the interrelation of *Willkur* and *der Wille* in the penal law.   As a noumenal being man recognises punishment as a rational consequence of his crime, but directed at his phenomenal being:

When...I enact a penal law against myself as a criminal it is the pure juridical legislative reason (*homo noumenon*) in me that submits myself to the penal law as a person capable of committing a crime, that is, as another person (*homo phaenomenon*) along with all the others in the civil union who submit themselves to this law.[56]

Finally, there is the *jus talionis*.   Aune argues that Kant did not 'offer an explicit defence for his principle'[57] but suggests that it can be gleaned with some difficulty from the justification of coercion in terms of a balancing out of the freedom of the criminal with that of the victim.   I agree with Aune that this is the source and nature of the justification of the *jus talionis* but it is much more clearly derivable than he supposes.

The doctrine of the unity of justice and coercion is represented by Kant as one of reciprocity[58] and he argues that it can be regarded *a priori* as based on the Idea of an equality of action and reaction.   Now, reciprocity entails returning like for like, and the coercive reaction could only be regarded as equal to the criminal action if the measure of coercion is somehow equal to the measure of the wrong done. Otherwise, any hindrance of freedom above and beyond that needed to match the initial hindrance of freedom would be unjust in itself.

This interpretation is confirmed in the section on punishment when Kant describes the *jus talionis* as 'the only principle of penal law that accords with the form stipulated a priori by the Idea'[59] and explains this in terms of a version of the categorical imperative.   He who steals acts on a non-universalisable maxim and thereby makes the property of everyone else insecure, including himself.   Thus 'any undeserved evil that you inflict on someone else among the people is one that you do to

---

[55] *Ibid.*, pp.44-45.
[56] *Ibid.*, p.105.
[57] *Op.cit.*, p.169.
[58] *M.E.J.*, p.36.
[59] *Ibid.*, p.132.

yourself.'[60]   It requires to be returned to you in equivalent form on 'the
principle of not treating one side more favourably than the other.'[61]   Just
punishment under the moral law, in other words, requires that
individuals be done to equally as they have done to others so as to hinder
their freedom to the extent that, but *only* to the extent that, they have
hindered others.   These ideas are integral to the law of the categorical
imperative and the pure *a priori* concept of coercion.   They have little to
do with the neo-contractarian schemes of modern commentators.   They
find their practical expression in the *jus talionis* alone:

> All other standards fluctuate back and forth and, because extraneous considerations
> are mixed with them, they cannot be compatible with the principle of pure and strict
> justice.[62]

3. 'A THEORY BUILT ON TENSION'

Kant's aim and achievement was an ideal metaphysical justification of
punishment which escaped the consequences of moral empiricism. The
natural empirical world is a negative point of demarcation for the
positive freedom embodied in the rational law, and law, coercion and
punishment are justified in accordance with the law of reason, the
categorical imperative.   Law may deal with the empirical world, and, in
accordance with the determined nature of that world, may seek to
influence individual actions, but as a morally necessary institution, it is a
pure concept derived *a priori* from reason.   Law aims to affect the
sensible will (*Willkur*) but is justified in terms of the rational will (*der
Wille*).   Noumenal, responsible individuals legislate for their own
punishment which they require as causally determined phenomenal
beings.
   There is an element of schizophrenia in this.   Are individuals
responsible and free, or are they determined?   Can they be both at the
same time?   If my crimes are the product of causally determined
circumstances can I be held responsible for them as a rational being?   If

---

[60] *Ibid.*, p.101.
[61] *Ibid.*
[62] *Ibid.*

laws are justified by the legislative will in man, which is always present in man, why does he ever commit crimes and need punished? Is Kant trying to have it both ways? Murphy expresses, albeit from his own standpoint, the problem in terms of a tension within Kant's theory:

On the one hand, it is a theory which respects human dignity, regards human beings as responsible agents and not merely as things or resources to be manipulated for the social good. On the other hand, it tends perhaps to encourage blindness to the way thing really are and to give rise to smugness and self-righteousness. It is a theory built on tension - tension between justice and utility, tension between ideal states and actual states, tension between righteousness and humility.[63]

The tension in question can be most clearly and generally expressed as one between ideal and actual states. In this section I will consider its manifestation in two well known problem areas for the Kantian theory.

(1)   The Gap between Theory and Practice[64]

In the Introduction to the *M.E.J.*, Kant considers a right (that he says is sometimes imagined to exist by lawyers) which 'is supposed to give me permission to take the life of another person when my own life is in danger, even if he has done me no harm.' No such right exists, although the circumstances of the crime must be taken into account in the determinations of the court, so that necessity is 'not to be understood objectively according to what a law might prescribe, but merely subjectively, as the sentence might be proposed in a court of law.' The law of murder remains the objective moral/juridical law, but the subjective position of the accused must be taken into account, for although his violence 'is not inculpable..., it still is unpunishable.' 'Subjective immunity from punishment' must however not be confused with 'objective (legal) immunity.' There are two possible ways in which one can take this argument.
    The first is given by Kant but is inconsistent with his overall position; the second can be fairly taken from what he says by implication, but opens up an interesting gap in his philosophy. Kant argues that the reason for not punishing the act done under necessity is that no punishment could effectively deter it for 'the threat of an evil that is still

---

[63] *Op.cit.*, p.90.
[64] See Murphy, *op.cit.*, p.86.

uncertain...cannot outweigh the fear of an evil that is certain.'[65]   Clearly this argument will not do for it abandons the basic principle of his philosophy that guilt is *the* necessary and sufficient condition for punishment in all cases.   No considerations of utility either for the individual or anyone else may be taken into account until guilt has been established.

The second possibility stems from the modern notion of an 'excusing condition'[66] which allows for mitigation of sentence even although a crime has been committed. Here one would say that although culpability existed, the circumstances in which the crime occurred were such as to diminish or excuse punishment. Kant points to the absolute nature of the threat to life in a situation of necessity, and although he does so in order to explain the uselessness of punishment, we might think it more consistent with his theory for him to see the individual as being, if not blameless, of diminished responsibility because of his circumstances. A situation like necessity drives a wedge between what is objectively right in a court of law and the subjective perception by the court of the circumstances of the crime.

If this second interpretation is plausible, it raises a problem within the terms of Kant's philosophy. His dualism allows either that man is determined by circumstances in the mechanism of nature or that man is rational and free; or rather, that man is both determined and free at the same time but from different standpoints.[67] But if that is so, then it is hard to see why necessity should be distinguished from any other set of circumstances, for all acts in the mechanism of nature are determined, and necessity only differs in terms of the starkness of the causal sequence in which the individual is located. If Kant is allowing an excuse for necessity, then in principle *all* acts within the phenomenal world should be excusable, and punishment should either always be mitigated or simply never occur. If on the other hand the principle of responsibility is based upon the existence of rational will unhindered by the phenomenal world, no excusing conditions should be allowed. Rational freedom and causal necessity are in competition as ways of understanding the same piece of behaviour, and they point in precisely opposite directions.

Support for this interpretation of necessity comes from Kant's discussion of mitigation of the death penalty in cases of the maternal murder of an illegitimate child or of a soldier who kills in a duel. In both

---

[65] *Op.cit.*, pp.41-42.
[66] H.L.A. Hart, *Punishment and Responsibility* (*op.cit.*), ch.1.
[67] *The Moral Law*, pp.116-118.

cases, the crimes involve a sense of honour which forces the mother or soldier to carry out the act. The problem is that in these cases society itself 'is responsible for the fact that incentives of honour among the people do not accord (subjectively) with the standards that are (objectively) appropriate.'[68] The sense of shame is real and in a state that is 'barbaric and underdeveloped' overrides the true requirements of moral behaviour. The result is that 'public legal justice as administered by the state is injustice from the point of view of the people.'[69]

We are here faced with the same problem as with necessity. If individuals commit crimes because society is not sufficiently developed morally, so that non-moral motives are cultivated in people, then they are not to blame for the actions that ensue. But all crime flows from false incentives among the people conceived as empirical beings, so on this basis punishment can never be justified. Equally, if society is responsible for these incentives existing among the people, then social reform which brings about an ideal society will not only remove the incentives to crime, it will also remove the need for punishment. Thus, *either* punishment is needed but morally unjustified, or it is morally justified but unneeded![70]

In different places, Kant acknowledged the paradox of his position. In a letter, he wrote:

In a world of moral principle governed by God, punishments would be categorically necessary (insofar as transgressions occur). But in a world governed by men, the necessity of punishments is only hypothetical, and that direct union of the concept of transgression with the idea of deserving punishment serves the ruler only as a prescription for what to do....[71]

Similarly in an observation in the *Critique of Pure Reason*, he argues that 'The more legislation and government are brought into harmony with [moral laws] the rarer would punishments become, and it is therefore quite rational to maintain, as Plato does, that in a perfect state

---

[68] *M.E.J.*, p.107.

[69] *Ibid.*

[70] Murphy argues ('Marxism and Retribution' in *op.cit.*, pp.93-116) that this is a paradox for a Marxist theory of punishment, which he sees as in its essence drawing upon Kant. It is however a Kantian paradox. Elsewhere, I have argued that Murphy has not read Marx in context in interpreting his views on punishment: see 'Marxism and the Critique of Criminal Justice' 1982 *Contemporary Crises*, 59. See also, below, ch.4 text at fn.54.

[71] Letter to J.B. Erhard, in A. Zweig, *Kant, Philosophical Correspondence 1759-99* (Chicago, 1967), p.199.

no punishments whatsoever would be required.'[72]   To the extent that
individuals are morally free, therefore, their punishment is just but never
required; to the extent that they are governed by natural necessity, their
punishment is required but never just. There is a gap between the theory
and the practice so that Kant's retributivism is, literally, a philosophical
white elephant.

The reason for this lies in the dichotomy between *Willkur* and *der*
Wille. The two ideas are not formally incompatible, but as ways of
understanding a single piece of behaviour, they are mutually
contradictory. Crime is *either* behaviourally determined as in *Willkur or*
rational and free as in *der Wille*. To argue that it is both from different
standpoints evades rather than resolves the problem.[73]

Before concluding this subsection, I will consider one possible
objection to the interpretation of Kant's work suggested here. In the
Groundwork, Kant suggests - although he does not develop the
suggestion - that while the rational man is responsible, he does not
answer for the desires and incitements provided by the sensible world of
nature. However, he 'does impute to himself the indulgence which he
would show them if he admitted their influence on his maxims to the
detriment of the rational laws governing will.'[74]   Precisely what concept
of will allows for the possibility of 'indulgence' is not made clear, but
this passage chimes with one in the *M.E.J.* where Kant also suggests that
the individual can somehow more or less resist the influence of the
sensible world. Here, he says that

the degree of imputability...of actions must be estimated by the magnitude of the
obstacles that have to be overcome....   [T]he less the natural obstacle[s of
sensibility] and the greater the [moral] obstacle from grounds of duty, so much the
more is transgression...imputed. Therefore, the state of mind of the subject, namely,

---

[72] Quoted by Ladd in *M.E.J.*, at p.107.

[73] Cf. Paton, *op.cit.*, pp.214-215, 276-277; Walker, *op.cit.*, pp.148-149. See Beck,
op.cit., pp.192-194 for an attempted resolution. He suggests that the two
ontological realms - the phenomenal and the noumenal - should be seen as two
methodological approaches to a common world, differing only with reference to
the *purposes* we hold in regarding the world in one way or another. Kant should
be seen as holding a 'two-aspect' rather than a 'two-world theory'. But if we take
this view, the problem of responsibility becomes harder not easier, for now it is
resolved in terms of the purposes of the observer rather than the nature of the
action, and we lose any independent guidance whatsoever as to the proper way of
regarding the action.

[74] *The Moral Law*, p.118.

whether he committed the deed with emotion or in cool deliberation, makes a significant difference in imputation.[75]

Now both these passages suggest a much less black-and-white, freewill- or-determinism approach. They indicate a grey area in between moral duty and sensible desires in which the subject is more or less responsible for his actions. It might be thought that within this conception, his comments on the mitigatory effects of necessity, and the shame of the unmarried mother and the soldier could be properly situated.

However, it must be said that nowhere does Kant develop this alternative account of human will or indicate in what way it is to be synthesised with the noumenal/phenomenal dichotomy. What sort of will is able to be 'indulgent' in relation to sensible impulses? Not *Willkur* for it is given over to such impulses already, nor *der Wille* which is simply a rational will. Kant is suggesting a third position here but in what way it is compatible with the overall approach is unexplained.[76]

(2)   Applying the Jus Talionis

We have seen that the necessity of the *jus talionis* can be derived *a priori* from the nature of the categorical imperative and the rational unity of justice and coercion. Like the idea of the 'hindrance of the hindrance', it is an ideal expression of a metaphysical relation between crime and punishment. However, at the same time, the *jus talionis* is a practical and very concrete principle - an 'eye for an eye' - and so it is possible to

---

[75] *M.E.J.*, pp.29-30
[76] See Paton, *op.cit.*, pp.213-215; Williams, *op.cit.*, pp.66-67. Beck, *op.cit.*, ch.XI, attempts to build on this position by arguing that while *Willkur* has only comparative freedom in the sense that 'the determining causes are internal to the agent and not compulsion from without' (p.190), it can also be free 'in the practical and phenomenological sense, as a faculty of spontaneously initiating a new causal series in nature....'(p.198). He does not explain how a will that is part of a causal series in nature can at the same time initiate such a series. This 'solution' appears simply to replicate the problem by using a dualistic definition of *Willkur* in place of the *Willkur/der Wille* duality. Cf. Walker, *op.cit.*, p.149: 'In his *Lectures on Ethics*... [Kant] recognises a gradation of different degrees of responsibility, saying for example that if a starving man steals food he is less responsible for his theft than a well-fed man would be, because he is less free; but this is incompatible with his official theory of freedom, whereby in each case the phenomenal choice is determined and the noumenal agents are equally free all the same.'

enquire to what extent the ideal and the concrete can be united through this concept.

As Kant recognises, there are severe problems in sticking to the letter of the *jus talionis*. 'A life for a life' may point to the necessity of capital punishment for murder, but there are other crimes for which no ready equation exists. Kant considers this a sufficiently serious problem to devote an addendum to what is to be done to the rapist, the pederast and the man who commits acts of bestiality. Here, we are forced to consider the spirit rather than the letter of the principle so that castration is the appropriate punishment for the first two, and banishment from human society appropriate for the third.[77]

Clearly in arguing for the spirit of the principle, Kant has already moved away from the 'principle of pure and strict justice' that he had advocated.[78]   This becomes more evident when he attempts to take account of class distinctions in order to achieve true equality of crime and punishment. In calculating punishment, one must have regard to 'the special sensibilities of the higher classes'.[79]   A fine for a rich man is much less serious to him than the same fine to a poor man.   But a rich man can be made as part of his punishment to kiss the hand of the poor man he has wronged in addition to his fine. Clearly, there is licence here for subjective opinion to run rings around the objective idea of equality of punishment.

How do you rigorously apply an ideal concept of equality to a world of concrete and infinite diversity? Every individual is different, so no two punishments (or crimes) will be alike. It is easy, as Hegel put it, 'from this point of view to exhibit the retributive character of punishment as an absurdity (theft for theft, robbery for robbery, an eye for an eye, a tooth for a tooth - and then you can go on to suppose that the criminal has only one eye or no teeth).'[80]   The point is valid for even the death penalty for murder achieves at best only a superficial equivalence. Would, for example, the execution of a young man for the murder of an octogenarian be an equal punishment?

The problem that Kant faces here concerns the translation of a metaphysical ideal (equality of punishment) into an actual practice. The *jus talionis* seems to make this possible because of the immediate

---

[77] *M.E.J.*, pp.131-133. In relation to bestiality, it is as well that utilitarian considerations do not enter into the determination of rightful punishment (but see *M.E.J.* p.104), for in this case the punishment seems designed to encourage the crime.

[78] *Ibid.*, p.132.

[79] *Ibid.*, p.101.

[80] *Op.cit.*, p.72.

identity of crime with punishment, but this is only at a very superficial level. The strength of the retributive doctrine of equality of punishment is that it flows from the metaphysical justification of punishment, and sets an ideal limit on what may be done to a criminal. But that is also its weakness, for the *jus talionis* is an attempt to cash in the practical world the ideal cheque of metaphysical justice. Between the two currencies - the ideal and the concrete - there is no adequate point of contact, no workable exchange rate.[81]   The ideal principle of equality is incommensurable with a world of infinite practical variation.

4. CONCLUSION: KANT'S JURIDICAL INDIVIDUALISM

Kant's achievement in the philosophy of punishment was that he rigorously separated the moral retributive justification of punishment from empirical questions concerning the material interests of the individual and society, in short the utility of punishment.   To be sure, utility had its place since legal punishment operated at the interface between the rational and the material wills, but punishment was justified in terms only of the former, that is, in terms of the conception of the individual as a rational being, abstracted from his worldly existence. Kant was able to achieve this separation because his metaphysic of morals is based upon an equally rigorous distinction between the noumenal and the phenomenal worlds of human life.

Comparing Kant with Hobbes, the latter had also interwoven an ideal political theory centred around a moral juridical image of man with an empirical theory of man's nature on earth. But at every turn, Hobbes's empirical materialist theory undercut and negated the ideal political theory in relation to crucial issues such as punishment. With Kant, the

---

[81] Murphy suggests (*op.cit.*, pp.84-86) that the best that can be hoped for from retributivism is a proportionality between crime and punishment in terms of seriousness, but he concedes that the measure of seriousness is a contentious issue. He therefore argues for an objective concept while acknowledging that no such concept exists. On the problem of proportionality, see the recent article by M. Davis, 'Harm and Retribution' (1986) *Philosophy and Public Affairs* 236. His alternative suggestion of grounding proportionality on the price people would be willing to pay for crimes seems equally susceptible to the problems of subjectivity. In *Past or Future Crimes* (Manchester, 1986), ch.6, A. Von Hirsch discusses the issue, but inconclusively.

process of abstraction of the ideal political theory is taken a stage further, so that man's empirical nature becomes only a negative point of contrast to his essence as a moral, rational being.   Kant does not rely on man's nature for natural laws in a moral sense or for the necessity of a transference of right in a contract.   The social contract becomes an Idea of reason, and man is governed by laws of reason which are pure and compelling regardless of his nature.   The moral theory of law, justice, coercion and punishment derives from the *a priori* application of reason.

Kant's rational individual is the counterpart of Hobbes's free, consenting individual.   Both stand in opposition to man conceived as determined by his nature.   Both entail a process of abstraction and idealisation of man (with Kant this is explicit) so that both are autonomous and responsible.   Just as Hobbes's man can commit himself in the social contract as a free individual, so can Kant's man legislate for himself as a free and rational individual.   *Der Wille* is the Kantian counterpart of the Hobbesian juridically free will. Therefore, as an abstract, ideal concept of human life, it too is a form of juridical individualism.

In designing a justification of punishment in terms of an abstract ideal being, Kant unavoidably only justifies punishment *of* abstract ideal beings - who never commit crimes anyway.   As soon as he descends to the world of phenomena and sensible experience - the realm of actual crimes and criminals - his justification of punishment is lost, for criminals, by definition, do not act according to rational laws but are governed by their natures.   Kant's dualism gives a special significance to his admission that while it is the rational individual who submits himself to the penal law, it is as 'another person' that he breaks it.[82]

Thus Kant and Hobbes share, albeit in different ways, a fundamental conflict between the *form* of their moral justifications of punishment and the *content* of human actions to which those justifications apply. This is so because in both cases moral agency is achieved by an idealisation of the moral will in contrast to the naturally determined will of the empirical world.   Both philosophers share a contradiction between the abstract juridical individualism of their moral theories and the concrete individuality of human nature.   Where they differ is in that Kant is able to postpone the clash between the ideal and the actual until after he has

---

[82] *M.E.J.*, p.105. Without tracing the reasons for the problem in the structure of the theory, Murphy hits the nail on the head when he writes 'We want an account of unjust actions and we want an account of what it is to deserve (or not to deserve) punishment for such actions; but it would seem that Kant's fondness for radical dichotomies (inner/outer, phenomenal/noumenal, justice/virtue, action/maxim) obscures rather than clarifies here' (*op.cit.*, fn.8, p.524).

constructed his justification of punishment. In a sense, Hobbes's justification of punishment never gets going because it is immediately negated by his conception of man's nature. Kant's retributivism at least gets off the ground. Indeed his problem is rather a matter of bringing it back down to earth! The metaphysical justification of punishment is achieved but is inapplicable to both criminals (the 'gap between theory and practice') and their crimes (the inapplicability of the *jus talionis*). Thus, at bottom, Kant has only succeeded in altering the terrain from the Hobbesian moral-juridical/natural being contradiction to that of his own noumenal/phenomenal schizophrenia. Both contradictions express that antithesis outlined in chapter I between juridical individualism and concrete individuality. To examine the further progress of this antithesis, we must now turn to Hegel.

CHAPTER IV

RATIONALISING JURIDICAL INDIVIDUALISM AND THE RISE OF 'THE IRRATIONAL' : HEGEL

1. INTRODUCTION

With Hegel, we reach the culmination of the philosophical developments outlined in the two preceding chapters and embodied in the construction of a modern classical retributive theory of punishment. That theory has two essential, related components. First, punishment of the individual is justified by reference to the individual, and not some extraneous source (society in general, the rights of others, etc.). This justification is based upon the individual's consent to, or rational willing of, punishment, which he therefore deserves. Punishment is given an individualistic justification in terms of the criminal's own will and actions.

Second, this justification of punishment is established in opposition to man's material nature by reference to an ideal source of political authority in the individual himself. For Hobbes, there exists, side by side with the nature-bound brute of the state of nature, a contractually bound juridical individual who, freed from the natural realities of life, can make commitments that his natural self would never consider. For Kant, the rough juxtaposition that Hobbes achieved between the ideal and the abstract on the one hand and the natural and the concrete on the other is transformed into a much subtler duality of reason and nature. Here, the ideal - man's reason - reigns supreme so that the justification of punishment is purified of recalcitrant reality. However, the suppressed contradiction between the ideal and the natural re-emerges as soon as the ideal justification of punishment is applied to practical questions concerning the material world of crime and criminality. Reason is eventually brought down to earth with a thud by unruly reality. In this chapter, I argue that the strength and importance of Hegel's theory of punishment lies in a philosophical method which avoids the gap between reason and reality, between the ideal and the material, in order to provide the most sophisticated version of the retributive philosophy of punishment.   In so doing, however, he evades rather than settles the fundamental problems of that philosophy.

English speaking philosophy has been badly served by its sometimes ill-concealed contempt for the work of Hegel[1] and by its popular assumption that words can be forced to reveal their meaning without regard to the context within which they were originally written. Honderich, for example, expounds at length and not unfavourably on Kantian retributivism before turning to 'another retribution theory of very secondary interest'.[2]   Hegel's philosophy of annulment of crime is regarded as 'obscure' and to reproduce it 'more faithfully and intelligibly [sic] would require a considerable and tedious excursus into the philosophy of Absolute Idealism.'[3] Although he does not seek to render the doctrine more intelligible, Honderich feels able to describe the idea that the criminal denies the rightness of a moral principle by his crime as nonsense.[4]   Similarly, the idea that the criminal demands his punishment as his right is regarded as so odd that its explanation might best be sought on the psychoanalyst's couch.[5]

Abuse aside, the substance of Honderich's criticisms are widely shared by modern philosophers.   As regards the criminal's right of punishment, Quinton observes that it is 'an odd sort of right whose holder would strenuously resist its recognition.'[6]   Furthermore, the stipulation of such a right reveals that Hegel's philosophy is not retributive at all, but is only a disguised form of utilitarianism since it holds that 'the sole relevant consideration in determining whether and how a man should be punished is his own moral regeneration.'[7] Similarly with the idea of punishment annulling crime, both Quinton[8]

---

[1] Thus, J. Plamenatz: 'There is, of course, nonsense and nonsense, some of it a credit to the heart and even the head of its author. Though the truth should lie far removed from both their systems, there will always be a world of difference between Kant and Hegel.' *The English Utilitarians* (Oxford, 1958), p.148.

[2] T. Honderich, *Punishment: The Supposed Justifications* (Harmondsworth, 1976), p.45.

[3] *Ibid.*, p.46.

[4] *Ibid.* Indeed, on his rendition it is nonsense.

[5] *Ibid.*, p.47.

[6] A. Quinton, *op.cit.*, p.57.

[7] *Ibid.*

[8] *Ibid.*, p.56: 'The doctrine of 'annulment', however carefully wrapped up in obscure phraseology, is clearly utilitarian in principle.'

and Benn agree that this involves a veiled utilitarianism. If punishment could annul wrongdoing, it could only be through 'the betterment of the victim of the crime or of society in general'.⁹ Then to add insult to injury, it is pointed out that on this interpretation of the Hegelian philosophy, it is an exceedingly weak justification of punishment since it can only be applied 'to a restricted class of cases, the order of nature is inhospitable to attempts to put the clock back'.¹⁰ While theft and wounding can be compensated (annulled), other crimes - most obviously murder - cannot.

The philosophical context within which Hegel wrote has been so lost to modern philosophers that even among those sympathetic to Hegel, there is often little real understanding of the nature of his philosophy of punishment.¹¹ Hegel's views have to be put into modern terms in order, it is supposed, to make them comprehensible. In reality, the opposite happens. Perhaps the best known modern account is that of David Cooper, who, rightly, begins by establishing Hegel's opposition to utilitarianism, but then proceeds to explain the doctrine of annulment in terms of the need to protect the rights of victims and of society in general. Rights are described as 'performatees' which 'logically depend for their felicitous existence upon the punishment of those who infringe them.'¹² The result of this is a rendition of the Hegelian philosophy which readily justifies the allegation of 'veiled utilitarianism': if people are not generally caught and punished for harming others in their affairs, then others cannot be said to have the right to pursue those affairs. Punishment prevents criminals from obstructing the rights of others.¹³ However, this interpretation is impossible to square with Hegel's actual words, for he makes it clear that annulment of wrong is only relevant from the point of view of the wrongdoer himself, and *not* from the point of view of the victim:

the injury from the point of view of the particular will of the injured party and of onlookers is only something negative. The *sole positive existence which the injury possesses is that it is the particular will of the criminal*. Hence to injure [or

---

⁹ S. Benn, 'An Approach to the Problems of Punishment' in H. Morris, *Freedom and Responsibility* (Stanford, 1961), p.519.

¹⁰ Quinton, *op.cit.*, p.57. C.f. Aune's criticism of Kant (above, ch.III, at fn.18).

¹¹ A good exception is P. Stillman, 'Hegel's Idea of Punishment' *Journal of the History of Philosophy* (1976) 14, pp.169-182.

¹² D. Cooper, 'Hegel's Theory of Punishment' in Z. Pelczynski, *Hegel's Political Philosophy* (Cambridge, 1971), p.163.

¹³ *Ibid.*, pp.162-3.

penalise] this particular will as a will determinately existent is to annul the crime, which otherwise would have been held valid, and to restore the right.[14]

We will have to explain the precise meaning of this passage in the next section, but for now, let us note the contortion it produces in Cooper's assessment of the doctrine. Taking his 'victim's rights' orientation, Cooper argues that what Hegel means here is that

The crime was, in intention, a demonstration that the victim had no rights. But the victim did have these rights, and so there never was such a thing as the demonstration that he did not have them. So to speak of annulling the crime is to speak of whatever it is that establishes that the victim did have those rights which were implicitly denied by the criminal.[15]

The passage is self-contradictory. If the victim did have rights so that 'there never was such a thing as the demonstration that he did not have them', why is it necessary to annul the crime so as to establish 'that the victim did have those rights'? If it was never demonstrated that he did not have them, why is it necessary to demonstrate that he did have them? Cooper here wrestles with the passage we have quoted from Hegel in which the injury to the victim is regarded as 'only something negative' and as having no 'positive existence'. Cooper, instead of seeing the significance of these comments in terms of Hegel's radical individualism, tries to blend them into his (not Hegel's) veiled utilitarianism.[16]

Thus what we must establish in examining Hegel's philosophy of punishment is, first, the way in which he justifies punishment in terms of the person to be punished (and not in terms of the victim, society in general, etc.), and second, the philosophical nature of his justification as a non-utilitarian, metaphysical account of the justice of punishment.

---

[14] G. Hegel, *The Philosophy of Right* (*op.cit.*), p.69, emphasis added.

[15] *Op.cit.*, p.164.

[16] Cf. Day's argument that 'annulment' means that a retributive right of punishment exists 'if and only if the good in the restitution outweighs the bad in the retribution. As Hegel says, this happens when the restitution restores some human right of the (victim).' Precisely where Hegel states that punishment restores a human right of the victim is not made clear: J.P. Day 'Retributive Punishment' *Mind* (1978) LXXXVII pp.498-516.

2. THE HEGELIAN JUSTIFICATION OF PUNISHMENT

(1)   Absolute Idealism and the Philosophy of Right.[17]

We must begin by understanding the context within which Hegel elaborated his views on right in general and punishment in particular. That context is given by the philosophy of absolute idealism and, as regards practical or moral philosophy, the starting point can be taken to be Hegel's objections to the Kantian categorical imperative.

For Kant, the universal is understood as a rational form which is imposed upon the content of the practical world and which thereby elevates elements of that world to the level of the rational and universal. The problem with applying a formal criterion of non-contradiction is that the content which is to be rationalised by such a procedure is not itself selected upon rational grounds. Rather it is drawn from the realm of contingency without further ado. Yet it is precisely the content which is to be rationalised which must first of all be established as *the* content to be rationalised. For example, if property is regarded as a universal principle, theft is wrong as being in contradiction to it. But the initial question as to why we should start with a concept of property and not, for example, its opposite, non-property, is not raised, far less answered:

The absence of property contains in itself just as little contradiction as the non-existence of this or that nation, family, etc., or the death of the whole human race. But if it is already established on other grounds and presupposed that property and human life are to exist and be respected, then indeed it is a contradiction to commit theft or murder; a contradiction must be a contradiction of something, i.e. of some content presupposed from the start as a fixed principle. It is to a principle of that

---

[17] Both Plant and Taylor in their works on Hegel discuss briefly his philosophical justification of punishment: R. Plant, *Hegel* (London 1973), pp.156-157; C. Taylor, *Hegel* (Cambridge,1975), p.429. I have found most useful, both for its discussion of the place of the *Philosophy of Right* in the Hegelian system as a whole and for its discussion of Hegel's account of punishment, the older work of H. Reyburn, *The Ethical Theory of Hegel* (Oxford, 1921); and the helpfully critical account of Hegel's moral philosophy by M. Inwood, *Hegel* (London, 1983) ch.XI. For a general introduction, I have used C. Taylor, *Hegel and Modern Society* (Cambridge, 1979). Both this and the next chapter are influenced by Marcuse's *Reason and Revolution* (London, 1949).

kind alone, therefore, that an action can be related either by correspondence or contradiction.[18]

How, then, to establish such a fixed principle on rational grounds? In the sphere of the philosophy of nature, Hegel had already established (again in response to Kant's dualism) the idea that the world of nature is not a world over against human subjectivity, although that is how it at first appears to man. On the contrary, nature is rather a second home for man once he realises through the speculative philosophy that it is permeated by man's thought. There is in nature an ideal rational order, which man discovers and which, in discovering, he recognises as part of himself as a rational being:

The study of nature sets mind free in nature; for mind develops in so far as it relates itself not to another but to itself. Similarly, it is the emancipation of nature. Nature is intrinsically reason, but it first obtains existence as reason through mind. Mind has the certainty which Adam had when he looked on Eve: 'This is flesh of my flesh, and bone of my bone.' Thus nature is the bride which mind weds.[19]

In the sphere of the philosophy of right, Hegel establishes a similar principle, for his method developes within the realm of social and legal institutions a rational order, already implicitly present, which it is the task of the speculative philosophy to render explicit. The truth about Right, Ethics and the State is 'as old as its public recognition and formulation in the law of the land' so that it only requires

to be grasped in thought as well; the content which is already rational in principle must win the form of rationality and so appear well-founded to untrammelled thinking.[20]

This principle of the speculative philosophy is summed up in Hegel's famous dictum that 'What is rational is actual and what is actual is rational.'[21] The unity of actuality and rationality is given in that the realm of the actual is shown to have, immanent within it, what is rational. Thus to read reason within (not *pace* Kant 'onto') the present is to grasp

---

[18] Hegel, *op.cit.*, p.90. Cf. Inwood, *op.cit.*, pp.474-476, Reyburn, *op.cit.*, pp.57-61, G. Lukacs, *History and Class Consciousness* (London, 1967) pp.124-125.

[19] G. Hegel, *The Philosophy of Nature* (transl. Miller)(Oxford, 1970), p.13. I have used Reyburn's translation at *op.cit.*, p.67 in preference to Miller's.

[20] *The Philosophy of Right, op.cit.*, p.3. See also, p.7.

[21] *Ibid.*, p.10.

the unity of form and content; for form in its most concrete signification is reason as speculative knowing, and content is reason as the substantial essence of actuality, whether ethical or natural. The known identity of these two is the philosophical idea.[22]

Like nature, then, law and state as social institutions represent a 'bride which mind weds', and the task of the *Philosophy of Right* is 'to look on at the proper immanent development of the thing itself.'[23] In this way, the justification of, first, coercion, then punishment, will be established as a rational necessity.

I have said that at the core of the justification of punishment is a regard for the right of the individual who is to be punished. It is indicative of this centrality of the right of the individual that the starting point of the *Philosophy of Right* as a whole is individual free will. Here we see both a similarity with, and a difference from, Kant:

The basis of right is, in general, mind; its precise place and point of origin is the will. The will is free, so that freedom is both the substance of right and its goal, while the system of right is the realm of freedom made actual.[24]

The realm of freedom made actual is established by means of the establishment of two modes of freedom of the will. Firstly, as with Kant, there is a moment of negative freedom, an element of 'abstraction and negativity' which constitutes the

pure reflection of the ego into itself which involves the dissipation of every restriction and every content either immediately presented by nature, by needs, desires, and impulses, or given and determined by any means whatsoever.[25]

Where Hegel parts company with Kant is in that for him, the element of 'positive freedom' is not understood as the abstract imposition of a universal form onto particularity but as the will 'positing...itself as something determinate, the ego step[ping] forth...into determinate existence.'[26] Then, as a third moment, so as not to dissolve freedom in determinate existence, there is the capacity of mind to comprehend in the particular that which is universal and rational:

---

[22] *Ibid.*, p.12.
[23] *Ibid.*, p.14.
[24] *Ibid.*, p.20.
[25] *Ibid.*, p.21.
[26] *Ibid.*, p.22.

Freedom is to will something determinate, yet in this determinacy to be by oneself and to revert once more to the universal.[27]

Whereas for Kant, the will withdraws from the flux of particularity in order to formulate and apply universal laws to it, Hegel presents the withdrawal of will as merely a prelude to its return to particularity as a rational will, able to comprehend that which is rational within the particular. The universal is not an abstraction over against the particular, it is something to be discovered within it. Where Kant and Hegel agree is that the foundations of Right lie in the freedom of the individual as a rational being. The *Philosophy of Right* can be seen as a kind of speculative voyage of the will through the particularities of social life with the navigational aid of reason. Coercion and punishment are two such facts of social life, and their necessity is a discovery of the rational will when it embarks upon determinate existence.

(2)   Coercion, Punishment and Proportionality

The *Philosophy of Right* is divided into three main sections corresponding to the three different stages in the development of the Idea of the absolutely free will.[28]   These three stages consist of the spheres of *Abstract Right, Morality* and *Ethical Life*.   In the sphere of *Abstract Right*, the will enters into particularity as an individual personality recognising only itself and its interests. The individual is in a position analogous to that of the individual in the state of nature, except that here, the questions of personality and rights are separated from questions of man's natural condition. This gives personality a double-sided character:

(i) I am completely determined on every side (in my inner caprice, impulse, and desire, as well as by immediate external facts) and so finite, yet (ii) none the less I am simply and solely self-relation, and therefore in finitude I know myself as something infinite, universal, and free.[29]

Whilst able to divest myself of my natural conditions, I am aware of myself as free - but only of myself as free. However, in the course of the logical development in the sphere of *Abstract Right* I ultimately become aware that in addition to my subjective freedom, there also exists as rational necessity in the world an objective universality and necessity

---

[27] *Ibid.*, p.229.

[28] *Ibid.*, pp.35-36.

[29] *Ibid.*, p.37.

which stands in opposition to my freedom. I realise this through the discovery that wrong exists in the world, and that coercion as a counteraction to wrong is a rational necessity. It is here that the fundamental groundwork of the justification of punishment is laid.[30]

The awareness that there exists a right and wrong - which is developed at the end of *Abstract Right* - concludes that sphere and entails the entry into the second sphere of *Morality*. Once I recognise the existence of right and wrong, I recognise that subjective freedom is not all that exists in the world. I now recognise that the morally right exists as an objective universal over against my subjective will, and this I incorporate into myself as conscience. But the opposition that is established between morality and conscience on the one hand and subjective freedom on the other is a false one, for both are expressions of what is universally right, and so the opposition must be overcome by revealing that subjective freedom and objective universality can be united in actual social relations, which embody both individual freedom and moral necessity.[31] This is the sphere of *Ethical Life*, and it is here that the institution of punishment, taking up the justification of coercion established in *Abstract Right*, is ultimately vindicated as a rational embodiment of individual freedom.[32]

Turning now to the detail of the justifications of coercion and punishment, the necessity of coercion is deduced from a development in the sphere of *Abstract Right* which begins with *Property* and leads through *Contract* to the concept of *Wrong*.

Property. Initially, when the will steps into determinate existence, it embodies itself in objects in the world, which constitute its property. Placing itself in things and making them an expression of itself, the will is implicitly universal but does not know itself to be such, for it simply enters into contact with its opposite - particularity. The act of occupying property is no more than the immediate grasp of a thing.[33]

Contract. A necessary consequence of property's existence is the exchange of property through agreement with other property owners. In entering into contracts, the particularised will meets other particular wills and accordingly realises that, where there was only one will before, will

---

30 *Ibid.*, pp.66-73.
31 *Ibid.*, pp.36, 103.
32 In *The Court of Justice, ibid.*, pp.140-141.
33 The argument is contained in *ibid.*, pp.40-57 and helpfully summarised by Knox at pp.332-4.

(*Verhürvend*) is in fact universal. Through a contract, the will recognises the existence of other wills, and so recognises that the *form* of the relationship of one will to another is universal. What was implicit in *Property* is explicit in *Contract*. However, while the form of the contractual relation embodies universality, its *content* does not. I exchange my *x* for your *y* so that we have in common the element of will but the objects of our wills remain particular and contingent. The content of will is not universal.[34]

Wrong. As in *Contract*, the *form* of wrong is a willed action and in this there exists universality. As in *Contract*, the *content* of the willed action is particular and contingent. Where they differ is that in *Contract*, while the content is not universal, it is not openly inconsistent with the principle of universality. In willing that I exchange my *x* for your *y*, I do not offend the principle that there should be willed acts. In doing wrong, I do offend that principle for an act that is wrong is an act of coercion of the will of another. To understand this, we need to recall that it is a fundamental feature of all human life for the individual to place his will in external objects, and that this is part of what it means to be free. Any act of will which seeks to force or coerce a will embodied in an external object not only negates the free will of another, it also negates the universal principle of willing, upon which it itself is based. A coercive will is therefore, viewed rationally, self-contradictory and thus, for a rational being, wrong:

Since it is only in so far as the will has an existence in something determinate that it is Idea or actually free, and since the existent in which it has laid itself is freedom in being, it follows that force or coercion is in its very conception directly self-destructive because it is an expression of a will which annuls the expression or determinate existence of a will. Hence force or coercion, taken abstractly, is wrong.[35]

Thus in doing wrong, the content of my willed act is in contradiction with the form of my act as a universal principle. Free will is the basis of right; coercion is the negation of free will and an opposition of right; coercion is therefore wrong.

What is to be done about this opposition to right? Logically, it cannot be allowed to stand for, although wrong is inherently, i.e. from the point of view of reason, nothing at all, it does have 'positive existence in the external world'[36] and therefore requires to be annulled. Otherwise, it would be held to be valid and it is accordingly necessary to

---

[34] *Ibid.*, pp.57-64; cf. Reyburn, *op.cit.*, p.143.
[35] *Ibid.*, p.67.
[36] *Ibid.*, p.69.

'restore the right',[37] by its annulment. Crime is an injury or negation of a free will by a free will acting coercively; coercion as punishment is the injury or negation of the free will acting coercively; coercion as punishment is, therefore, 'the negation of the negation'.[38]

This analysis, however, raises a question; if crime is 'inherently ...nothing at all', why is it necessary to annul its positive existence in the world? If from the point of view of what is rational, crime is a mere 'nullity',[39] why is it necessary to negate it? Hegel's answer is that from the point of view of onlookers and even the victim, there is no need to annul the wrong act. The implicit will of the victim cannot in itself be injured 'except insofar as it fails to withdraw itself out of the external object in which it is held fast'[40] and so the injury 'is only something negative'.[41] But from the point of view of *the criminal*, it is necessary to annul the wrong and restore the right,[42] for *his* will is in contradiction with the universal principle of willing, and this contradiction needs to be overcome by punishment. As a rational being the criminal demands this as his right. The justice of punishment is therefore justice from the point of view of the criminal:

The injury [the penalty] which falls on the criminal is not merely implicitly just...it is also a right established within the criminal himself....The reason for this is that his action is the action of a rational being and this implies that it is something universal and that by doing it the criminal has laid down a law which he has explicitly recognised in his action and under which in consequence he should be brought as under his right.[43]

Thus, we can now see the error of those who would argue that punishment is justified in terms of the rights of the victim or of society. Hegel maintains the radical individualism of Kant in relating the justification of punishment to the criminal and to him alone, as a rational being. Similarly, we can also understand that Hegelian punishment is in no way a veiled utilitarianism, for it has nothing whatever to do with the protection of the victim and his rights, or the betterment of the criminal himself. What is at stake is not individual improvement but the logical progression of 'the Idea':[44] a rational development of speculative

---

[37] *Ibid.*
[38] *Ibid.*, p.246.
[39] *Ibid.*, p.69.
[40] *Ibid.*, p.66.
[41] *Ibid.*, p.69
[42] *Ibid.*
[43] *Ibid.*, p.70.
[44] *Ibid.*, p.35, and translator's introduction, p.ix.

philosophy which deals with individuals, but from the point of view of
their rationality.[45]

We have now seen the way in which coercion is justified as the
annulment of wrong in the sphere of *Abstract Right*. This does not
mean, however, that punishment *by the state* has been justified.
Abstract Right, as I have said, can be regarded as an analogue of the
state of nature, that is, as a *pre*-political sphere. Thus any punishment
which occurs in it occurs prior to the establishment of the institutions of
the state, and is really, viewed in a social context, no more than
individual (albeit justified) revenge. It is necessary that punishment
should receive an adequate social form, and this it achieves within the
sphere of *Ethical Life* wherein the Court of Justice removes the
'subjective feeling of private interest'[46] and introduces, in place of the
injured party, the 'injured universal [which] now comes on the scene.'[47]

State punishment entails not only that the criminal is put to rights
with himself, but also that the laws of the state, as expressions of what is
universal, are also re-affirmed. State punishment unifies both social and
individual right and is both subjectively and objectively just:

Objectively, [punishment] is the reconciliation of the law with itself; by the
annulment of the crime, the law is restored and its authority is thereby actualised.
Subjectively, it is the reconciliation of the criminal with himself, i.e. with the law
known by him as his own and as valid for him and his protection; when this law is
executed upon him, he himself finds in this process the satisfaction of justice and
nothing save his own act.[48]

Finally, we come to the question of the distribution of punishment. We
saw in the last chapter that Hegel exposed the weaknesses in Kant's use
of the concrete standard of the *jus talionis* as a principle of equality
between crime and punishment. Yet Hegel was as clear as Kant that
just punishment required an equal injury for the injury done. How was
this to be established? Both crimes and punishments are quantitatively
and qualitatively determinate in their existence so that no immediate
identity or equality between them can be established. This can only be
achieved 'in respect of their implicit character, i.e. in respect of their
'value' ',[49] which Hegel defines as 'the inner equality of things which in

---

[45] Cf. Stillman (*op.cit.*, p.172.): 'Criminals are punished in order to ratify in the
objective world the truth within the conceptual world: that crime is null.'

[46] *Ibid.*, p.140.

[47] *Ibid.*, p.141.

[48] *Ibid.*

[49] *Ibid.*, p.71.

their outward existence are specifically different from one another in every way.'⁵⁰
This way of measuring the equality of crime and punishment does, however, not allow for complete exactitude for 'in the field of the finite, absolute determinacy remains only a demand' which the Understanding must attempt to meet by means of approximations.⁵¹ Similarly, in the *Administration of Justice*, while the concept lays down maxima and minima for sentencing, it must be left to the judge to affix the precise sentence in an individual case:

> In this sphere, the concept merely lays down a general limit, within which vacillation is still allowed. This vacillation must be terminated, however, in the interest of getting something done, and for this reason there is a place within that limit for contingent and arbitrary decisions.⁵²

We have now considered the main lines of Hegel's justification of coercion, punishment and the measure of punishment and demonstrated the general character of this justification as individualistic and rationalistic. In the next section, we proceed to assess Hegel's achievement in the light of those problems which, we have seen, bedevilled the work of his predecessors.

3. 'FROM THE POINT OF VIEW OF ABSTRACT RIGHT'

In an essay on capital punishment, Marx wrote of justifications of punishment that

> From the point of view of abstract right, there is only one theory of punishment which recognises human dignity in the abstract, and that is the theory of Kant especially in the more rigid formula given to it by Hegel.⁵³

There can be no doubt that for Marx the prefatory qualifier of his praise for Hegel's (and Kant's) work is crucial since he proceeds, in far from complimentary terms, to describe Hegel's justification of punishment as

---

⁵⁰ *Ibid.*, p.72.
⁵¹ *Ibid.*, pp.72-73.
⁵² *Ibid.*, p.137.
⁵³ M. Cain and A. Hunt, *Marx and Engels on Law* (London, 1979), p.194.

a 'transcendental sanction to the rules of existing society' entailing the
delusionary substitution 'for the individual with his real motives, with
multifarious social circumstances pressing upon him, the abstraction of
'freewill' - one among the many qualities of man for man himself.'[54]   In
order to understand the significance of these comments, we must first
understand what Hegel has done, and we can do this, once more, by
making reference to Kant.

(1)   The Gap between Theory and Practice

For Kant, there is a division between noumenal and phenomenal reality,
but both are recognised within his discussion of punishment.   Reality
from the former point of view is the rational reality of a system of laws
and punishment is derived from the imposition of laws of reason on the
world of phenomena.   But, here the noumenal encounters its opposite,
for reality from the point of view of phenomena is a contradictory affair
of social and natural determinations of behaviour - of dishonoured
mothers and honourable soldiers.   The problem for Kant is that he cannot
exclude phenomenal aspects from his analysis, he can only impose
rational forms upon them, so that the phenomenal is exhibited as a
contradictory presence in the face of laws of reason.

    For Hegel, this contradiction - the gap between theory and practice -
is avoided because his speculative method is able to appropriate reality
from the standpoint of reason while at the same time excluding those
aspects of reality which do not accord with reason.   The task of the
speculative philosophy is to bring out, within the flux of the particular
(phenomenal) the 'light of the essence glinting in it.'[55]   Reason has to be
discovered within 'an infinite wealth of forms, shapes and appearances',[56]
but this 'infinite variety of circumstances' is not, says Hegel, 'the subject
matter of philosophy.'[57]   To touch upon external and contingent matters

would be to meddle with things to which philosophy is unsuited; on such topics it
may save itself the trouble of giving good advice.[58]

Now, it is true that in making these comments, Hegel has in mind the
need for philosophy to exclude from consideration the ephemeral and

---

[54] *Ibid.*, p.195.
[55] *Op.cit.*, p.11.
[56] *Ibid.*, p.10.
[57] *Ibid.*, p.11.
[58] *Ibid.*

trivial,[59] but it is also true that it is of the nature of his speculative method that it excludes *all* reality other than that which is regarded as an embodiment of the rational and is therefore accorded the status of the actual. What is defined as actual derives its reality not from the essence of the thing itself, but by fiat of reason, and no further explanation is given.[60] Thus, for Hegel, there is no need to consider the dishonoured mother or the proud soldier, because such phenomenal affairs are simply irrelevant to the workings of reason and can therefore be ignored. Hegel's reason, unlike Kant's, is no external form imposed upon reality; it is something developed out of reality and which, as the infinite in the world of the finite, must select those phenomena adequate to itself, but *only* those phenomena.

We can see this exclusive, appropriative method at work in the *Philosophy of Right* if we consider Hegel's discussion of individual personality. We have already seen that in *Abstract Right*, the starting point is not the individual who is 'completely determined on every side' but rather the person who knows himself as 'something infinite, universal, and free'.[61] Similarly in *Ethical Life*, while there must be a realm of contingency,[62] the realm of the *Administration of Justice* is concerned with the ego 'as a universal person in which all are identical' and in which 'A man counts as a man in virtue of his manhood alone.'[63] While in relation to the State, it is essential 'that the universal be bound up with the complete freedom of its particular members and with private wellbeing',[64] in considering freedom

the starting point must be *not individuality*, the single self-consciousness, but *only the essence of self-consciousness; for whether man knows it or not, this essence is*

---

[59] For example, Plato's advice to nurses on how to handle babies and Fichte's recommendations on the design of passports: *ibid.*

[60] Cf. Inwood, *op.cit.*, p.502: 'Hegel provides no satisfactory criteria for distinguishing what is actual from what is not. Nor does he supply any guarantee that the various marks of the nonactual - contingency, transience, triviality, and so on - will inevitably coincide.' See also K. Marx, 'Critique of Hegels Doctrine of the State' in *Early Writings* (Harmondsworth, 1975), pp.58-74.

[61] *Op.cit.* p.37.

[62] 'The concrete person...is, as a totality of wants and a mixture of caprice and physical necessity one principle of civil society.' *Ibid.*, p.122. C.f. Inwood, *op.cit.*, p.488.

[63] *Ibid.*, p.134.

[64] *Ibid.*, p.280.

externally realised as a self-subsistent power in which single individuals *are only moments*.[65]

In relation to coercion and punishment, this same exclusionary logic is evident in Hegel's insistence that punishment is the criminal's right as a rational being, regardless of whether or not a particular criminal might will it or not:

> What is involved in the action of the criminal is not only the concept of crime, the rational aspect present in crime as such *whether the individual wills it or not*, the aspect which the state has to vindicate, but also the *abstract rationality of the individual's volition*. *Since that is so*, punishment is regarded as containing the criminal's right and hence by being punished he is honoured as a rational being.[66]

We can now see how Hegel successfully closes the gap between theory and practice. He does so not by bringing reality in all its practical forms and concrete determinations under the wing of reason, but by using reason to filter out all the recalcitrant elements. Hegel is able to avoid - or rather evade - the social and natural causation of crime by simply declaring it irrelevant from the point of view of reason. It does not matter whether the criminal wills his punishment in practice or not, nor whether he is an honourable soldier, or she is a dishonoured mother: all such questions of particularity concerning man as 'completely determined on every side' can be ignored as not concerning the work of reason. Thus Hegel resolves the dichotomy of the ideal and the material, of reason and nature in a very particular way. He unites theory and practice - but on theory's terms, for, in the speculative philosophy, mind looks on nature not as an independent reality but as an immanent self-embodiment.[67] The consequence of this is that in sealing off reason from recalcitrant reality, Hegel unifies reason and reality within theory while shutting out any elements which do not fit. His philosophy is a kind of intellectual double-glazing. The gales may blast outside, but inside all is calm and undisturbed. One can say that Hegel succeeds in establishing two realities - one inside and one outside philosophy. Put another way, the gap between theory and practice is overcome *within* philosophy, but only by transposing it *outwith* philosophy.

---

[65] *Ibid.*, p.279, emphasis added.
[66] *Ibid.*, p.71, emphasis added.
[67] Cf. L. Feuerbach: 'If the reality of thought is merely thought reality, then the reality of thought is still merely a thought and we are still imprisoned within the identity of thought with itself, inside idealism.' Quoted in D. McLellan, *The Young Hegelians and Karl Marx* (London, 1969) p.99.

As illustration of this process, we may compare the Hegelian reality of punishment with that of our experience. For Hegel, criminals rationally demand punishment as their right, yet experience tells us that this is by no means the way in which criminals habitually regard their punishment. It is true that the occasional prisoner has expressed sentiments apparently consistent with the *Philosophy of Right* (and these are keenly snapped up by the modern retributivist),[68] but in general we can agree with those who, like Quinton, point out that it is 'an odd sort of right whose holders would strenuously resist its recognition.'[69] It is this gap between *theoretically understood* reality and reality itself (not simply theory and practice) which underlies Marx's ambivalence towards Hegel's retributivism for at the end of the day, philosophical admiration must be tempered with sociological realism. In the end, Hegel justifies punishment, but only 'from the point of view of abstract right'.

(2) Proportionality of Punishment

That Hegel avoids the gap between theory and practice by a philosophical method which establishes in its place a gap between thought reality and empirical reality can be seen in his analysis of proportionality of punishment. We have already seen that for him, the Idea (thought reality) cannot determine the precise amount of punishment (its empirical manifestation). There is a gap between the Idea of punishment as rational reality and as empirical reality. Hegel admits as much when he concedes that while just punishment requires exact measurement, such justice is unattainable in practice:

Reason cannot determine...any principle whose application could decide whether justice requires for an offence (i) a corporal punishment of forty lashes or thirty-nine, or (ii) a fine of five dollars or four dollars ninety three, four, etc., cents.... And yet injustice is done at once if there is one lash too many, or one dollar or one cent...too many or too few.[70]

However, the problem is not just one of determining punishment with absolute precision within a given set of maxima and minima as Hegel suggests. The impossibility of absolute precision and justice is symptomatic of a more fundamental failing of the system. Crime and

---

[68] Both J. Mabbott ('Punishment' in Acton, *op.cit.*,) and Stillman (*op.cit.*) quote an ex-prisoner who wrote: 'To be punished for an offence against rules is a sane man's right.'

[69] Above, fn. 6.

[70] *Op.cit.*, p.137.

punishment are measured according to the 'concrete and determinate existence' of the act[71] and the 'qualitative and quantitative characteristics of crime and its annulment fall, then, into the sphere of externality.'[72] As such, there is no possible equation of crime with punishment, for each act has only its own particular and different qualities.

What provides the possibility of an equation is, as we have seen, the equality between crime and punishment which stems from their 'value', that is, from 'their universal property of being injuries.' Value is the 'inner equality of things which in their outward existence are specifically different from one another in every way',[73] and this inner equality of crimes and punishments as injuries allows for a proportional reciprocity between the two.

But this is inadequate, for we need to know not only wherein equality lies but also what the measure of that equality is. If crime x and punishment y can in principle be equalised because both are injuries, we still need to know how much of x equals how much of y, and here the Idea cannot help us, for the amounts of x and y can only be regarded from the point of view of what they are, i.e. concrete and determinate existents in the sphere of externality. Thus, on the one hand, Hegel differentiates crimes and punishments as external concrete existents,[74] and on the other, he identifies a principle of the Idea as their measure ('value'). But he can provide no means of establishing a concrete allocation of punishments on this basis for there exists a gap between the ideal reality of equality and value and the practical reality of crimes and punishments. It is not that equal punishment for crime cannot be *exactly* established, but that it cannot be established at all, for the practical business of measuring crimes and punishments can only occur in the sphere of external reality, whereas the principle of equality occurs in the sphere of thought reality. The gap between the two, which had been to Hegel's advantage in establishing a right of punishment regardless of the particularity of the criminal's will, *i.e.* when he wanted to exclude recalcitrant empirical realities from the philosophical realm, now becomes a problem when he turns to the question of establishing punishment's particular measure, *i.e.* when he wants to move outward from the philosophical concept to the empirical reality.

---

[71] *Ibid.*, p.68.

[72] *Ibid.*, p.72.

[73] *Ibid.*

[74] E.g.: 'The distinction between robbery and theft is qualitative; when I am robbed, personal violence is done to me and I am injured in my character as consciousness existing here and now and so as *this* infinite subject.' (*ibid.*, p.68).

4. REASON, REALITY, AND THE IRRUPTION OF 'THE IRRATIONAL'

Ultimately, Hegel's philosophical strategy of sealing off unseemly social realities from rationally understood reality begins to fall apart, and empirical reality irrupts into the world of reason as an irrational and contradictory force. This occurs in relation to both the nature of criminality and the measure of crime.

(1)   The Nature of Criminality.

Civil society is 'an association of members as self-subsistent individuals'[75] so that the administration of criminal justice within it is both the 'reconciliation of the criminal with himself' and 'with the law known by him.'[76]   However the harmony brought about through the rightful interplay of individual interests within civil society is undermined from within by its own internal dialectic. The division of labour leads to 'the dependence and distress of the class tied to [unskilled] work' and to an 'inability to feel and enjoy the broader freedoms and especially the intellectual benefits of civil society.'[77] There develops 'a large mass of people [which] falls below a certain subsistence level', and it becomes apparent that civil society is unable 'to check excessive poverty and the creation of a penurious rabble.'[78] ⟶ *nob*

The polarisation of individual life into class society cannot but have implications for criminal justice. The role of the police becomes not the enforcement of individual right but to

diminish the danger of upheavals arising from clashing interests and to abbreviate the period in which their tension should be eased through the working of a necessity of which they themselves know nothing.[79]

---

[75] *Op.cit.*, p.110.
[76] *Ibid.*, p.141.
[77] *Ibid.*, pp.149-150.
[78] *Ibid.*, p.150.
[79] *Ibid.* pp.147-148. Hegel himself was not terribly clear as to how this 'necessity' would resolve the existing tensions. See *ibid.*, pp.150-151.

In this situation, right and wrong are no longer perceived as logical stages in the dialectic of individual right, for poverty leads to a 'loss of the sense of right and wrong',[80] or rather to its refocus not upon individual transgressions but upon social wrongs:

Against nature man can claim no right, but once society is established, poverty immediately takes the form of a wrong done to one class by another. The important question of how poverty is to be abolished is one of the most disturbing problems which agitate modern society.[81]

Thus the dialectic of the *Philosophy of Right* and of right and wrong within it are explicitly threatened by the social developments occurring within civil society, which tend to throw over the developments of the Idea.

(2)   The Measure of Punishment

In measuring punishments, we have already seen that it is impossible for the idea of reason to establish a concrete gradation of external crimes and punishments. For this reason, any discussion of the actual nature of punishments is, as it were, thrown upon its own resources, and must establish its own criteria of measurement.   We see this in Hegel's discussion of the liberalisation that had occurred in punishments as a result of the work of penal reformers such as Beccaria. Hegel applauds this development, and argues that a penal code is 'primarily the child of its age and the state of civil society at the time.'[82]   As civil society has become more stable, there is less need for severe punishments.[83]

These observations by Hegel, while surprising in the light of his arguments for a strict proportionality between crime and punishment, are interpreted by Stillman[84] as evidence of his essential liberalism in matters of penal policy.   However, it must be noted that the gradation of punishments according to the nature of social stability cuts both ways as regards harshness or mildness, and Hegel recognises both sides of the coin:

If society is still internally weak, then an example must be made by inflicting punishments.... But in a society which is internally strong, the commission of crime

---

[80] *Ibid.*, p.150.
[81] *Ibid.*, pp.277-278.
[82] *Ibid.*, p.140.
[83] *Ibid.*
[84] *Op.cit.*, p.178.

is something so feeble that its annulment must be commensurable with its feebleness.[85]

While Hegel was against 'super-erudition' in relation to matters of contingency,[86] this did not stop him from observing that variation in the strength of society

> is the *justification* for sometimes attaching the penalty of death to a theft of a few pence or a turnip, and at other times a light penalty to a theft of a hundred or more times that amount.[87]

Here, Hegel has admitted the possibility of those 'fluctuating standards' that both he and Kant had warned against. His previous opposition was based upon the requirements of individual justice, but now Hegel overrides his earlier concerns in favour of *raison d'etat* pure and simple. From the point of view of the *Philosophy of Right*, this is irrational, for since the State is the ultimate embodiment of individual freedom, it is also the incorporation of the earlier moments in the dialectic of right, including the dialectic of individual freedom from the sphere of *Abstract Right*.

Thus behind the rationality of punishment and the justice of proportionality in punishment, established as the philosophical reality of that institution in society, we observe another, empirical, reality responding to a different and contradictory logic. Against the recognition of the abstract right of punishment for wrong done, the impoverished proletarian sees only social injustice and wrongdoing, and against the just measurement of punishment, the weak state applies punishment to save itself. These are realities nonetheless, and Hegel is ultimately forced to take account of them even if they cannot be rationally incorporated within his system. The empirical reality of social classes and class conflict follows a material logic far removed from the ideal logic of the Philosophy of Right. It exists as a 'corruptive invader'[88] within the dialectic of thought reality.

---

[85] *Op.cit.*, p.140.

[86] Above, fn.59, and accompanying text.

[87] *Op.cit.*, p.140, emphasis added.

[88] *Ibid.*, p.10. Hegel uses the phrase to describe Plato's attitude to the emerging principle of subjective freedom in Greek society.

5. CONCLUSION

Hegel takes the same essential raw materials as Kant - free, rational (juridical) individualism; determined natural individuality - and weaves them into a philosophical theory which unites reason and reality. But he does so in such a way that he selects those aspects of reality which are consistent with reason while excluding those other aspects which are not. His philosophy of punishment can avoid the kind of contradictions concerning criminality which we saw in Kant, for where the empirical world is concerned, reality is only on the agenda to the extent that it conforms with reason.

The method is not so successful in relation to the *measure* of punishment, for having sealed theory off from empirical reality, the actual grasp of that reality as a reality external to reason itself is impossible. However, as regards the realities of criminality, Hegel can ignore the plight of the unmarried mother or the honourable soldier with a clear conscience (or, more precisely, a clear mind). The price of this clarity is a certain empirical implausibility, on which modern philosophers have been quick to pounce (even if they have failed to understand why Hegel should have thought in these terms).

Hegel's philosophy of punishment can be seen as a final attempt to avoid the terms of the antithesis between juridical individualism and concrete individuality discussed in previous chapters. For him, concrete individuality is sealed off from the triumphant rule of rational, abstract individualism. The gap between reasoned reality and empirical reality ensures that concrete human individuality is kept at bay. Yet towards the end of the *Philosophy of Right*, Hegel is sufficiently worried about the reality of concrete individuality within civil society to open the door just enough to allow it in. It is interesting to compare his pessimism with the more optimistic views of Hobbes and Kant. Hobbes had argued that the 'common people' had to be educated in the ways of civil society in order to eventually play their part as citizens.[89] Kant had argued that social forces shaped people's perceptions of right and wrong, and looked forward to the day when society would develop the enlightenment that

---

[89] Above, ch.II, text at fn.63.

would bring conformity between perceptions and reason.[90]   For both, then, civil society _could_, at some future point in time, embody reason universally.

Hegel, however, with a clearer picture of how civil society was in reality developing, is more pessimistic. Society is divided into rich and poor, and he sees no immediate solution to the problem of poverty.[91] The possibility of good citizenship is tied up with this problem, hence Hegel evinces no optimism as to the future law-abidingness of a large section of the people. He simply notes the creation of a penurious rabble who have lost the 'sense of right and wrong'.[92] The juridical individualism/concrete individuality antithesis is forced back into the reckoning by the strength of modern developments, breaking through the chains of reason with which Hegel sought to bind it.   But it now clearly takes the form of materially determined social antagonisms.

At this point in the argument, we see, emerging from the engagement with the first contradiction of juridical ideology (see above, Chapter I), the development of the second contradiction: between individual right and state power.   What solution to this problem of class conflict could Hegel have?   The rabble is a potential threat to the state, for it interprets its poverty as wrong done to it.[93]   Hegel has already admitted that severe punishments are possible when the state is challenged. The logic of his position is to argue (as indeed happened in reality in Germany in the 1830s)[94] for a more vicious penal code in order to scare people into obedience. But if that is the logic of Hegel's position on the amount of punishment, it is a logic which leads him to fall foul of our second modern juridical antithesis.   To argue for over-punishment in order to protect the state (_raison d'etat_), while abandoning the standard of individual justice, is to adopt a position which expresses the contradiction between juridical individualism and political power. This is what happens when Hegel justifies the execution of petty thieves. Thus in seeking to manage the first contradiction of juridical individualism, the logic of Hegel's position leads him ultimately to confront the second.   Recalcitrant material reality proves to be that of a class society, and the state comes to be acknowledged as the defender of

---

[90] _M.E.J._, _op.cit._, p.107; above, ch.III, text at fn.68.

[91] _Op.cit._, pp.150 and 277-278. The drive to colonialism discussed on pp.151-152 is seen as an effect of domestic poverty, rather than as a solution to it.

[92] Above, fn. 80.

[93] Above, fn. 81.

[94] G. Rusche and O. Kircheimer, _Punishment and Social Structure_ (New York, 1939), pp.99-100.   (Das int eluran ordu global)

Für Hegel
f.h.d.

class, not universal, interest. Individual right ceases to be an absolute demand. It passes into the realm of contingency at the moment that state intervention in the defence of particular social interests causes it (the state) to abandon its formal respect for the individual embodied in the idea of proportionate punishment.

In the further development of the retributive philosophy of punishment, we will see how this emergent reality, admitted at the edges of Hegel's *Philosophy of Right*, came to achieve a much more central position in the formulation of a justification of punishment in the work of subsequent philosophers, particularly in the work of the so-called English Idealists to whom we now turn.

CHAPTER V

ABSTRACT RIGHT AND THE SOCIALISATION OF WRONG: RETRIBUTIVISM'S ENGLISH DECLINE AND FALL

1. INTRODUCTION

In the last three chapters, we have traced the development of the classical retributive theory of punishment. We have seen how the contradiction between juridical individualism and the reality of individual life slowly develops. In the first place, material realities are understood in the atomised form of an actual individual determined by his psychic and physiological nature. Gradually, however, the view of the isolated natural individual becomes inflected with the recognition of the role of *social* determinations on individual life. In Hobbes, this occurs, minimally, with his discussion of the ability of the common people to become citizens. In Kant, we noted the influence of social mores which he saw as determining certain types of person to commit some kinds of crimes. With Hegel, we noted the philosophical and methodological exclusion of this kind of consideration, but we also saw how the social reality of civil society ultimately intruded rather dramatically upon the later sections of the *Philosophy of Right*.

In turning now to the work of the English Idealists, those Victorian Hegelians who sought to synthesise Idealism with the conditions of late nineteenth century Britain, we see much more clearly the impact of social conditions upon the philosophy of abstract right and juridical individualism. In their work, the antithesis between abstract individualism and concrete (social) individuality is ⟨writ large⟩ as a contradiction embodied within. In the work of T.H. Green, with whom we will be in the main concerned, the aim is not to avoid this contradiction but to revise the theory so as to *reconcile* the philosophy of abstract right with the social nature of wrongdoing.

[handwritten note: Lehsa: in derselbichen Handschrift ?]

As regards the second antithesis between juridical individualism and state power, we saw how in the work of Hegel, the defence of individual right was exposed to the contrary logic of *raison d'etat* as a result of the failure to develop a method of establishing proportionality between crime and punishment.   The strong state punishes weakly while the weak state punishes strongly not so as to respect individual rights and desert but in order to protect the state and the social interests it reflects. With the English Idealists, we will see the way in which this second antithesis emerges as a direct and central consequence of their incorporation of the first antithesis within their work.   For the recognition of the social nature of wrongdoing implies the need for an *interventionist* state with new functions of prevention and reform *as well as* the need to punish retributively.   But state intervention on the basis of principles other than those of individual right is incompatible with individual right, so that the English Idealists express this second contradiction as a central feature of their philosophy alongside the first. This is particularly apparent in the work of Bradley and Bosanquet, to whom I turn later in the chapter. The important point to note is that the revisions   brought   about   by   these   philosophers   reflected   real developments in the nature of the state in late Victorian England, and that these developments were themselves a response to social problems associated with the poverty of Victorian capitalism - crime, delinquency, and the rest. The recognition of these problems, however, only served further to *activate* the contradictions within the classical theory of punishment, so that attempts philosophically to rationalise such social problems and their interventionist solutions only ended in tearing the classical theory apart.

2. REVISING THE CLASSICAL TRADITION: T. H. GREEN

(1)   Green's Philosophy of Punishment

For Green, there is truth in Hegel's view that 'freedom, as the condition in which the will is determined by an object adequate to itself, or by an

object which itself as reason constitutes, is realised in the state.'[1]
Green's own work seeks

to show how the self-distinguishing and self-seeking consciousness of man, acting
in and upon those human wants and ties and affections which in their proper
character have as little reality apart from it as it apart from them, gives rise to a
system of social relations, with laws, customs and institutions corresponding....[2]

But if society, laws and the state are objects of reason and individual
freedom, Green differs from Hegel in arguing that, until now, societies
have never embodied freedom for all. There is 'something in all forms
of society that tends to the freedom *at least of some favoured
individuals*',[3] and in modern society, 'The number of individuals whom
society awakens to interests in objects contributory to human perfection
tends to increase.'[4] But nonetheless, the realisation of freedom in all
societies, including Green's own, remains 'most imperfect':

To an Athenian slave, who might be used to gratify a master's lust, it would have
been a mockery to speak of the state as a realisation of freedom; and perhaps it
would not be much less so to speak of it as such to an untaught and under-fed
denizen of a London yard with gin-shops on the right hand and on the left.[5]

Green suggests, echoing the concluding point of the last chapter, that
'What Hegel says of the state in this respect seems...hard to square with
the facts.... [T]he difference between the ideal and the actual seems to
be ignored....'[6]   In truth, the nature of modern society is not that of a
unity of free individuals but the development on one side of a 'shiftless
population [in] the centres of industry',[7] the 'multiplication in recent
times of an impoverished and reckless proletariat.'[8]
    The solution to this contrast between free individualism and the
reality of social conditions is the development of the state as an active
agency of intervention. There is 'a work of moral liberation, which
society, through its various agencies, is constantly carrying on for the
individual'[9] and this in modern times takes the form of 'positive

---

[1] T. H. Green, *Lectures on the Principles of Political Obligation* (London, 1901).
[2] *Ibid.*
[3] *Ibid.*, p.7, emphasis added.
[4] *Ibid.*
[5] *Ibid.*, p.8.
[6] *Ibid.*
[7] *Ibid.*, p.228.
[8] *Ibid.*, p.225.
[9] *Ibid.*, pp.8-9.

reforms...which involve an action of the State in the way of promoting conditions favourable to modern life.'[10]   However, Green also points out that in overcoming the reality of social conditions, these state reforms entail impinging upon the boundaries of individual freedom: 'advancing civilisation brings with it more and more interference with the liberty of the individual.'[11]

Comparing Green with Hegel, we might say that while Hegel transposed the gap between theory and practice *outwith* philosophy (thought reality), Green brings it back in and attempts to rationalise it *within* philosophy by a process of theoretical revision. Thus he draws a distinction within his system between the particular, *egoistic* will and the *rational* will without suggesting that the former is the latter viewed from a different angle or that it is in some way implicitly rational. On the one hand the egoistic will is conceived as 'the effort of a self-conscious subject to satisfy itself'[12] as it pleases; on the other, the rational will alone seeks satisfaction in objects that allow for self-perfection. The contrast between the two is seen in that the immediate objects of self-satisfaction sought by the egoistic will may actually obstruct the ultimate goal of self-perfection so that there is no necessary coincidence between the object of will and the object of reason.[13]   To render egoistic will rational - to bring theory and practice together - requires an external principle, which Green describes as the 'organisation of life' or 'conventional morality',[14] in order to guide and educate the individual to his own self-perfection.

Thus Green seeks to reconcile theory and practice within theory by recognising the role of a collective principle (the 'organisation of life', the state) as the means of rendering individual wills rational.   The uncomfortable gap between theory and practice is actually engaged within his theory by reference to the interventionist role of the 'social organisation'. But an important feature of Green's argument that should be noted at this point is his characteristic, yet contradictory, tendency of reasserting the autonomy of individual reason or right almost in the same breath as he denies it. For example, he writes of moral education by the state as involving a

---

[10] *Ibid.*, p.39.
[11] *Ibid.*
[12] *Ibid.*, p.20.
[13] *Ibid.*, p.21.
[14] *Ibid.*, p.24.

determination of the will as in the individual by objects which the universal or rational will, of which the will of the individual is a partial expression, has brought into existence, and is thus a determination of the will by itself.[15]

Thus the individual will requires to be determined by objects provided by the rational will, but the individual will is an expression of the rational will, so education is *of* the individual will *by* the individual will. This attempt to have it both ways, to affirm the role of social organisation *against* individual will, yet to legitimate social organisation *in terms of* individual will is, as we shall see, a central feature of Green's philosophy of punishment.

As regards punishment, it is in this overall context that Green breaks from the classical retributive position by arguing that the justification of punishment should not only be retributive, but should also be preventive and reformatory. This is not just a matter of adding preventive or reformative effects to a fundamentally retributive theory in the manner of Kant,[16] but of recasting the justification of punishment in accordance with his general revision of the classical tradition. The key concept for Green is, as it was for Hegel, that of right, but in Green's work, rights are inherently *social*. No one can have a right save as a member of a society in which 'some common good is recognised by the members of the society as their own ideal good, as that which should be for each of them.'[17] For Green there is no possibility of conceiving of rights as pre-social, as, for example, in Hegel's sphere of *Abstract Right*. Rights are *ab initio* both socially recognised and socially justified:

The right (i.e. the power secured by social recognition) of free life in every man rests on the assumed capacity in every man of free action contributory to social good ('*free*' in the sense of determined by the idea of a common good...).[18]

Punishment entails the forfeiture of rights and just as rights are conceded only to the extent that action *contributes* to social good, so are they retracted to the extent that action *prejudices* social good. The right of punishment is a

right on the part of associated men [which] implies the right on their part to prevent such actions as interfere with the possibility of free action contributory to social good.[19]

---

[15] *Ibid.*
[16] See above, Chapter III, fn.1.
[17] *Ibid.*, p.44.
[18] *Ibid.*, p.180, emphasis added.
[19] *Ibid.*

Thus the right of punishment is not the right of the individual criminal as it was with both Kant and Hegel. It is the right 'belonging to a society of persons recognising a common good, and belonging through membership of the society to the several persons constituting it.'[20] It is because of this change from individual to collective right that the nature of punishment changes. Because the aim of punishment is to prevent *Hegel punb* actions interfering with social good, the intellectual fulcrum of the moral justification of punishment shifts from the right of the criminal to the prevention of crime in the general interest. In the *first* place:

[Punishment's] proper function is, in the interest of rights that are genuine..., to prevent actions of the kind described by associating in the mind of every possible doer of them a certain terror with the contemplation of the act, - such terror as is necessary on the whole to protect the rights threatened by such action.[21]

If punishment is primarily preventive and deterrent, it is also reformatory, for two reasons. First, and more importantly, if punishment is genuinely to prevent harm to the social good, it should reform as well as deter the criminal. A secondary reason is that the criminal has the 'assumed capacity...of free action contributory to social good' and punishment must take account of all rights 'including the suspended rights of the criminal himself..., must tend to qualify the criminal for the resumption of rights.'[22] Punishment, in this reformatory aspect, entails not the recognition of individual right by a rational being, as in Hegel, but the integration of the criminal into the community of rightfulness through a penal education. However, the principal aim of punishment is preventive, and Green holds that the added possibility of individual rehabilitation is a sort of moral bonus.[23]

Third, there is the question of retribution. Given that Green has recast the philosophy of punishment as a matter of social rather than individual right, what role could the individual desert of the criminal possess within his philosophy? Initially when Green confronts this question, it appears, consistently with his general analysis, as if he has completely transformed the classical retributive account, for he treats the element of retribution as an aspect of social condemnation, not individual right. While the state is not motivated by revenge, taking a 'purely social

20 *Ibid.*, p.183.
21 *Ibid.*, p.188. Cf. Cooper's account of *Hegel's* philosophy of punishment in the previous chapter.
22 *Ibid.*, p.204.
23 See *ibid.*

interest'[24] in punishment, public indignation takes the form, if not the substance, of vengeance. Such *collective indignation* is an expression of that public interest 'on which the system of rights with the corresponding system of punishment protective of rights depends.'[25]   Retribution here is understood in terms of a moral-social function, not a criminal's right, and therefore has a quite different meaning than in Kant or Hegel.

But Green than veers back towards the classical account by arguing that public indignation also takes the form of an insistence that 'the criminal should have his due, should be dealt with according to his deserts, should be punished justly.'[26]   Just punishment is then defined as entailing two elements, one philosophical, one practical. As regards the philosophical element, the criminal must possess

a capacity for determination by the conception of a common or public good, or in other words a practical understanding of the nature of rights as founded on relations to such public good.[27]

Because the criminal possesses this capacity and has this understanding, punishment can be not only defensive of collective rights, it can also be legitimated in terms of the individual right of the criminal; punishment can be the criminal's due:

[The criminal] being susceptible to the idea of public good, and through it to the idea of rights, though this idea has not been strong enough to regulate his actions, sees in the punishment its natural expression. He sees that the punishment is his own act returning on himself, in the sense that it is the necessary outcome of his act in a society governed by the conception of rights, a conception which he appreciates and to which he does involuntary reverence.[28]

We shall have cause to come back to this passage, but for the present, let us also note the practical element in just punishment. There must be

an actual violation of a right or omission to fulfil an obligation, the right or obligation being one of which the agent might have been aware and the violation or omission one which he might have prevented.[29]

These then are the three components of Green's philosophy of punishment: the preventive, the reformative and the retributive.   Green

---

[24] *Ibid.*, p.184.
[25] *Ibid.*, p.185.
[26] *Ibid.*
[27] *Ibid.*, p.186.
[28] *Ibid.*, pp. 186-187.
[29] *Ibid.*, p.180.

has attempted to justify punishment from the points of view of both
collective social-moral well-being and of the individual criminal's right.
Is he successful in this, or is it a question of trying to have his
philosophical cake and eat it?

(2)   Contradictions in Green's Account   (vielleicht: Schweise)

In this section, I discuss three areas in Green's philosophy of punishment
which highlight the relative importance of individual right and social
well-being in his account, and consider the extent to which he is able to
reconcile these two standpoints.

(1) Green's philosophical retributivism.   Given the general positions
that he has adopted on individual rationality and the social nature of
rights, is it possible for Green to justify punishment in terms of
individual desert?   We have seen that punishment is just for Green
because the criminal possesses 'a *practical understanding* of the nature
of rights as founded on relations to public good.'[30]   But criminals by
their actions reveal - *ex hypothesi* - no such practical understanding for
their behaviour is not determined by a concept of the public good.
Green recognises as much when he concedes the need for, and
possibility of, reform of the criminal.   The aim of reform is to restore to
individuals their rights by *returning to them* their practical understanding
of the nature of the common good through their 'recovery of criminal
habits'.[31]   If the commission of crime is a mark of the *absence* of
practical understanding, Green cannot logically justify punishment on
the basis of its presence.   He cannot have it both ways.

If we consider the passage quoted above[32] in which Green most
clearly explains the retributive justification of punishment, we can now
see the reason why his argument appears equivocatory.   He writes that
the individual is '*susceptible* to the idea of public good', not determined
by it, and he concedes (indeed he must do so) that such an idea 'has not
been strong enough to regulate his actions.'   If this is so, in what sense
has the criminal been 'susceptible' to it in the first place?   How can
Green go on to say that the criminal sees in punishment the 'natural
expression' of the idea of public good since his crime revealed, by

---

[30] Above, fn.26. emphasis added.
[31] *Ibid.*, p.202.
[32] At footnotes 25-27.

definition, his lack of understanding of that idea? Why does the criminal see his punishment as 'his own act returning on himself [as] the necessary outcome of his act in a society governed by the conception of rights'? Green writes that the criminal 'appreciates' this conception, but we have no means of knowing why or how, and he ultimately concedes that if the criminal does revere it, he does so in an 'involuntary' way. Precisely what this means is not clear.

(2) Individual Responsibility and the Measure of Punishment. We have seen that just punishment entails both a moral capacity and a practical act on the part of the criminal, and this might lead us to suppose that individual criminal responsibility would be a central feature of Green's discussion of punishment. However in considering the allocation of punishment, Green makes it clear that prevention is the aim, not just deserts. The state is not concerned with the 'inward' aspect of crime, only its 'outward' aspect, by which he means the effect of a man's conduct on 'the security and freedom in action and acquisition of other members of society.'[33] For this reason, the rationale of mitigating circumstances is not to be understood in terms of the moral guilt of the criminal, but in terms of the requirements of prevention.

The retributive approach of establishing individual guilt is fundamentally flawed in practice, for 'the degree of moral depravity implied in any crime is unascertainable.'[34] The degree of moral depravity within the inner character of the criminal is an imponderable and in any case, it must be recalled that the aim of the state is not to punish individual wickedness but 'the protection of rights, and the association of terror with their violation [as] the condition antecedent of any general advance in moral well-being,'[35] so that mitigation of punishment must be understood in these terms.

Similarly, in discussing criminal negligence, Green acknowledges that, although this is legitimately punished, it is not on the basis of the individual's guilt. Criminal negligence from the criminal's point of view is 'on a level with multitudes of actions and omissions which are not punished at all.'[36] Its justification rests upon the general social well-being. But what then of justice for the individual? Green attempts to 'sell' the punishment of negligence to the individual by arguing that such punishment will be seen as just by him 'in proportion to his sense of

---

[33] *Ibid.*, p.196.
[34] *Ibid.*, p.194.
[35] *Ibid.*, p.195.
[36] *Ibid.*, p.197.

justice, which means his habit of practically recognising true rights.'[37] But this is not the justice of individual desert, it is the justice of the prevention of social harms which the individual _ought_ to recognise, for true rights are social, not individual.

As regards the amount of punishment, Green's argument here follows the general trend of his thought away from retributivism. There is no possibility of a true equivalence between crime and punishment for 'neither a crime nor its punishment admits of strictly quantitative measurement.'[38] In any case, the idea of proportionality is made quite impossible because crime is no longer seen as a wrong done to an individual, for which requital can take the form of another wrong done to a criminal. Crime is, in Green's philosophical system, a wrong done to society, and this cannot be measured in the same scales as punishments to individuals:

A hurt done to an individual can be requited by the infliction of a like hurt upon the person who has done it; but no equivalent of wrong done to society can be paid back to the doer of it.[39]

In keeping with his general orientation, Green argues that since the primary aim of punishment 'is not to the effect of the punishment on the person punished but to its effect on others,' the 'considerations determining its amount should be prospective rather than retrospective.'[40]

If we put these positions on individual responsibility and the amount of punishment together, we may raise the question whether, on Green's account, punishment would in practice be just to individuals. For example, on his analysis, would the innocent be safeguarded from punishment, or could the guilty be punished in draconian fashion? If the aim of punishment is prevention, and social rights are to be protected, does this not suggest (as indeed the example of criminal negligence implies) that individuals may well be treated as a means to a social end?

In a long, meandering passage, Green attempts to get to grips with this question. While claiming that punishment is preventive and this is the basis for its allocation and measure, he argues that it should not be seen as '_merely_ preventive' for this leads to the notion that 'any action which any sufficient body of men find inconvenient may justifiably be prevented by any sort of terror that may be convenient for the purpose.'[41]

---

[37] _Ibid._
[38] _Ibid._, p.190.
[39] _Ibid._, p.183.
[40] _Ibid._, p.192.
[41] _Ibid._, p.188, emphasis added.

This notion needs to be guarded against 'by substituting for the qualifying 'merely' a statement of what it is which the justifiable punishment prevents and why it prevents it.'[42] However, his own general elaboration of what such a statement would entail is unenlightening for it consists in the assertion that punishment is only just where it protects rights that are 'necessary to the well-being of society on the whole, and [where] the terror which the punishment is calculated to inspire is necessary for their maintenance.'[43] This takes us no further forward, for what we want to know is not whether the rights protected are necessary for social well-being, nor whether the terror involved is necessary for the maintenance of such rights. We want to know whether there are any limits on terror given that rights and punishment are both necessary.

Green comes nearest to answering this question when he talks of the punishment of sheep-stealers and starving men. As regards the former, it is wrong to hang the sheep-stealer

because, though it is a genuine right that sheep-stealing violates, in a society where there was any decent reconciliation of rights no such terror as is caused by the punishment of death would be required for the protection of the right.[44]

This idea of reconciliation of rights appears again in relation to the crimes of the starving man. While it might be thought 'that, so far from the hunger of the thief being a reason for lightening his punishment, it is a reason for increasing it' so as to deter such theft, this would be wrong as a one sided application of the principle. This is because the state must protect all rights, including those of the starving.

It is not the business of the state to protect one order of rights specially, but all rights equally. It ought not therefore to protect a certain order of rights by associating special terror with the violation of them, when the special temptation to their violation itself implies a violation of right ... of those who are so tempted....[45]

Now, this notion of the reconciliation of rights appears to provide a means of controlling the operation of the social good against the individual, for it suggests a role for the state of balancing individual

---

[42] *Ibid.*, pp.188-189.
[43] *Ibid.*, p.189. This, Green concedes, is an 'abstract and negative' kind of criterion. A 'positive and detailed criterion of just punishment' must wait until the rights of men have been truly harmonised and experience has shown which punishments are required for which crimes. Of course, we still await this ideal state of affairs, although some still cling to the possibility of its achievement: see A. Von Hirsch, *Past or Future Crime* (Manchester, 1986), ch.6.
[44] *Ibid.*, p.188.
[45] *Ibid.*, p.193.

rights against each other, so that draconian punishments or punishment of the innocent is impossible. However these suggestions must be weighed against Green's general position on the nature of rights and the position of the individual vis-a-vis the social good. Here it is made clear that the social good retains primacy, and that individual rights are dependent upon their coincidence with social well-being:

> If laws are passed interfering with [the freedom of the individual], he says that his rights are being violated. But he only possessed these...rights through membership of a society which secured them to him, and of which *the only permanent bond consists in the reference to the well-being of its members as a whole....* [I]f...the reference to social well-being suggests the necessity of some further regulation of the individual's liberty to do as he pleases, *he can plead no right against this regulation,* for every right that he has possessed has been dependent on that social judgement of its compatibility with general well-being which in respect to the liberties in question is now reversed.[46]

Clearly on this principle, the punishment of the innocent would be justified. But surely, it might be suggested, the individual as a member of society may make claims upon that society, and those claims must be reconciled with the claims of all other individuals, so that in any laws that are passed, the individual's interest will be recognised and reflected? Such a suggestion runs against the general formulation of Green's theory in which the social interest is not just an amalgam of individual interests, but rather is a superior interest having higher claims. Thus no assertion of individual right - for example, the right of the innocent - may be advanced purely in terms of individual freedom. All such assertions 'must be founded on a reference to an acknowledged social good' because it is *only on that basis* that a right will be acknowledged:

> however abstractedly desirable for the promotion of human good it might be, [no exercise of a power] can be claimed as a right unless there is some common consciousness of utility shared by the person making the claim and those on whom it is made. It is not a question whether or no it ought to be claimed as a right; it simply cannot be claimed except on this condition.[47]

Thus the social well-being always has primacy, always negotiates on its own terms. The individual's rights are always precarious and secondary so that any talk of the state as the reconciliator of individual rights must be a sham. Individual rights *may* be recognised if the social well-being indicates the value of so doing, but they may just as readily not be for the same reason. There is nothing in Green's position to indicate that

---

[46] *Ibid.,* p.147, emphasis added.
[47] *Ibid.,* pp.148-149.

the innocent may not be punished or the guilty over-punished where this
is of value to the general good.[48]

(3) Capital Punishment. Green's ambivalence on individual rights is
nowhere more clearly seen than in his discussion of capital punishment.
At first, he appears reasonably 'liberal' in that he strictly limits the
exercise of the death penalty. The state has the right to punish but ought
to recognise 'the reversionary rights of the criminal, rights which, if
properly treated, he might ultimately become capable of exercising for
the general good.' Clearly, this can only happen if the criminal remains
alive, and so Green insists that capital punishment can only occur where
either it is necessary to 'preserve the possibility of a social life' or the
nature of the crime committed 'affords a presumption of a permanent
incapacity for rights on the part of the criminal.'[49]   The former type of
situation is confined to cases of treason and breach of war discipline,
while Green argues with piety that 'in our ignorance' the latter
presumption is one 'which we ought not to make.'[50]
      Thus in the interest of the reversionary right of the criminal, capital
punishment is strictly delimited. Yet at the very end of the chapter on
punishment, Green argues that capital punishment, far from being the
negation of the criminal's reversionary rights, is in fact...the means of his
moral rebirth! In the following passage, Green exhibits a complacent
disregard for the value of individual life which jars with and negates the
'liberal' humility and moderation of his earlier view on the death penalty:

Ultimately, therefore, the just punishment of crime is for the moral good of the
community. It is also for the moral good of the criminal himself..., it is morally the
best thing that can happen to him. It is so, even if the true social necessity requires
that he be punished with death. The fact that society is obliged so to deal with him
affords the best chance of bringing home to him the anti-social nature of his act. It
is true that the last utterances of murderers generally convey the impression that
they consider themselves interesting persons, quite sure of going to heaven; but
these are probably conventional. At any rate if the solemn infliction of punishment
on behalf of human society, and without any sign of vindictiveness, will not breed

---

[48] Of course, this is not to say that Green would intend that the state should act in
   such a way, only that the logic of his theory is open to such things happening:
   'Strictly speaking, a theory of rights, defined purely as socially acknowledged
   claims, says nothing about their content. If the members of a society recognised
   cannibalism as a practice, not only justified but mandatory in certain
   circumstances, no one using Green's criterion would have a right to object to
   being eaten under such specified conditions.' M. Richter, *The Politics of
   Conscience* (London, 1964), p.264.
[49] *Ibid.*, p.203.
[50] *Ibid.*

the shame which is the moral new birth, presumably nothing else within human reach will.'⁵¹

(3)   Juridical Individualism, Concrete Individuality and State Power

How does one classify Green's philosophy of punishment? According to Ewing, Green 'is no retributionist',⁵² while according to Acton, he did 'not reject retribution altogether, but [tried] to give some acceptable account of it.'⁵³   In a note in the *International Journal of Ethics*, Rashdall claims that in conversation, Green explained that while he once held to the retributive view, he had given it up as untenable.⁵⁴   One can see an element of truth in all these perspectives within Green's *Lectures*. A retributive element is present, and so Acton's comment seems valid, although we must note that the modifications undertaken by Green are not in order to provide an acceptable account of retributivism *per se*, but rather an acceptable account of retributivism within a wholly novel and revised idealist context.   But it is also that new context which so undermines the retributive theory as to render it little more than vestigial in Green's work as a whole.   Thus there is a sense in which Ewing's comment is true too.   As for Green's own admission, we do not know whether he already regarded himself as having given up retributivism in his position in the *Lectures*, but we can say that he might as well have done, given the insignificant and contradictory role that the philosophy plays therein.

(?)   Essentially what has happened in the *Lectures* is that Green, while starting out from Hegel's idealist individualism, has so revised the classical doctrine that when he comes to punishment, his position is much closer to utilitarianism than retributivism.   The emphasis upon prevention and reform indicate that this is so.   Of course, this is not to say that Green has abandoned idealism in favour of the simple materialism of the early utilitarian tradition; rather that his philosophy can be seen as a kind of ideal (idealist?) utilitarianism.

Support for this view can be drawn from Green's own discussion of natural rights theory and utilitarianism.   Green argues that the former theory had gained real political reforms through its stress upon the

---

⁵¹ *Ibid.*, pp.204-205.
⁵² A. Ewing, *The Morality of Punishment* (London, 1929), p.34.
⁵³ H. Acton, *op.cit.*, p.16.
⁵⁴ H. Rashdall, *International Journal of Ethics* (5) 1894-95, p.243.

liberty of the individual and the minimal role of the state, but that it now stands in the way of further advancement for the individual by way of positive social reforms. Utilitarianism, on the other hand, presents no such obstacle and is therefore preferred to natural rights theory. Indeed, utilitarianism 'may be presented in a form in which it would scarcely be distinguishable'[55] from his own doctrine. Green differs from the utilitarian position not because of its social interventionist standpoint, but rather because it 'recognises no vocation of man but the attainment of pleasure and avoidance of pain.'[56] Green's position is in substance utilitarian, it is with the non-ethical *form* of the theory that he is in disagreement.

But if this is a key to understanding the revisions that Green makes within the theory of punishment, it is also important to recognise the contradictory and inconsistent nature of his thought. The authoritarian conclusions of his philosophy of punishment stem from the logic of his revisionism but they are accompanied by attempts - throughout his work[57] - to temper state intervention by means of a defence of individual rights.[58] Similarly, it must also be borne in mind that part of the reason for his authoritarianism is his recognition of the need for positive social reforms to benefit individuals.

Green's position can be grasped once one understands his ambiguous and ambivalent attitude to the two antitheses entailed by a philosophy based upon juridical individualism. Green's work describes a circle. He begins by rejecting juridical individualism because of the first antithesis we have identified between the doctrine's abstract individualism and the concrete individuality of social life; this leads him to reject it again in favour of a philosophy of state intervention (the second antithesis); but ultimately, he returns to juridical individualism in order to seek to evade the authoritarian consequences of his own position. However, this return proves impossible because his system is premised upon the doctrine's rejection.

To expand on this: Green's starting point is his refusal to accept the Hegelian doctrine of abstract individualism. He recognises the contradiction between that doctrine and the reality of the social

---

[55] *Op.cit.*, p.42.
[56] *Ibid.*, p.43.
[57] See Richter, *op.cit.*, chs. 7 and 8.
[58] Cf. Richter, *op.cit.*, p.201: Green engaged in a 'massive effort' to 'prove that Idealist metaphysics when applied to the sphere of politics did not subordinate the individual to the state. Throughout his ethics there are signs of the strain produced by his merger of conservative concepts with liberal and even radical values.' See also *ibid.*, p.211.

conditions of individual life within Victorian England. His solution is to attempt a synthesis between abstract individualism ('the theory') and the reality of concrete individual life ('the practice'). He seeks to reconcile the 'gap between theory and practice' *within* philosophy, and not to place it outside, as Hegel did. He begins, therefore, by rejecting the doctrine of abstract individualism as the fundamental basis for political authority, and seeks to recast it by reconciling it with the reality of individual life.

This attempted reconciliation takes the form of a revised role for state intervention as a means of synthesising individual liberty and moral (social) life. The state will merge these divergent aspects through positive reforms. In so doing, however, it will override individual liberties in the name of the common good. Thus Green is forced to confront the limits of juridical individualism once more, this time in the form of the second antithesis between individual liberty and state power. Again, Green must reject juridical individualism, this time in order to create the new interventionist role of the state.

But now he is caught on the horns of a dilemma. He wishes to give the state this new role, but he also resists the logic of his own philosophical position, seeking to affirm state intervention *and* to defend individual freedom. Individual freedom must constitute both the end of state intervention *and* its moral foundation stone. In order to achieve this position, Green returns to the doctrine of juridical individualism, seeking to base his philosophy on the discarded doctrine of individual right. But there is no way back for Green, for his system is premised upon a rejection of this old doctrine.

This is the significance of Green's retributivism in the philosophy of punishment. Punishment is for Green really a form of (idealist) utilitarianism emphasising prevention and deterrence for the public (moral) good. Yet Green seeks also to justify punishment *to the criminal* by means of a vestigial retributivism. Given his overall doctrine of social prevention, the retributive defence of individual right can only appear as a secondary and subservient doctrine; and given his conception of the moral inadequacy of the individual will, such a will as manifested in criminality cannot form an adequate basis for an individualistic, retributive justification of punishment. Having discarded juridical individualism, there is no way back for Green from the logic of his own philosophical system.

3. REVISING THE CLASSICAL TRADITION: BRADLEY AND BOSANQUET

(1) F.H. Bradley

In considering Bradley's views on punishment, it is interesting to compare the crude and stark manner in which he confronts the same issues as Green. Bradley wrote two essays on punishment with a gap of almost twenty years between them.[59] However the gap is not just temporal, it is a gap between two philosophical outlooks: one in which juridical individualism is still dominant, the other in which social authoritarianism predominates.

In the earlier essay, Bradley discusses punishment in the context of a dispute about free will and individual responsibility. His justification of punishment follows closely the argument of Hegel when he writes that 'I' deserve punishment where

I have done 'wrong'. I have taken into my will, made a part of myself, have realised my being in something which is the negation of 'right', the assertion of not-right. Wrong can be imputed to me. I *am* the realisation and the standing assertion of wrong....[60]

He rejects prevention and reform as justifications of punishment, although he admits these more openly into calculations of the nature and quality of punishment than Kant or Hegel would have done. In the following passage, he separates the question of the justification of punishment (a retributive question) from that of the amount of punishment (a utilitarian question):

---

[59] F. H. Bradley, 'The Vulgar Notion of Responsibility' in *Ethical Studies* (Oxford, 1927), (originally published in 1876); 'Some Remarks on Punishment' *International Journal of Ethics* 4 (1893-94), p.269. Reprinted in *Collected Essays I* (Oxford, 1935). References are to the original journal publication. For a recent discussion of the two essays which attempts to rescue a revised retributive philosophy from them, see P. Johnson, 'Bradley and the Nature of Punishment' in A. Manser and Stock, *The Philosophy of F. H. Bradley* (Oxford, 1984).

[60] *Ethical Studies, op.cit.*, p.27.

We pay the penalty, because we owe it, and for no other reason; and if punishment is inflicted for any other reason whatever than because it is merited by wrong, it is a gross immorality...and not what it pretends to be....Having once the right to punish, we may modify the punishment according to the useful and the pleasant; but these are external to the matter, they cannot give us a right to punish, and nothing can do that but criminal desert.[61]

This division between justification and amount is extremely dubious, for if punishment is a matter of desert, its amount must be graded according to desert so that any *particular* punishment is deserved. If I have parked my car illegally, I do not deserve to be punished by *any* punishment that the state deems useful or pleasant.

Nevertheless, it is clear that here, Bradley is adopting an essentially individualistic, retributive position. It is true that he identifies a *collective* desire for punishment ('*we* annihilate the wrong and manifest the right')[62] but this is not a move away from an individualistic approach. The social annihilation of wrong, the collective desire for punishment, stems not from any posited superiority of the collective will over the rights of the individual, but from a recognition that individual wrong, if unpunished, falls upon all individuals in the manner of Kantian bloodguilt.[63]

When we turn to the later essay, we note a radical change in focus. Here Bradley aims to consider the role of punishment in the light of Darwinism and his emphasis falls upon 'the welfare of the community realised in its members.' In this 'organic view of things', individuals 'have rights and duties only as members of the whole'.[64] In this view, as with Green, retributive considerations rank on a par with preventive and reformatory effects of punishment. Over all three doctrines, however, Bradley places a new and overriding principle: 'the right and duty of the organism to suppress its undesirable growths' which derives from 'the moral supremacy of the community, its unrestricted right to deal with its members' as 'a Providence to itself'.[65] This new principle Bradley designates as 'social surgery'.[66]

Within this new context, Bradley identifies a positive and a negative side to the old theory of retributivism. The positive side 'declares punishment to be essentially the supplement of guilt' and he claims still

---

[61] *Ibid.*, pp.26-27.
[62] *Ibid.*, p.28.
[63] *Ibid.*, pp.27-28; see above, ch.3, text at fn.4.
[64] 'Some Remarks on Punishment', *op.cit.*, p.270.
[65] *Ibid.*, pp.272-273, 278.
[66] *Ibid.*, p.272.

to hold to this view. However, when he expands on what this means, he transforms the doctrine from one based upon individual desert to a collective principle in which retributivism is defined as the 'doctrine that punishment is moral reaction, the reaction of the moral organism against a rebellious member.'[67]

On its negative side, retributivism is the doctrine that the individual is sacred save insofar as he is guilty of a crime. Bradley attacks this view by a rather circuitous route. He takes up Green's argument that it is impossible to estimate the inward guilt of the individual as the basis for calculating the amount of punishment. In practice, we are thrown upon other devices in calculating the amount of punishment. The retributive principle ceases to be absolute, and cannot be held to have overriding authority: the principle of individual justice has become 'an inferior and subordinate duty', albeit one with which one cannot play 'fast and loose'.[68]   Following through his logic, however, Bradley argues that innocence is no moral barrier to punishment, for it has become a thing conditional:

the sacred rights of innocence [continue to] exist, so far as the rule of justice is not overruled, and they are intact, if anywhere, there where punishment corresponds to desert.   But, *where the good of the whole may call for moral surgery, mere innocence is certainly no exemption or safeguard.*[69]

Thus Bradley rushes in where the comparatively more angelic Green feared to tread. The sole value of these vulgarised arguments is to reveal in stark and crude form the nature of the change that took place in retributivism at the end of the nineteenth century. For Bradley in his later essay, retributive principles are secondary and conditional; their position is less than vestigial where the social good demands it. While the difference between his arguments and those of Green is really one of form and expression rather than content, Green at least sought to temper the logic of his position with a residual individualism; for Bradley such caution is thrown to the wind with a ruthless logic.

It is also worth noting that, from the first to the second essay, Bradley actually alters the *definition* of retributivism, which becomes a collective principle ('the reaction of the moral organism against a rebellious member') and he does so apparently without being aware that he has

---

[67] *Ibid.*, p.273.
[68] *Ibid.*, p.275.
[69] *Ibid.*, p.275, emphasis added.

effected a fundamental transformation.   He seems to be of the view that
the content of his two essays are fundamentally compatible.[70]

(2)   Bernard Bosanquet

Bosanquet's position is little different from that of Bradley, although he
reaches it by a different route.   Writing after Green, at the very end of
the nineteenth century, Bosanquet presents the state simply as the
representative of an organic unity.   Comparing himself to his one-time
teacher, he writes that the 'time has gone by for the scrupulous caution
which Green displayed in estimating the value of the State to its
members.'[71]   The 'gap between theory and practice' is ruthlessly brushed
aside and a division is opened up between those who are part of the
organic unity of the State, and those who are simply beyond the pale.   It
is in principle open to the English labourer to 'have touch with the
connection which Hegel represents as that between the Bourgeois
Society and the State proper.'[72]   The poor, 'omitting the definitely
criminal quarters'[73] are as capable of citizenship as any, and those who
are not are designated 'the 'dangerous classes', virtually outlawed by
[themselves].'[74]
        This assertion of the primacy of the organic state together with the
contempt expressed for those who do not fit in is reflected in
Bosanquet's discussion of punishment which, while following Green,
emphasises the authoritarian element in his philosophy.   Whereas for
Green, retribution was the sense of public indignation that took the form
of a demand that the criminal should have his due, for Bosanquet,
retribution is the necessity that the State 'should strike down the hostile

---

[70] *Ibid.*, p.284: 'In short, I should have little to correct in the old statement of my
view except a certain number of one-sided and exaggerated expressions.'

[71] B. Bosanquet, *The Philosophical Theory of the State* (London, 1965) p.ix.   This
is a reprint of the 3rd edition (1919) which differs little from the original of 1899.

[72] *Ibid.*, pp.272-273.

[73] *Ibid.*, p.ix.

[74] *Ibid.*, p.272.   Interestingly, Bosanquet is in fact quoting the words of Green
(*op.cit.*, p.129).   That Green could write thus indicates the ambivalence in his
work between compassion and compulsion.   Compare this comment with his
pity for the 'denizen of the London yard' (above, text at fn.5).   The difference
between Bosanquet and Green is that for the former, no such ambivalence is
apparent.

will which has defied the right by doing harm.'[75] Bosanquet concedes that the strength of retributivism is its 'definite idea of the offender' as a 'responsible person, belonging to a certain order which he recognises as entering into him and as entered into by him.'[76] He notes, however, that such an ideal representation of the criminal may well not coincide with the reality, which may involve, on the criminal's part, 'a furious hostility against the whole recognised system of law,'[77] but he simply and peremptorily brushes aside this objection to retributivism: 'after all, we are dealing with a question of social logic and not of empirical psychology.'[78] Quite so. Thus the point of view of the individual is peremptorily discarded. Where the individual rejects the demands of the 'social logic', he is simply regarded as unfit for membership of the social organism:

[It] must be laid down that, in as far as any sane man fails altogether to recognise in any form the assertion of something which he normally respects in the law which punishes him..., he is outlawed by himself and the essentials of citizenship are not in him.[79]

Whereas Green envisages only the insane as having a permanent incapacity for rights, and doubts whether society is ever able even to make that assumption, for Bosanquet, any wholesale rejection of the state as an ideal organic unity can only mean a total lack of the 'essentials of citizenship.'

Finally, in a later essay for popular consumption, Bosanquet makes even more explicit the move away from individual right. Retribution becomes 'a reaction of the general moral will, stimulated by an action of a personal bad will', a 'formal verdict or censure of the social authority'.[80] The aim of *retributive* punishment is not to give the individual his due, but to ensure that even

the dullest capacity, including that of the guilty person if dimmed and hardened by sin, shall not fail to apprehend the intensity of the annulling act.[81]

---

[75] *Ibid.*, p.208.
[76] *Ibid.*
[77] *Ibid.*, p.210.
[78] *Ibid.*
[79] *Ibid.*
[80] 'On the Growing Repugnance to Punishment' in *Some Suggestions in Ethics* (London), 1919, pp.198, 191.
[81] *Ibid.*, p.193.

Thus, as with Bradley, here all sense of retributivism as a justification of punishment based upon individual right is lost. Retributivism is defined as a collective social principle of vengeance.[82]

4. CONCLUSION

With the English Idealists, retributivism fell into careless hands. In the work of Green it became transformed into an incoherent addendum to an essentially utilitarian theory; in the work of Bradley, it was relegated to secondary status behind the principle of the totalitarian state, and was indeed conflated with that principle at one point; and with Bosanquet, all notions of individual right were negated in favour of the organic unity of the whole. Whereas Green retained a liberal 'intention', no such qualm obstructed the totalitarian rigour of the work of Bradley and Bosanquet. In their work, retributivism was given a bad name, and it was not therefore surprising that when the philosophy of punishment of the twentieth century came to be written (in the Anglo-American world at least), much of it was 'by way of reaction' to the English Idealists.[83] When Mabbott attempted in 1937 to recast the retributive doctrine itself, he anticipated 'deep suspicion and hostility' from philosophers among whom the prevailing view was that it had 'been definitely destroyed by criticism'.[84]   But as we shall see in the next chapter, it was in essence this scrambled, decayed and inverted version of retributivism that, taken to be the real thing, was destroyed by criticism.

This was so because another apparent consequence of the work of the English Idealists, particularly Bradley's earlier essay, is that it seems to have acted as a kind of distorting prism by means of which comprehension of the classical retributive accounts of Kant and Hegel was impaired.   For example, in Rashdall's telling critique of retributivism, it is not only Bradley but also Kant who is seen as holding

---

[82] 'The violation of right within the moral community has called forth a shudder of repudiation which is at the same time a reflex stroke and shock directed against the guilty person.' *Ibid.* At least one of Bosanquet's critics was aware that his theory was not really retributive at all: see H. Rashdall, *The Theory of Good and Evil, Vol I* (Oxford, 1907), pp.300 - 301 (fn.).

[83] H. Acton, *op.cit.*, p.9.

[84] 'Punishment' in Acton, *op.cit.*, p.39.

to a theory based upon a 'mysterious demand that moral guilt should be atoned by physical pain,'[85] This point is also taken up by Ewing in what proved to be a pivotal essay on punishment.[86] It appears, therefore, that not only did the English Idealists squander the classical inheritance, they also made it more difficult for modern writers to understand what that inheritance was. Kant's retributivism, whatever else it was, was no 'mysterious demand' for punishment. It was a rational deduction of the legitimacy of coercion on the basis of individual right, admittedly dressed from time to time in rather florid language. The critics take what was superficial in Kant as his essence. But if the proponents of retributive punishment had themselves discarded this essence without, in Bradley's case at least, being even aware that they had done so, it would perhaps not be surprising if its opponents should equally fail to make the connection. The matter is essentially conjectural, but there is no doubt that the classical tradition of individual right was lost at the turn of the century, and has not, as chapters III and IV claim, been properly recovered to this day.

Finally, it should be noted that the English Idealists opened the philosophical route to the kind of shallow eclecticism that has been the lot of punishment theory in the twentieth century. For Kant and Hegel, the moral unity of the individual subject was the core of the intellectual unity and coherence of the philosophy of punishment. It was the moral individual who anchored the justification of punishment and decisively allocated considerations of deterrence, reform and social revenge to their proper epiphenomenal status. Once that core had gone, the way was open for fifty seven varieties of penal function to take the place of the proper philosophical justification of punishment. In particular, the decay of the classic individualist accounts of punishment opened the door to a pervasive and overarching utilitarianism, the consequences of which philosophers were to spend the next century trying, without much success, to evade.

But that is the story of the next chapter. For the moment, let me conclude by pointing out that these final observations are not the prelude to a 'back to the Enlightenment' move in the argument. The past in the philosophy of punishment (as generally) genuinely is another country. What separates us from Kant and Hegel is not just a series of intellectual differences and misinterpretations, but rather a gulf of social history mediated through the ideas of the more recent past and the present. Green and the others were genuinely attempting (from one particular

---

85 Rashdall, *op.cit.*, pp.284 - 287.
86 A. Ewing, *The Morality of Punishment* (London, 1929), p.17.

political perspective, it must be said) to interpret the social and political problems and developments of their time within the Hegelian Idealist canon. What stopped them from simply replicating Hegel was the social reality that stood in their way. There could be no going back to the revolutionary enthusiasm of Enlightenment thought. Too much development (and underdevelopment) had occurred in the meantime for the dreams of the past to be simply replayed. The revolutionary abstract individualism of a Kant or a Hegel would have sounded as a hollow echo in a mass society of acknowledged and acute social problems. The only answer was to revise the classical theory, and the only way to do this was to destroy it through the incorporation of new ideas that could not possibly gel with the old.

The 'social problems' associated with the existence of Green's 'impoverished and reckless proletariat'[87] forced a radical revision in a doctrine that placed the abstract rational individual philosophically at the heart of the state. In the late nineteenth century, the state, and 'public spirited individuals' acting on its behalf, began to adopt new interventionist policies designed to neutralise a social residuum regarded as dangerous and irrational, and likely to 'contaminate' the better off sections of the working class. This broad historical move in which the state began to be perceived in a new 'welfarist' light did not leave political philosophy untouched.[88] Green and the other English Idealists in their different ways sought to revise the Hegelian individualist philosophy to accommodate and legitimate this new reality of social control, with the kinds of contradictory intellectual results we have explored. What was at stake was the place of juridical individualism within philosophical theory. To the abstract, 'free' individual, Green opposed, first, the social, concretely determined individual in need of reform and education, and, second, the 'benign' authoritarian state designed to do the reforming. Green's work is thus no more than a convoluted historical play upon the two antitheses of juridical individualism identified in Chapter I.[89] It is these antitheses that ultimately wrecked the classical tradition and left the way open for the twentieth century eclecticism to which we now turn.

---

[87] Above, fn.8.
[88] On these historical developments, see G. Stedman Jones, *Outcast London* (Oxford, 1971,) and D. Garland, *Punishment and Welfare*, *op.cit.*, at ch.1, fn.32, parts I and II. On Green and the philosophy of public service, see M. Richter, *op.cit.*
[89] Above, pp.8-11.

CHAPTER VI

JURIDICAL INDIVIDUALISM AND STATE POWER: UTILITARIANISM IN THE TWENTIETH CENTURY

1. INTRODUCTION

In Chapter I it was argued that the relationship between law and the historical development of the state in the era of monopoly capitalism meant that philosophical ideologies developed from the nature of juridical ideology in that period would exhibit an uneasy coexistence and tension between contradictory elements of individualistic and interventionist doctrine. Pashukanis argued that in the sphere of legal theory, the result of the historical development of the state was that the principle of legal subjectivity was no longer seen as 'an absolute attribute of the human personality' but rather 'as a purely technical determinant' or as a 'speculative hypothesis lacking any material basis'. This led to particular problems in the area of public law, where an overweening state had undercut the classical individualism of the law:

the more consistently the principle of authoritarian regulation is applied, excluding all reference to separate autonomous wills, the less ground there remains for applying the category of law. This is particularly noticeable in the realm of so called public law. It is here that legal theory encounters the most serious difficulties.[1]

In the eminently public arena of state punishment, we have already seen the value of applying this perspective on legal theory to the work of the English Idealists, where the principle of state intervention, glorified by their philosophical idealism, comes to relegate the position of the individual to a secondary and vestigial role. In turning now to twentieth

---

[1] Pashukanis, *op.cit.*, p.101.

century discussions on punishment, we will be applying this perspective
to the modern debate on the end and justification of punishment. It will
be argued that while the major positions within that debate have
developed from a rejection of the work of the English Idealists, they
nonetheless share a similarly problematic standpoint in relation to the
contradiction between individual right and state power. / Furthermore, it
will be argued that the standard debates which occupied philosophers for
the middle part of the twentieth century, with their typically sterile focus
on an unsynthesised amalgamation of utilitarian and 'weak' retributivist
arguments, owe their intellectual structure and character to the decay of
idealism revealed in the previous chapter.   In the absence of a
transcendental philosophical basis for the justification of punishment,
little remained to the twentieth century other than some rather dull
consequentialist generalities, onto which were tacked, contradictorily,
some rather prosaic half-truths about the nature of law which were meant
to do the work of philosophical enquiry.   The result, which was a
historical one, in the sense that the intellectual context was formed in the
crucible of the real socio-political developments indicated at the end of
Chapter V, was an arid and unstimulating set of discussions in pursuit of
an uncatchable will o' the wisp; the reconciliation of individual right and
the general social interest in the context of the justification of
punishment.

2. THE TRIUMPH OF UTILITARIANISM

The trajectory of utilitarianism from its early beginnings in Hobbes's
materialism has not been traced in detail in this work for, unlike the
retributive philosophy, its development has already been well charted[2]

---

[2]   See, for example, J. Plamenatz, *The English Utilitarians* (Oxford, 1966); E.
Halevy, *The Growth of Philosophical Radicalism* (London, 1972). It is not the
aim of this chapter to provide a *tour d'horizon* of utilitarian theories of
punishment. I focus on the twentieth century debate, which I argue has
developed on the back of the revision of late nineteenth century retributivism,
and which has had to confront the question of the justice of punishment in a
particular way because of retributivism's decline and fall. Of course,
utilitarianism is very important as a theory of state activity from the early
nineteenth century onwards, but in the earlier period, it remains essentially
individualistic in its approach. Bentham's *Introduction to the Principles of*

and is fairly easy to follow. The transition from Hobbes's individualistic psychological hedonism to the collective principle of the 'greatest happiness of the greatest number' was achieved by Bentham, with some assistance from earlier philosophers such as Hume.[3]   Utilitarianism was then developed and modified into a more complex doctrine by later philosophers such as John Stuart Mill and G.E. Moore.[4]   By the beginning of the twentieth century, the predominant theme within the utilitarian philosophy of punishment was of an ideal utilitarianism in which the justifying consequences of punishment could take a variety of forms, including, alongside the more traditional ideas of prevention and reform, that of moral education.

In this section, we consider the way in which this approach came to pre-eminence at the same time as it finally laid to rest the classical retributive philosophy.   The culminating work of this period is undoubtedly Ewing's thorough analysis of the main philosophies of punishment, *The Morality of Punishment*[5], and it is this book which forms the main focus of this chapter. But in many ways Ewing has done no more than to amalgamate a number of different approaches which represented philosophical orthodoxy in the early part of this century. It will therefore be useful to spend some time considering the various strands feeding into the orthodox position before examining Ewing's work as its final outcome.

Morals and Legislation (New York, 1962) and *Theory of Legislation* (New York, 1975) are essentially *juridical* formulae for the resolution of social problems since they rely on the activities of calculating individuals confronted by the threat of punishment, rather than the effects of extended state intervention.

[3]   And not without some confusion on Bentham's part. See Plamenatz, *op.cit.*, pp.70-82. On Hume, see *ibid.*, ch.2 and J. Mackie, *Hume's Political Theory* (London 1980), pp.151-154. Nor was the development of a consistent utilitarian theory of punishment easily achieved.   Adam Smith, for example, elaborated a theory in which utilitarian and retributive elements vied with each other in a highly contradictory way.   See Norrie, 'Justice and Punishment in Adam Smith' (1989) *Ratio Iuris*, pp.227-239.

[4]   See in general J. Smart and B. Williams, *Utilitarianism For and Against* (Cambridge, 1973) pp.3-27.

[5]   (London, 1929). A short version is contained in 'Punishment as a Moral Agency', *Mind* (1927) XXXVI, pp.292-305.

(1)   The Utilitarian Context

In the foreword of *The Morality of Punishment*, Ewing acknowledges a debt to four earlier authors.   The first two, indicating the continuity between the old Idealists and their realist critics, are Green and Bosanquet.   From Green, he draws the idea that punishment is necessary in a society in order to prevent interference with rights: punishment has value as a deterrent.   He also affirms the importance of Bosanquet's view in his later essay that punishment is a way of annulling a precedent that would otherwise be held valid in society.   The criminal act must be met with punishment not as a requital of the individual criminal but so that society may declare certain acts to be wrong.   Punishment is a form of social/moral condemnation.   Ewing correctly argues that this position, its author's view to the contrary notwithstanding, is not a retributive one.

These two views of the consequences of punishment clearly fit into a utilitarian framework without difficulty.   The other two sources, which Ewing acknowledges have similar implications, have an added impact in that they complete the rejection of the retributive doctrine in its classical form begun by the English Idealists.   In *The Theory of Good and Evil*, Rashdall advances a critique of retributivism, which reduces it virtually to nought.   Retributivism is, he claims, no more than a form of the 'old world cry of blood for blood'.[6]   It refuses to justify punishment in terms of its effects but rather because it wipes out 'in some mysterious way'[7] the offender's guilt through his punishment.   Looked at realistically, this doctrine amounts to no more than the claim that to the pain in the crime should be added an additional pain of punishment regardless of any consequences, good or bad:

A wrong has been done - say, a crime of brutal violence; by that act a double evil has been introduced into the world. There has been so much physical pain for the victim, and so much moral evil has polluted the offender's soul. Is the case made any better by the addition of a third evil, - the pain of the punished offender, which *ex hypothesi* is to do him no moral good, whatever.[8]

This argument begs the question, for it depends upon how one defines 'moral good'.   If it means the same thing as 'moral right', then Rashdall's claim is invalid.   For clearly, a retributivist could argue that to have one's right respected in punishment is the only moral good that can exist. Of course, Rashdall is not talking about 'moral good' in this sense. He is talking about moral *improvement* or *reform*, and it is certain that the

---

6   H. Rashdall, *The Theory of Good and Evil (Vol.1)* (Oxford 1907) p.284.

7   *Ibid.*, p.285.

8   *Ibid.*, p.286.

classical retributivists had no philosophical interest in such a doctrine. But in order to criticise the retributivists, Rashdall must come up with something more than a definitional difference of opinion.

He is on stronger ground when he attacks the abstract nature of the retributive philosophy. This he does in two ways. First, he criticises the whole notion of an overarching moral or rational law as a piece of meaningless idealism. Retributivism, he claims

> shows a disrespect for human personality by proposing to sacrifice human life and human well-being to a lifeless fetich [sic] styled the Moral Law, which apparently, though unconscious, has a sense of dignity and demands the immolation of victims to avenge its injured amour propre.[9]

Now we have seen that the failing of the moral-rational doctrines of Kant and Hegel lies in the gap that they open up between the realities of individual life and the abstraction entailed in their philosophical systems. There is a real contradiction within their philosophies stemming from the ideological nature of their premises. Rashdall recognises this much in his criticism of the moral fetishism of classical retributivism, but he fails to understand the nature of the method which established the fetish. Instead he explains it in terms of personal intuition - whether one 'does or does not in [one's] best moments feel this mysterious demand that moral guilt should be atoned by physical pain.'[10]

Second, Rashdall attacks the abstraction implicit within the doctrine of proportionality between crime and punishment. How can one measure moral guilt against physical pain? We have already seen that both Green and Bradley had conceded that it was impossible to measure guilt, and this had led Bradley to argue that the amount of punishment could be varied according to what was socially useful.[11] Rashdall seizes on this concession, claiming that it reveals that punishment can *only* be fixed according to the ends for which it is used, thus revealing a fundamental inadequacy in the retributive doctrine:

> If punishment is 'modified' for utilitarian reasons, does not that mean that it is inflicted partly for retribution and partly for some other reason? If so, we do not pay the penalty because we owe it, and for no other reason.[12]

Thus the abstraction of the retributive doctrine, while its philosophical source is not recognised, is rightly stressed by Rashdall in its two

---

[9] *Ibid.*, p.304.
[10] *Ibid.*, p.286.
[11] Above, ch.V, text at fn.59.
[12] *Ibid.*, p.288.

principal forms - the justification and measure of punishment - in order
to, on the one hand, reduce it to no more than moral intuition, and, on the
other, reveal its collapse into utilitarianism. All that remains positive in
it can be described as certain moral effects which punishment possesses
both for the criminal and for society as a whole. As regards the former,
punishment keeps the individual's 'lower self' in check, allowing his
'better self' to thrive[13], and as regards society, punishment acts as an
outlet to the community's moral indignation (cf. Green) and gives
expression to its moral sentiments, helping to promote moral education
(cf. Bosanquet).

Thus all that is of value in the retributive philosophy is not in fact
retributive at all in the proper, classical meaning of the term. Still,
Rashdall builds on this demolition of retributivism in order to formulate
an ideal utilitarian justification of punishment which rests on the added
values of several kinds of good consequence. Deterrence and reform
have their place but must be supplemented by an 'educative' element,
that is an ethical aspect which he imagines to be the rational kernel of
retributivism, but which is not retributivist at all in the classical sense.
The resulting amalgam is described as 'teleological' in that punishment
can deter, reform and morally educate.[14]

Before moving on to Ewing's fourth source, it will be useful to
consider one important question raised by this position. If the
punishment of individuals is to be seen teleologically, i.e. if individuals
are to be used as a means to an end, could this not lead to their unjust
treatment? Rashdall agrees that individuals are to be treated as means
within his approach, but this does not entail that the individual is not also
treated as an end 'if his good is treated as of equal importance with the
end of other human beings.'[15]

But this begs the question, for what we want to know is whether on
the teleological view, the individual's good *is* to be treated as of equal
importance. Rashdall concedes that his theory may require some
unwarranted sacrifice of the individual to the common good:

---

13 *Ibid.*, pp.292-293.
14 *Ibid.*, p.302-303: 'Both the 'deterrent theory' and the 'reformatory theory' are no
   doubt inadequate to express the whole truth about punishment. There is a side of
   punishment which might perhaps be best expressed by the term 'educative
   theory'; or, perhaps, we may simply say that the end of punishment is partly
   deterrent or utilitarian, and partly ethical. Both sides of punishment would be
   summed up in the assertion that our view of punishment must be a teleological
   one.'
15 *Ibid.*, p.303.

Social life would not be possible without the constant subordination of the claims of individuals to the like claims of a great number of individuals; and there may be occasions when in punishing a criminal we have to think more of the good of society generally than of the individual who is punished.[16]

Ewing's fourth source is an essay by the Hegelian, McTaggart, who had, significantly, developed an interpretation of the Hegelian philosophy of punishment which brought it into line with the ideal utilitarian concerns of the early twentieth century. McTaggart's aim is, in the light of the unpopularity of retributivism (the 'vindictive' theory of punishment, as he calls it),[17] to interpret Hegel's philosophy in a non-retributive fashion. While Hegel clearly rejected the deterrence and reform theories of punishment, he argues that he did not follow the vindictive/retributive approach, which is described as the view that

if a man has done wrong it is right and just that he should suffer for it, even if the pain does no good, either to himself or others. The punishment is looked on as a satisfaction of abstract justice, and he is said to deserve it.[18]

Whereas Rashdall simply attacked the retributivists for holding to this kind of view, McTaggart seeks to rescue Hegel from the opprobrium associated with it. Hegel held to a fourth theory which rested upon the fact that man was 'potentially moral'[19] and that punishment was a means of reform having the effect of 'purifying'[20] his mind of its wrongfulness:

In sin, man rejects and defies the moral law. Punishment is pain inflicted on him because he has done this, and in order that he may, by the fact of his punishment, be forced into recognising as valid the law which he rejected in sinning, and so repent of his sin - really repent, and not merely be frightened out of doing it again.[21]

But is this not a kind of reformatory theory? McTaggart adopts a distinction between the reformatory effects of the act of punishment *per se*, and the use of the duration of punishment in order to reform. The reformatory theory involves the latter, for the *period* of punishment is used to extend reforming influences to the individual. In McTaggart's view, the actual act of punishment can be reformatory by 'emphasising some moral tie which the offender was all along prepared to admit, although it was too faint or incomplete to prevent the fault,...work[ing]

---

16 *Ibid.*
17 J. McTaggart, *Studies in Hegelian Cosmology* (Cambridge, 1901), p.131.
18 *Ibid.*, p.130.
19 *Ibid.*, p.132.
20 *Ibid.*, p.145.
21 *Ibid.*, p.133.

on him as, at any rate potentially, a moral agent.'[22]   He describes this theory of punishment as 'purificatory'.

Let us consider the effects of this account of Hegel's philosophy. First, it clearly entails a radical revision of the meaning of the original doctrine. The individual is seen as only '*potentially*' moral, and needs to be '*forced*' to be good. The state therefore has an important role to play. The 'vindictive theory' as it is called is rejected and along with it the central elements of abstract justice and criminal desert. It does not appear to me that these revisions are justified on the basis of any reading of Hegel's philosophy of punishment. In chapter IV, it was pointed out that the fundamental justification of punishment as a matter of individual right is already established *prior* to the rational recognition of the state and Hegel's discussion is based upon the inherent - not potential - rationality of the individual.[23]   Hegel's criminal does not require to be forced to recognise anything: he demands his punishment as the right of an already rational being.

Second, we may note what McTaggart loses through this reinterpretation of Hegel.   Most obviously, he loses the central connection between punishment and desert: punishment (in Hegel's theory!) is now understood as reformative:

There seems no reason why we should enquire about any punishment whether the criminal deserved it.... Of course, a punishment is only to be inflicted for a wrong action, for the effect of all punishment is to discourage the repetition of the action punished, and that would not be desirable unless the action were wrong. But to enquire how far the criminal is to be blamed for his action seems irrelevant. If he has done wrong, and if the punishment will cure him, he has, as Hegel expresses it, a right to his punishment. If a dentist is asked to take out an aching tooth, he does not refuse to do so, on the ground that the patient did not deliberately cause the toothache, and that therefore it would be unjust to subject him to the pain of the extraction.   And to refuse a man the chance of a moral advance, when the punishment appears to afford one, seems equally unreasonable.[24]

To modern eyes, this invocation of a 'medical model' is all too familiar. If desert is no longer relevant to punishment, why should we only punish those who have committed crimes?   Could not the state anticipate the commission of crimes and therefore punish in a pre-emptive fashion? There appears to be no reason why not on McTaggart's reasoning. If wrong acts can be predicted, why wait until they have been committed in order to educate the criminal by punishment? Dentists not only extract

---

[22] *Ibid.*, p.142.
[23] See above, Chapter IV, text at footnotes 43,46.
[24] *Ibid.*, p.140.

teeth, they also drill and fill them at earlier stages so as to avoid the ultimate pain of extraction. We will return to this point shortly in our discussion of Ewing's work.

Third, McTaggart argues that Hegel's great mistake in formulating his theory was to imagine it to be relevant to the operation of legal punishment by the state. It really is only relevant to the operation of the educational system. The main aim of state punishment is deterrence not reform, for its deterrent effect 'is far more certain than its purifying effect',[25] and also because the criminal is generally too callous and disrespectful of the state to be much persuaded by his punishment of his moral wrongdoing.[26]

Thus just as Rashdall had discarded retributivism in favour of a blend of utilitarian influences, so too does McTaggart. The only difference between them is that the latter resurrects the corpse of Hegelian philosophy, dressing up the mouldering remains in modern clothing. In the process, he not only manages to lose the central connection between punishment and desert, he also succeeds in rendering the doctrine largely irrelevant to the question of state punishment. With such philosophical friends, Hegel had little need of enemies. Still, McTaggart has confirmed that at the beginning of the twentieth century, there was only one direction available for philosophical thought: all roads, even those allegedly sympathetic to the classical positions, led to a utilitarian philosophy of punishment, in which, in keeping with the spirit of the age, the 'benign' purposes of an interventionist state superceded the classical foundation of state punishment in individual right.

(2)   A Utilitarian Morality of Punishment

We have seen how the final retributive pretensions of the Victorian Idealists were stripped away by the realists to reveal underneath a common utilitarian standpoint emphasising the significance of the state over against the individual. Rashdall and McTaggart merely carried through the logic of the English Idealists to its conclusion. Because of this common standpoint, the tension between individual right and state power was carried over from the one to the other, so that the position of the individual in the work of Rashdall and McTaggart remained precarious. If we turn now to Ewing's more complete and sophisticated

---

[25] *Ibid.*, p.145.
[26] *Ibid.*, pp.146 - 148.

realist work, we can examine the ways in which he aggregates the various arguments that circulated in this period, and see how he tries to come to terms with the question of individual right.

With Rashdall, Ewing agrees that Kantian retributivism is an intuitive doctrine, the value of which has to be measured against the other more important intuitions of the deterrence and reform theorists.   With McTaggart, he agrees (with some degree of ambivalence) that whatever Hegel intended, his views can best be understood as a philosophy of 'moral improvement or a necessary stage in moral development'.[27]   From Green he takes the emphasis on the value of deterrence; from Bosanquet, he takes the aspect of moral declamation and suppression; from McTaggart, he takes the concept of moral reform; and from Rashdall, he takes the general idea of punishment as an amalgam of practical and moral effects. Punishment deters, but individuals are not psychological hedonists alone. There is a moral aspect to their actions so that to 'deter men by pain or fear of pain from doing a certain act is not the same as condemning the act as morally wrong'.[28]

However, where Ewing strikes out on his own is in his recognition that no matter what the valid ends of punishment may be, no theory of punishment of a teleological kind is going to be acceptable unless and until it can take account of a deeply held feeling held by 'the natural man'[29] that punishment, whatever else, should be deserved.   The retributivist philosophy has been unceremoniously rejected in its entirety, but it cannot be denied that, however inadequately, it did express a 'natural' sentiment of mankind:

The ideas of desert, of 'justice' as a good-in-itself, and even of proportion between guilt and penalty, are too deeply rooted in our ethical thought to be dismissed lightly, however hard they may be to rationalise.[30]

This recognition of the importance of individual right marks Ewing out as the initiator of a new debate, familiar to all modern students of the philosophy of punishment, in which, on the basis of the rejection of retributive philosophy - the natural home of individual right - the retributive effect is to be achieved 'by other means': as Ewing puts it, 'without the *prima facie* irrationality'[31] of the old philosophy. This in

---

[27] Ewing, *op.cit.*, p.22.
[28] *Ibid.* p.60.
[29] *Ibid.*, p.14.
[30] *Ibid.*, p.45.
[31] *Ibid.*, p.100.

effect means that Ewing sets out to establish the effect of individual justice within a utilitarian philosophical framework. The first stage of his argument follows McTaggart in asserting that punishment is 'pain inflicted because of wrong done and after a judicial decision involving moral condemnation by an organ representing society.'[32] Punishment is therefore morally educative, *but it can only be so for the guilty*. If the individual to be punished had not committed an offence, there would be no point in punishing him, for to express moral disapproval of what is not wrong will not reform, only corrupt.

The second stage of his argument is to concede that while moral education may benefit few *criminals*, it can have a general educative effect in society as a whole. If punishment 'may help the offender to realise the badness of his action, may it not help others to realise this badness before they have committed the kind of action in question at all?'[33] Once again, such moral condemnation must be of a past criminal act. This is because

The moral object of a punishment as such is to make people think of a certain kind of act as very bad, but, if it were inflicted otherwise than for a bad act, it would either produce no affect of this sort at all or cause people to think an act bad which was not really bad, and this is why we must first of all ask - is a punishment just? Is it inflicted for a wrong act?[34]

In this way, Ewing also explains the proportionality between crime and punishment. The state must not only educate people as to the nature of what is wrong, it must also show them the relative seriousness of different wrongs. Different quantities of punishment can achieve this. It is not possible to fix an exact proportion between the two as the retributivists had claimed, but it is possible 'to compare the degrees of badness presupposed on the average by different offences, and, having done that, we can lay down the principle that a lesser offence should not be punished so severely as a greater one.'[35]

In a number of ways, this search for retributivism by other means is inadequate. Firstly, as with McTaggart, Ewing has only sought to establish *some* connection with a past criminal act, he has not established a connection between punishment and individual desert *per se*. His discussion is designed to show that the identification of punishment with past crime can be based on something *other than* individual guilt. But

---

[32] *Ibid.*, p.83.
[33] *Ibid.*, p.94.
[34] *Ibid.*, p.104.
[35] *Ibid.*, p.106.

124   CHAPTER VI

this then raises the question of the value of the connection he has established in place of the retributive account.

If the aim of punishment is the moral education of the criminal, is it impossible to conceive of such education being achieved through the punishment of one who has not committed a crime but who, let us say, might be considered a potential criminal?   Indeed, might not the potential criminal be *more* convinced of the moral wrongness of crime if he is punished in advance of the commission of a crime? Might not the ordinary individual? One cannot exclude *a priori* the possibility that this would be so since the goal of education is as conceivable through prior admonitory chastisement as through *post hoc* punishments. Nor can one assert *a priori* that pre-emptive punishment would have a corruptive effect. It might have, but it might equally - on the rationale of this theory - serve to convey the very serious moral view that society takes of certain kinds of behaviour.

Ewing's reply to this is to argue that if one does punish an act that is not wrong, this is bound inevitably to have a corruptive effect, for one is then punishing an act which is '*ex hypothesi* right'.[36] But this misses the point, for one can concede that the punishment of a right act would be corruptive without avoiding the objection raised. The proposal for pre-emptive or admonitory punishment covers not the punishment of right acts but the punishment of the potential for future wrong acts.[37]

A second problem for Ewing's account stems from his recognition of a *general* educative effect of punishment. In relation to the goal of deterrence, Ewing points out that the punishment of the innocent would be permissible where the deterrent effect was operative. But what is true of a general deterrent effect is also true of a general educative effect. One might have to ensure that the punishment of an innocent man occurred under certain conditions (most obviously, as regards his innocence, of secrecy),[38] but provided that this was done, punishment

---

[36] *Ibid.*, p.91.

[37] T. Honderich, *Punishment: The Supposed Justifications* (London, 1976) misses this point, although he correctly identifies the second problem noted below.

[38] Mabbott's famous injunction to 'keep it dark', (in Acton, *op.cit.*, p.44). J. Hampton, 'The Moral Education of the Criminal' (1984) *Philosophy and Public Affairs*, 208 is a recent attempt to tread this ground, but she cannot avoid these same problems. Her argument that the punishment of the innocent would send a wrong message to the community assumes that its wrongness will not be kept dark. The further argument that we know the criminal needs a lesson but are less sure about the community, and that therefore punishing the *guilty* individual has lexical priority, assumes that society can be divided in advance into two discrete groups of criminals and non-criminals. If society contains potential

would have an educative effect in the same way that it has a deterrent effect. Finally, there is Ewing's treatment of the question of proportionality between crime and punishment. He concedes that a rough, not precise, proportionality is possible on the basis of his criterion of education. But he also agrees that the determination of the proportions of crimes and punishments depends not upon any intrinsic value between the two but upon the particular view of a particular crime or punishment held by society at any given time:

Not that the punishment suited to express a given degree of disapproval will be eternally the same; what punishment is suited to convey disapproval depends not on the badness of the act to be punished alone, but also on the way in which the society in question is likely to interpret a given degree of punishment.[39]

Here we are back to the fluctuating standards against which Kant had warned and which retributive philosophy had centrally sought to avoid.[40] On Ewing's account, both crime and punishment are subject to changes in social perception as to their seriousness. Accordingly, there can be no intrinsic proportionality such that the individual may feel he is getting his due - no more and no less.

3. UTILITARIANISM AND INDIVIDUAL RIGHT

Ewing's unsuccessful attempt to establish retributive principles 'by other means' set the scene for the great majority of contributions to the philosophy of punishment which were to follow. The question of how to secure individual rights on the basis of a general utilitarian doctrine has dominated much of the mid-twentieth century debate on punishment, and in this section, I will examine the principle contributions. To begin with, I consider, fairly briefly, three approaches which have had their proponents, but which have not generally been regarded as being particularly successful in defending the individual against the general interest. Thereafter, in a second subsection, I consider the influential argument of Mabbott, that retributivism should be re-cast as a legal

criminals, which must be a premise, then a general educational function cannot be denied or given a lower priority on the educational theory.

[39] *Op.cit.*, p.106.
[40] See above, ch.III, text at fn. 62.

rather than moral doctrine; and then, thirdly, I consider a number of 'two-stage' approaches to the problem which retain a fair measure of support today.

(1) Refining Utilitarianism and the 'Definitional Stop'

One approach to the problem of individual right is to argue that utilitarian philosophy itself can be formulated in such a way that it does not entail injustice for individuals. Thus Rawls suggests a rule-utilitarian position in which the punishment of the innocent is regarded not as an isolated act but as an institution, and argues that the institutionalised punishment of the innocent could hardly conceivably have beneficial consequences.[41] However, he concedes that such an approach does not exclude the institutionalised punishment of the innocent, but only makes it less likely to be justified on utilitarian grounds.[42]

A more telling argument against this approach, however, is the logical one that a consistent rule-utilitarianism, that is, a rule-utilitarianism which remains true to the utilitarian command to maximise benefits, would collapse into act-utilitarianism. The application of a rule-utilitarian approach to the manifold situations presented by circumstances would result in rules so flexible and individualised that they would not amount to more than a series of *ad hoc* decisions no different in form from an act-utilitarian approach.[43] In the context of Rawls's argument, the point of this is that it indicates that the problem with an institution of what he calls 'telishment' is not that such an institution is practically inconceivable, but rather that its institutional design must be such as to allow maximum flexibility as to the circumstances in which punishing the innocent could be justified. The

---

[41] J. Rawls, 'Two Concepts of Rules' in Acton, *op.cit.*
[42] *Ibid.*, p.114.
[43] Cf. Smart in Smart and Williams, *op.cit.*, pp.11-12: '...an adequate rule-utilitarianism would not only be extensionally equivalent to the act-utilitarian principle (i.e. would enjoin the same set of actions as it) but would in fact consist of one rule only, the act-utilitarian one: 'maximise probable benefit'. This is because any rule which can be formulated must be able to deal with an indefinite number of unforeseen types of contingency. No rule, short of the act-utilitarian one, can therefore be safely regarded as extensionally equivalent to the act-utilitarian principle unless it is that very principle itself.' See also Honderich, *op.cit.*, pp.85-86.

problem in this theory is not with the institution of 'telishment' *per se*, but with the best way of designing it so as to maximise its efficacy. Such an institutional design would, no doubt, be quite different from that of, say, the criminal justice system as it stands, for it would emphasise *ad hoc* decision-making and secrecy. It would, however, remain an institution, justified on utilitarian grounds.

A second utilitarian approach is to impose factual limits upon the practical situations which a utilitarian philosophy would be likely to confront.[44] A recent example of such an approach is that of Hare, who argues that in the real world, no cases where breach of a principle such as non-punishment of the innocent

are likely to arise in practice, and it is for the world as it is that prima facie principles have to be selected and firmly inculcated. The good judge will not consider the possibility of the case before him being of such a sort. If he could consider it, he would certainly be a worse judge - one who would not act for the best in *other* cases. Only in extreme situations in which the system was disintegrating could such considerations come in, and probably not even then.[45]

The argument is not clear. The reference to 'the good judge' is either a piece of question-begging (for we want to know what the good judge *should* do) or part of a different argument concerning the value of rule-utilitarianism (he 'would not act for the best in *other* cases') with which we have already dealt. To the extent that it is a denial of the practical value of punishing unjustly in the world as it is, it is clear that even Hare concedes the *possibility* of unjust punishment, although he leaves the matter open.[46] His ambivalence affirms Acton's conclusion that there are good but not conclusive arguments against the punishment of the innocent on the basis of a utilitarian approach alone.[47]

Finally, and very briefly, a third position that has enjoyed some popularity is the definitional argument that the word 'punishment' means

---

44 T. Sprigge, 'A Utilitarian Reply to Dr. McCloskey', *Inquiry* (1965) 8, p.264, and see Honderich's response in *op.cit.*, pp.72-74.
45 R. Hare, *Moral Thinking* (Oxford, 1981), pp.163-164.
46 He continues: 'Perhaps the sheriff should hang the innocent man in order to prevent the riot in which there will be many deaths, if he knows that the man's innocence will never be discovered and that the bad indirect effects will not outweigh the good direct effects; but in practice he never will know this' (*ibid.*, p.164). However, the problem is not whether or not the innocent should be punished but the general question of knowing what the future effects of one's acts will be, a question that applies to *all* utilitarian calculations, and which is not, therefore, a specific objection to punishing the innocent.
47 Acton, *op.cit.*, p.21.

the infliction of pain on an offender for an offence.[48]   The counter-
argument to this is well-known: that definitions cannot take the place of
justifications, and that, in any case, the 'definitional stop' relies upon a
standard definition that ignores other non-standard meanings, whose
existence is a necessary consequence of the vague and open-textured
nature of language.[49]

This third argument, however, does begin to push us away from
utilitarianism *per se* and towards the qualification of utilitarian principles
by reference to extraneous concepts. It is in the area of compromise
between utilitarianism and some kind of quasi-retributive approach that
the most significant attempts to defend individual rights have occurred.
In   the   next   subsection   we   consider   Mabbott's   apparently
uncompromising defence of retributivism before moving on to some
more explicit compromises.

(2)   Retributive Punishment as a Legal Requirement

In an influential paper, Mabbott announces his intention 'to defend a
retributive theory of punishment and to reject absolutely all utilitarian
considerations from its justification.'[50]   There is no sense of compromise
in this claim. At the same time, however, he wishes to reformulate the
traditional retributive approach so as to avoid the problems, described
above, that are associated with it, and in so doing, an element of
compromise does creep in.

He argues, first, that 'a 'criminal' means a man who has broken a law,
not a bad man'.[51]   Punishment is not for moral or social wrongdoing, but
because an individual has broken the law.   Only God can punish moral
wrongs, and social wrongs are only punished to the extent that they are
contained within law.

Second, if punishment is not intended to negate moral wrong, then the
balancing of moral wrong and physical pain is an issue that can be
avoided. Instead of this hopeless quandary, the legal retributivist may
retain a proportionality between crime and punishment by grading

---

[48] The linguistic approach has some early support in the work of Bradley, Rashdall
and Ewing (see Acton, *op.cit.*, p.16), but is best argued by A. Quinton in 'On
Punishment' in Acton, *op.cit.*

[49] See A. Flew, 'The Justification of Punishment' and K. Baier, 'Is Punishment
Retributive?', both in Acton, *op.cit.*, and Honderich, *op.cit.*, pp.62-64.

[50] J. Mabbott, 'Punishment' in Acton, *op.cit.*, p.39.

[51] *Ibid.*, p.41.

'crimes in a rough scale, and keep[ing] our heaviest penalties for what are socially the most serious wrongs....'[52]
With this requirement that punishment be scaled according to the social seriousness of wrongdoing, a utilitarian element creeps into the picture. Mabbott does not deny this; what he suggests is that utilitarian considerations are relevant to the establishment of a legal system with sanctions, but that the individual decision to punish depends upon the infraction of a law by the criminal, who 'brings it on himself':

> Punishment is a corollary of law-breaking by a member of society whose law is broken.... Considerations of utility come in on two quite different issues. Should there be laws, and what laws should there be? Legislators do not *choose* to punish. They hope no punishment will be needed. Their laws would succeed even if no punishment occurred. The criminal makes the essential choice; he 'brings it on himself'.[53]

It should be made clear, his own claim to the contrary, that Mabbott is not defending a solely retributive theory of punishment. He defends a theory as to the conditions under which punishment should be allocated to individuals, and on this question, his answer is retributive. He also defends a theory as to the general considerations which make a system of punishment valid - regardless of how that system is administered in individual cases; and that defence rests upon considerations of utility. Thus, Mabbott's position is in essence a compromise one along lines not that different from the later work of Hart, with his distinction between punishment's 'General Justifying Aim' and the principles involved in 'retribution in distribution'.[54]

But if this is a compromise position, then it is important to consider whether it works: whether, that is, the defence of individual right is coherently maintained within Mabbott's approach. To do so, it is instructive to consider a criticism of Mabbott's original paper, and his response to it. The criticism concerns the nature of his multiple justification of punishment. Once we see that he has justified punishment as an institution or system by one set of criteria (utilitarian) and particular applications of punishment by another (retributive), then we must recognise that the justification of punishment is, depending on the particular case, either overdetermined or contradetermined. It is overdetermined in those situations in which punishment is justified on both utilitarian and retributive grounds; it is contradetermined where there is a conflict because utilitarian criteria point in one direction and

---

52 *Ibid.*, p.50.
53 *Ibid.*, pp.48-49.
54 On Hart, see next subsection.

retributive criteria point in another. This must be so, because to justify a *system* of punishment must also be to justify, in part, particular acts of punishment falling within the system. The system of punishment cannot be regarded in total isolation from the acts and effects of individual punishments which comprise it.[55]   But if this is so, would not the situation of contradetermination entail the possibility in properly specified circumstances of overriding the retributive requirement in favour of the utilitarian; of, for example, punishing the innocent?

Mabbott accepts the principle but not the conclusion. In his response to this objection, he concedes that retributive punishment is only a conditional obligation, which may be overridden in certain circumstances: the judge has 'a prima facie obligation or a responsibility to inflict punishment.   There are other ethical claims which may contradetermine my decision (and justify me in letting the criminal off).'[56]   But, if another ethical claim may override the retributive claim in order to justify letting the criminal off, what, logically, prevents such an ethical claim from doing the opposite; i.e., punishing the innocent? Mabbott does not address this question, but it is a relevant one to ask, as becomes clear in the following parallel discussion of telling the truth:

For Kant truth-telling was a claim which no counter-claim could override. Most of us would hold that other claims can override this one.   When it would cause great suffering to tell the truth there is contra-determination.[57]

The weakness in Mabbott's position can be seen if for 'truthtelling' and 'to tell the truth' in this quotation, we substitute the words 'not to punish the innocent'.

Thus, given that Mabbott's position is a compromise one, and therefore one which entails over- and contradetermination of moral claims, it must be conceded that in logic, his approach cannot avoid the injustice associated with utilitarianism in particular cases.   The possibility of contradetermination is given in his distinction between systems and acts of punishment. But we can go further than this, for it is possible to claim that the logic of Mabbott's approach leads not just to the possibility, but to the *necessity* of individual injustice in appropriate

---

[55] The original argument is Flew's: 'though Mabbott claims to 'reject absolutely all utilitarian considerations from its justification', he is prepared to appeal to these to justify *systems* of punishment.   But if a *system* is to be justified even partly on such grounds, some cases within that system must be partly justifiable on the same grounds: the system surely could not have effects to which no case within it contributed'. ('The Justification of Punishment' in Acton, *op.cit.*, p.94).

[56] 'Professor Flew on Punishment' in Acton, *op.cit.*, p.124.

[57] *Ibid.*, p.123.

cases. The reason for this lies in the structure of his ethical thought and the relation within it between his general utilitarian standpoint and his legal account of retributivism.

Again, we may approach this point by reference to a criticism levelled against Mabbott. If retributive punishment is a legal matter, has he not produced simply a *description* of the punishment process rather than a justification of it? Does he not need to go on to explain why punishment for law breakers is *justified*? His response to these questions is to concede that moral justification *is* required on top of legal description, and to seek such justification in the obligation on a judge to punish an offender where the judge has voluntarily accepted his position and because of 'his recognition of the value of a legal system which has rules and penalties'.[58]

Let us explore the two parts of this supposedly moral justification of punishment. First, the judge's voluntary acceptance of his position is a sort of promise to do his job; it is a kind of agreement akin to the idea of a contract: the judge promises to do his job in return for his appointment to a position. But there is nothing particularly *moral* in this reference to promise-keeping. In effect, this part of Mabbott's justification of punishment rests the legal obligation to punish upon a quasi-legal (contractual) obligation to do one's job. This 'justificatory' element gives no additional moral purchase. Were judges in Nazi Germany morally bound to punish opponents of the regime because of their voluntary acceptance of their position? The point is that the voluntary acceptance of a position says absolutely nothing about the moral justifiability of the position itself.

As regards the argument concerning 'the value of a legal system which has rules and penalties', this, at best, justifies the system of punishment as a whole and that system alone, which, as we have seen is justified in utilitarian terms. So, Mabbott can hardly justify the retributive demand for punishment of the guilty on this basis. On the contrary, his argument amounts to no more than a utilitarian justification of punishment as a whole, onto which is grafted a legal description of the way in which the system works. To the extent that Mabbott is a retributivist, his position is purely descriptive; to the extent that he attempts to justify his retributivism, his argument collapses into his overall utilitarianism.

Finally, Mabbott's position is further confused by a misunderstanding of the nature of the judicial function when he discusses the measure of punishment. When it comes to sentencing, he argues that the proportion

---

[58] *Ibid.*, pp.121-122.

of punishment should be, and is, fixed by the legislature on the basis of utility according to the social seriousness of crime. However, he acknowledges that the legislature usually fixes maxima which give judges discretion as to particular sentences. Does this then mean that judges also employ a utilitarian discretion in sentencing, thus breaking down the division that Mabbott has erected between the utilitarian functions of the legislature and the retributive functions of the judge? He rejects this argument on the basis that it is not the *effects* of punishment that determine the precise sentence but retributive issues concerning 'the degree of guilt (in the past) or the degree of responsibility (also in the past)'.[59] Mabbott must argue in this way if he is to avoid the conclusion that judges sentence according to utilitarian criteria, but his argument is inadequate, for while it is true that retributive questions concerning individual responsibility do help to determine sentence, it is also the case that utilitarian criteria do too. We need only think of the idea of 'exemplary sentencing' to see that this is so.

(3)   Two-Stage Approaches to Retributivism

In effect, Mabbott's position breaks down into a two-stage approach, in which the moral primacy of his utilitarianism effectively overrides what amounts to no more than a(n ideal) description of the operation of the legal system. This then leads us on to the similar positions adopted by a number of philosophers, whose work entails a duality of approach in their analysis of punishment.

To my knowledge, the first philosopher to adopt this kind of analysis was Ross[60] who distinguished in 1930 between 'two stages which are not usually kept apart in discussions of [punishment].' He distinguishes the stage of 'the affixing of the penalty, from that of its infliction' and asks 'on what principles the state or its officials should act at each stage.' At the stage of legislation, he argues that 'a large place must be left for considerations of expediency',[61] but once a law has been promulgated, the judge must simply apply it. Admittedly he must consider expediency where the law merely sets down maxima and minima of punishment, but in general his role is to apply the law to those who have broken it.

---

[59] *Ibid.*, p.122.
[60] W.D. Ross, *The Right and the Good* (Oxford University Press, 1930), pp.56-65.
[61] *Ibid.*, pp.61-62.

Ross's approach accordingly rests upon a demarcation of legislative and judicial roles, with a division of philosophical principles resting thereon. While such an approach is implicit in Mabbott's 1937 essay, it is also explicit in an influential paper of Rawls, which we have already considered in relation to rule-utilitarianism. In the first half of that paper, before advancing the rule-utilitarian argument, Rawls claims to explain and avoid the conflict between retributivist and utilitarian views by virtue of 'the time-honoured device of making them apply to different situations.'[62]   Their confusion can simply be dispelled once one distinguishes the roles and attitudes of judges and legislators;

...the judge and the legislator stand in different positions and look in different directions: one to the past, the other to the future. The justification of what the judge does, *qua* judge, sounds like the retributive view; the justification of what the (ideal) legislator does, *qua* legislator, sounds like the utilitarian view. Thus both views have a point...; and one's initial confusion disappears once one sees that these views apply to persons holding different offices with different duties, and situated differently with respect to the system of rules that make up the criminal law.[63]

Can it be this simple; can an institutional demarcation do the work of a philosophical analysis? Plainly not. While Ross's two stage approach distinguishes different kinds of philosophical principle, he recognises that the clash of principle is not resolved thereby. Thus the state's obligation solely to punish the guilty is only (like Mabbott) a conditional one, for

There may be cases in which the *prima facie* duty of punishing the guilty, and even that of not punishing the innocent, may have to give way to that of promoting the public interest.[64]

But once Ross has conceded this, the distinction he draws between legislative and judicial functions is itself undermined, for the duty of punishing the innocent remains a function of the administrator of the law (the judge) and not the legislator.   As with Mabbott, the mere identification of a particular judicial function is no bulwark against the philosophical logic of a general utilitarian scheme.

Similarly, with Rawls, the 'time honoured device' of making philosophical principles apply to different situations dispels no confusion whatever, it merely compounds it. If individual rights could be so easily defended from the logic of the utilitarian approach, why is it

---

[62] Acton, *op.cit.*, p.109.
[63] *Ibid.*, p.108.
[64] Ross, *op.cit.*, p.64.

necessary for Rawls to consider the possibility of a rule-utilitarian defence of the individual in the second half of his paper? How is it, if the separation of questions is an answer to the clash between retributivism and utilitarianism that Rawls must still confront the charge that utilitarianism justifies too much?[65]   Finally, we come to Hart's distinction between punishment's 'General Justifying Aim' and 'Retribution in Distribution'. Again, the problem is seen in terms of the need to recognise different philosophical principles at work at different points in the legal system:

> Much confusing shadow-fighting between utilitarians and their opponents may be avoided if it is recognised that it is perfectly consistent to assert both that the General Justifying Aim of the practice of punishment is its beneficial consequences and that the pursuit of this General Aim should be qualified or restricted out of deference to principles of Distribution which require that punishment should only be of an offender for an offence.[66]

But it is not 'perfectly consistent' to operate in this way, as Hart concedes when he later admits that the penal system is a 'compromise between partly discrepant principles'[67] and that individual justice may on occasion have to give way to official fraud on the basis of utilitarian calculation.[68] What is surprising in this concession is that Hart should acknowledge only a *partial* discrepancy between retributive and utilitarian principles, for as concepts they are in complete opposition to each other.

The reason that Hart must acknowledge lack of consistency and discrepancy in his approach is that, like Mabbott, his position is based upon an overdetermination of the justification of punishment. Individuals are punished according to principles of retributive justice, but they are also punished as individual instances of the pursuit of the General Aim. It could not be otherwise for it would be impossible to conceive of a general effect of punishment which was not instantiated in (at least some) of its particular incidents. But if overdetermination is present, then contradetermination is also potential, so that Hart has not resolved the clash of philosophies, he has merely expressed it within his approach. Since the principles of retribution in distribution serve to qualify the general aim of punishment, the possibility of contradetermination indicates that these subsidiary principles of individual right remain conditional upon the overall requirements of the system. To avoid this conclusion, Hart would have to provide a meta-

---

[65] Acton, *op.cit.*, p.111.
[66] H.L.A. Hart, 'Prolegomenon to the Principles of Punishment' in *op.cit.*, p.9.
[67] *Ibid.*, p.10.
[68] *Ibid.*, p.12.

theory to establish a means of choosing between the utilitarian and retributive principles in individual cases.[69] This, he does not do.

4. CONCLUSION

Our analysis of the predominant debate within the philosophy of punishment this century confirms the theoretical propositions established in Chapter I, and outlined at the beginning of this chapter. The tension between state intervention and individual right is wholly apparent in the work of all but the most single-mindedly utilitarian[70] but the one doctrine which embodied individual right in a fundamental and wholehearted way - retributivism - has been thrown over so that individual right appears as a secondary addendum to the utilitarian principles of state action.

In relation to legal theory, Pashukanis argued that the more the principle of authoritarian regulation takes over from reference to individual autonomous wills, the less room there is to apply the individualist categories of law. This point is fundamental not just for an understanding of legal theory but for all doctrines which have their roots in juridical ideology. The more the philosophies of Green, Bradley, Bosanquet, Rashdall, McTaggart and Ewing start out from a position of the general well-being, and the less they refer to the autonomy of the individual, the more they are unable to defend individual right against state intervention.

In the process, we have seen, the principle of individual subjective right is transformed from 'an absolute attribute of the human personality' to a 'speculative hypothesis lacking any material basis'. We need only compare Kant and Hegel's retributivism with Rashdall's denunciation of it as a 'moral fetich' or his and Ewing's characterisation of retributivism

---

[69] Cf. N. Lacey, *State Punishment* (London, 1988), pp.47-49. For criticism of Lacey's own solution to the problem of individual justice, see my review essay of her book in (1990) *International Journal of the Sociology of Law*, 18(1). For a recent two stages discussion in the spirit of Ross and Hart, but employing a neo-Kantian weak retributivist argument, see A. Goldman, 'The Paradox of Punishment' (1979) *Philosophy and Public Affairs*, 42. Goldman's use of rights as both a side-constraint on punishment and as the basis for its social justification only replicates the problem of the twin justificatory standpoint in the typical Hartian analysis.

[70] For example, see J. Smart (Smart and Williams, *op.cit.*, pp.67-73).

as no more than an intuition of the ordinary man. Having adopted such a position, it is no surprise that the defence of individual right offered by Ewing should be inadequate, for it is grounded in its opposite, the utility of state intervention.

When we come to the mid-century attempts to compromise between utilitarianism and retributivism, we find again that individual right is regarded not as an inherent quality of individuals, but as 'a purely technical determinant' in the practice of law. It is not surprising that those seeking to defend the individual should return to legal practice as a source of individual right, for individual right is an inherent - though partial and contradictory - feature of the bourgeois legal form.[71] However, such attempts are doomed to failure. The reason for this is that a technical practice cannot do the work of a philosophical defence against an overriding philosophical principle. Inevitably in the positions taken by Mabbott, Ross, Rawls, and Hart, contradetermination remains a possibility, so that the rights of the individual remain secondary and contingent, to be overridden in the general interest when need be.[72] The classical retributivists had employed juridical ideology at the heart of their moral theory, elevating the legal form to a transcendental metaphysical status. Having destroyed that status, the twentieth century utilitarians still resort to legal form as the basis for individual justice, but now in the shape of an idealised picture of legal practice itself. Having thrown over the moral individualism of retributivism, founded on the doctrine of individual right, in favour of a utilitarian justification of state power, modern philosophers of punishment have necessarily found it impossible to defend the rights of the individual in any absolute or consistent fashion.[73] They remain caught in the antithesis between state

---

[71] See above, Chapter I, pp.10-11.

[72] In Chapter VIII, it will be argued that criminal justice cannot provide a bulwark against utilitarian actions because criminal justice itself, as a legal form, is founded upon the antithesis between individual right and state power. Criminal justice is implicated in political compromise. The simple example of exemplary sentencing illustrates this, but I will also argue that the existence of this antithesis makes any rationalistic account of the nature of legal reasoning in the criminal law untenable. A further dramatic illustration of the contradictory character of the criminal justice process is revealed in the recent exposure of the judicial role in the UK in relation to 'miscarriages of justice', in which the judges have consistently defended 'the system' against claims of false conviction by individual prisoners. See B.Woffinden, *Miscarriages of Justice* (Sevenoaks, 1989) for a summary of cases.

[73] As a final illustration, consider Mundle's amendment of Mabbott so as to avoid his 'legal descriptivism': ....'punishment of a person by the State is morally justifiable, if and only if he has done something which is both a legal and a moral

power and individual right.   Their residual individualism well earns the title 'weak retributivism'.

Utilitarian theory was the natural successor to retributive ideology in the twentieth century.   The English Idealists had already heralded the demise of an individualistically based philosophy of punishment through their support for an interventionist role for the state.   In so doing, they gave philosophical expression to contemporary political developments in the role of the state at the turn of the century.   Criminality and delinquency became ready foci for the exercise of paternalistic state intervention through the ideologies of 'treatment' and 'welfare'.[74] Together with the general dynamic of society towards what was to become Keynesian intervention and the welfare state, these developments formed the context in which thinking about punishment would start from the perspective of the 'general social interest'.   Where the legitimating ideology of capitalist societies was strongly moving in the direction of 'social eudaemonism',[75] it was to be expected that the justification of punishment would follow suit.

But it is important to note the persisting practical and ideological significance of juridical concepts throughout this period.   Legal philosophers in particular, keen to retain a liberal outlook within the overarching utilitarian culture, opposed *exclusively* utilitarian practices such as rehabilitation or treatment in place of punishment.[76] Consequently the philosophical task set, as it were, by history was to achieve a reconciliation between an overall predominant role of the state on the one hand and principles of individual justice on the other.   This is seen in the almost totemic status enjoyed by Hart's discussions of punishment in the 1960s and 70s.   Hart's theory, which was the culmination of the work of a series of philosophers from the 1930s onwards, and therefore not particularly original, precisely reflected the historical movement of institutions and ideas in this period, and it was this rather than its novelty or intrinsic intellectual power that gave it its

offence, and only if the penalty is proportionate to the moral gravity of his offence.' ('Punishment and Desert' in Acton, *op.cit.*, p.79).   But this provides no better defence of individual right, for Mundle argues for *both* the moral right of the individual to disobey an unjust law *and* for his moral duty to obey the law, since legal regulation 'is a necessary condition of civilised life' (p.78).   Thus he only succeeds in re-establishing the clash between individual right and state power, for the individual has a right to disobey at the same time as he has a duty to obey.

[74] N. Kittrie, *The Right to be Different* (London, 1971).
[75] G. Poggi, *The Development of the Modern State* (London, 1978), p. 134.
[76] See for example Hart's response to Wootton's attack on the principles of criminal liability in *op. cit.*, chs. 1 and 7.

significance.   The whole debate from Ross onwards involved the
historically set task of resolving a contradiction that remained stubbornly
irresoluble. The scene was set by two completely interlinked processes:
historically, by developments in the state's role; intellectually, by the
decay of idealist thought. Shorn by the development of history of the
high, but flawed and contradictory, ideals of classical liberal
individualism, launched upon a process of intellectual fragmentation and
eclecticism by the decline of idealism, the twentieth century search to
square the utilitarian circle became a dry, pettifogging trip through the
by-ways of analytic philosophy and legal positivism.   Nothing much
else remained for philosophers to do.

CHAPTER VII

JURIDICAL INDIVIDUALISM, INDIVIDUAL FREEDOM
AND CRIMINAL JUSTICE

1. INTRODUCTION

The characteristic positions in the modern debate about punishment are
essentially concerned with the second of the two antitheses identified in
the first chapter between juridical individualism and state power, in the
form of the attempt to reconcile a utilitarian philosophy of punishment
with principles of individual justice. Because the modern philosophy of
punishment is founded on the rejection of the principles of individual
right, from the time of the English Idealists onwards, the ideology of
juridical individualism must play second fiddle to the ideology of the *\l*
collective wellbeing. The ensuing 'reconciliations' of utility and
individual right are attempts to have it both ways which must fail
because of the antithetical nature of the two positions that are to be
reconciled. What, it may be asked, has the modern philosophy of
punishment done with the first antithesis between abstract individualism
and concrete individuality? Has it, as perhaps the preceding two
chapters suggest, simply been quietly buried and forgotten? Were it
possible so to ignore one of the two major antitheses of law in capitalist
society, the fundamental connection between law, legal ideology and
capitalism posited in chapter I would be considerably undermined, for it
would suggest that the antithesis is not so fundamental as has been
indicated. Happily, this has not been the case, for the abstract
individualism/concrete individuality contradiction has not gone away:
displaced, it has re-emerged in debates about the nature of criminal
responsibility and, in particular, in the shape of the freewill/determinism
controversy within jurisprudence. In this chapter, I shall argue that the
two terms of this controversy, freewill and determinism, represent the

two contradictory poles of the first antithesis of legal ideology. On the one hand, the concept of freewill, as the basis for the idea of individual responsibility, is a development of the ideology of abstract individualism in which a central element is the idea of the free individual; on the other hand, the individual viewed as a being determined by circumstances (of whatever kind) represents an embodiment of the idea of concrete individuality. I will also argue that, as with the last chapter, attempts to reconcile the two poles of the antithesis - this time through the ideas of 'compatibilism' or 'soft determinism' - fail, for they too attempt to reconcile the irreconcilable. The result is a serious gap in the philosophical justification of punishment with important negative implications for the legitimation of the criminal law.

(2.) The chapter has the following structure. In the next section, I outline four modern attempts to evade the contradiction between freewill and determinism. Three of these take the form of claims that freewill and determinism are compatible, whereas the fourth seeks to abolish the contradiction by rejecting certain forms of determinism as incoherent. At this point, I would enter the caveat that, for reasons of space and in line with the general ambit of the argument, I have had to limit myself to *jurisprudential* discussions of the freewill/determinism issue, although clearly there is much within the general philosophical area that could be made relevant to the legal discussion. However, that said, the positions examined here are developed within an overall philosophical context, so that a substantial overlap exists between what is discussed here and what would be considered central within the broader area.[1]

(3.) Thereafter, in a third section, I return the discussion to the nature of law itself through an analysis of certain aspects of legal discourse generated by the actual practice of law in the criminal courts. My aim in this section, through analysis of the notions of excuse and mitigation, is to show that law does itself generate in practice the contradiction between abstract individualism and concrete individuality in order to confirm that the apparently high-flown discussions of legal philosophy

---

[1] See also T. Honderich, *op.cit.*, ch.5, G. Watson, *Free Will* (Oxford, 1982), and M. Moore, 'Causation and the Excuses' (1985) *California Law Review*, 73, 1091. Moore's position is odd in that it is presented as a fundamental critique of attempts to reconcile freewill and determinism (pp.1114-1128) and is very effective as such, yet ends up defending such a reconciliation through arguments that voluntary action and causation are not incompatible (pp.1132-1137) and a functionalist argument that 'our moral life' requires that causation and responsibility be compatible, evidence to the contrary notwithstanding (pp.1144-1148). I take these arguments up below. Moore's further difference with the causation theorists, that they fail adequately to rationalise the standard legal excuses, is not a central focus of this chapter, but see below, fn.53.

have their material roots in the particular social practice of the law.
Finally, in a concluding section, I make some general comments about (4,)
the nature of the freewill/determinism controversy as it relates to legal
practice and human agency.   In what remains of this introductory
section, I outline the nature of the freewill/determinism controversy
within jurisprudence.
     Modern orthodoxy has it that it is of the nature of criminal law that
while it is concerned with social control through the deterrence of crime,
that general function is qualified by the requirement that justice be done
to the individual. In particular, according to Hart, this requirement is
embodied in the need to establish the subjective fault of the individual
for his criminal actions,[2] and this need presupposes a particular
conception of human agency in which human beings are regarded as
potentially free. Before the law may take its course a 'moral licence is
required in the form of proof that the person punished broke the law by
an action which was the outcome of his free choice.'[3]
     It is this connection between freewill and justice that underlies the
existence of certain excusing conditions for Hart. When a person acts by
mistake or accident, under provocation or duress, or when insane, he
cannot be said to have acted freely and therefore cannot be said to be
responsible for his actions.   This conception of the nature of legal
responsibility appears to be shared by practical judges who, while not
given to jurisprudential discourse in normal circumstances, have been
forced in consideration of at least one excusing condition - duress - to
lay their philosophical cards on the table. According to Lord Simon of
Glaisdale in the case of Lynch, the law accepts

as an axiom the concept of the free human will - that is, a potentiality in the
conscious human mind to direct conscious action - specifically, the power of choice

---

[2] In general, see H. Packer, *The Limits of the Criminal Sanction* (Stanford, 1968).
     In relation to criminal responsibility, see H.L.A. Hart, *Punishment and
     Responsibility* (*op.cit.*); H. Gross, *A Theory of Criminal Justice* (New York,
     1979), ch.1.
[3] Hart, *ibid.*, p.22. Strict liability offences are seen as an exception to this rule and
     are not considered here. Hart's later more concrete statement of this principle,
     that 'unless a man has the capacity and a fair opportunity or chance to adjust his
     behaviour to the law its penalties ought not to be applied to him' (*ibid.*, p.181)
     has found considerable support among academic lawyers. See A. Smith, 'On
     Actus Reus and Mens Rea' in P. Glazebrook (ed.) *Reshaping the Criminal Law*
     (London, 1978), and A. Ashworth, 'Reason, Logic and Criminal Liability' (1975)
     Law Quarterly Review, pp.102-130.

in regard to action. Even the most devout predestinarian puts off his theology when he puts on his legal robe.[4]

Not only does Lord Simon pin his colours to the mast of freewill, he also recognises the possible implications of determinism for the law. Admittedly, he sees determinism in a theological rather than behavioural light, and he deals with it in cavalier fashion. Nonetheless, the problem is there, and unless the law is going to follow the suggestion that one tailors one's philosophy to suit one's clothes, then it is necessary for law to come to terms with Kenny's succinct rhetorical question:

Supposing, then, that determinism is true - and surely many intelligent and well-informed people believe that it is - how can we any longer uphold the notion of responsibility in our courts of law?[5]

According to Hart, the claim of the determinist has two elements. First, 'it may be true - though we cannot yet show that it is true - that human conduct [is] subject to certain types of law... in the sense of a scientific law.' The second element relates the first to the operation of the law:

if human conduct so understood is in fact subject to such laws (though at the present time we do not know it to be so), the distinction we draw between one who acts under excusing conditions and one who acts when none are present becomes unimportant, if not absurd. Consequently to allow punishment to depend on the presence or absence of excusing conditions, or to think it justified when they are absent but not when they are present, is absurd, meaningless, irrational, or unjust, or immoral, or perhaps all of these.[6]

The important point here is not whether or not 'laws' of human behaviour exist in the same way as, say, the law of gravity; rather it is whether or not human behaviour can be seen as caused by conditions external to the will of the actor. If so, then to talk of individual responsibility in any situation is to talk nonsense, and to distinguish between situations is absurd.   The doctrine of determinism thus poses a problem for the ideology of law with which it must seek to come to terms.

---

4   *Lynch v D.P.P.* [1975] AC 653 at 689.
5   A. Kenny, *Freewill and Responsibility* (London, 1978), p.21. In this chapter, I am concerned only with the essentially 'Kantian' problem posed by Kenny's question. There may be other ways of conceiving of the nature of criminal justice, for example, that of the pure utilitarian, which do not consider responsibility as an essentially retributive issue. But here, I concentrate solely upon what may be called the predominant view of the nature of criminal justice. Cf. M. Bayles, 'Character, Purpose, and Criminal Responsibility' *Law and Philosophy* 1 (1982) pp.5-20.
6   *Op.cit.*, p.29.

2. DEFENDING FREEWILL

As might be anticipated from our consideration of the decline and fall of retributivism, the leading positions within the modern debate on freewill and responsibility stem from the materialist and empiricist doctrines of British moral philosophy begun with Hobbes and developed by Hume. We have already seen[7] that for Hobbes, liberty was consistent with necessity, so that he could analogise the freedom of human action with that of water which 'hath not only liberty, but a necessity of descending by the Channel'. Hume adopted a similar position which distinguished between 'liberty of spontaneity' and 'liberty of indifference'.[8] 'Liberty of spontaneity' is that liberty which is consistent with necessity, and is possessed by men. 'Liberty of indifference', on the other hand, entails freedom *from* necessity, contracausal freedom, and this, argued Hume was a delusion. We shall return to the consequences that Hume drew from this distinction once we have examined the modern debate, but for now, let us note that this position, sometimes called soft determinism, in which liberty and determinism are regarded as consistent, represents the predominant view within modern Anglo-American philosophy, and has indeed been replicated in fundamentally the same terms by a stream of leading philosophers.[9] It is the position from which at least three of the four philosophers I am now going to examine start: they maintain that the soft determinist position is compatible with the freewill required to found a satisfactory concept of criminal responsibility.

(1)   Determinism and Freewill as Compatible Doctrines

In the three positions examined here, it is argued that even if determinism is true, legal responsibility is justified on the basis of freewill because of, first, the notion of individual choice; second, the

---

7   See above, ch.II, text at footnotes 41, 42.
8   D. Hume, *A Treatise of Human Nature* (Oxford, 1888), pp.407-412. See also A. Kenny, *op.cit.*, at ch.III, fn.29.
9   The list includes Mill, Russell, Schlick and Ayer: see J. Glover, *Responsibility* (London, 1970), ch.3.

notion of a capacity to choose; and third, the idea of an action. I shall argue against these three positions that while all three concepts legitimately describe facets of human behaviour, they do not establish a conception of freewill adequate to the idea of legal responsibility, but are all undercut by the fundamental premise of determinism.

First, we may consider Hart's argument that even if determinism is true, it is not absurd, or anything else pejorative, to talk of freedom of choice as the basis for legal responsibility. The individual is a choosing being, and law is a choosing system, which stipulates that the individual will only be held responsible for those acts he consciously chooses. Thereby, under the law, the individual determines his own future by his choices, and this is true whether or not his choices are determined:

> No form of determinism that I, at least, can construct can throw any doubt on, or show to be illusory, the real satisfaction that a system of criminal law incorporating excusing conditions provides for individuals in maximising the effect of their choices, within the framework of coercive law. The choices remain choices, the satisfactions remain satisfactions, and the consequences of choices remain the consequences of choices, even if choices are determined...[10]

Even if determinism is true, it is not incoherent to talk of freedom of choice except in those situations where some overt form of coercion interferes with that freedom. What is in question is not that behaviour is caused, but the nature of the causes at play. Freedom for Hart is not contracausal freedom, that is the freedom to act against the causes determining one's behaviour, the freedom to choose otherwise than one does; rather it is the ability to follow one's desires no matter what their causes might be. To be unfree is to be unable to follow one's desires. Thus, provided that no form of external compulsion exists, individuals are choosing beings. Even if choices are determined, they remain choices, consciously undertaken by rational actors.[11]

This argument, however, rests upon a confusion between the experiential description and the philosophical explanation of choice. Where behaviour is determined, it is hard to see in what philosophical sense the individual possesses any element of free choice. Logically, indeed, it is doubtful whether Hart's account is coherent. If choices are determined, then choices are not really choices at all. It is questionable whether the idea of a 'determined choice' is anything other than a

---

[10] *Op.cit.*, p.48.

[11] Hart uses this argument to explain why excusing conditions are allowed in those situations where no rational choice is made either because there was simply no intention to commit an act (mistake, accident), or compulsion (duress, necessity). In the third section, I examine this claim more carefully.

contradiction in terms. What remains of choice if determinism is true - and this Hart's compatibilism does reflect - is no more than the *feeling* of choice. We may feel that we have freedom to choose, but in reality, our every choice is preselected according to a determining cause, and so our feeling is no more than a psychological or social illusion.[12] The sense of having choices and the reflection of that sense within law may give, as Hart suggests, a feeling of satisfaction, but that in no way entails that the concept of individual freedom upon which the satisfaction is premised is in any way justified.

Contra Hart, it is an inherent part of the concept of choice not only that the individual's choice was unimpeded by external constraints, but also that his choice was, in itself, free. The individual must not only have chosen his action, he must have chosen his choice. He must have been able to choose otherwise than he did.[13] So much is conceded by another compatibilist, Jonathan Glover, who focuses not upon choice but upon the individual's *capacity* to make choices in any given situation. Glover, however, concedes that a focus on capacity to choose will not in itself evade the determinist's argument:

But it may be objected that questions of capacity cannot be so clearly separated from questions of causation. Surely, it may be said, determinism must entail that, in any situation as it is, I do not have the capacity to take any course of action except the one predictable on the basis of the causal laws? That I stayed indoors yesterday does not show that I lack in general the capacity to leave the house: I am neither paralysed nor a prisoner. But does determinism not perhaps show that, with circumstances as they were yesterday, I lacked the capacity to leave the house on that particular day?[14]

The claim of determinism is not only that our actions are determined, but also that our capacity to choose and act, while not analytically the same thing as any given choice or action, is equally determined in individual cases.

Glover's strategy against this claim is to argue that while my choice to stay in may have been caused by the circumstances on one particular

---

[12] Cf. David Hume: 'We may imagine we feel a liberty within ourselves; but a spectator can commonly infer our actions from our motives and character; and even where he cannot, he concludes in general, that he might, were he perfectly acquainted with every circumstance of our situation and temper, and the most secret springs of our complexion and disposition. Now this is the very essence of necessity....' *A Treatise of Human Nature* (*op.cit.*), pp.408-9.

[13] Cf. P. Edwards, 'Hard and Soft Determinism' in S. Hook, *Determinism and Freedom in the Age of Modern Science* (New York, 1961); A. Kenny, *Freewill and Responsibility* (*op.cit.*), pp.25-26.

[14] J. Glover, *Responsibility* (*op.cit.*), pp.76-77.

day, 'if I had chosen to go out I would have succeeded in going out'.[15] The capacity to leave the house has two component parts: first the capacity to take a decision to leave the house, and second, the capacity to put the decision into effect. Now, the determinist's claim affects the first but not the second of these two components of the capacity to act, for while determinism may affect our capacity to choose otherwise than we do, it does not affect our ability to put our choices into effect:

So, given that, if I had chosen to act differently, I would have succeeded in so acting, the claim that determinism abolishes our capacities to act differently from how we do act can be narrowed down. This can only have plausibility when it is suggested that what determinism shows us to lack is the capacity to take decisions that we do not take. It may be said that, while yesterday I was capable of executing any decision to go out, I was not then capable of taking such a decision.[16]

How does this narrowing down of determinism avoid the conclusion that determined choices are not free choices, whether choice is regarded as a particular choice or as an instance of a general capacity to choose? Glover concedes that while determinism might mean that any decision could not have been other than it was, this

does not show that I lacked *the capacity* to decide otherwise. I may decide to have a drink in a pub, and so may an alcoholic. The fact that a statement that this will be my decision is entailed by certain other statements does not seem sufficient to show that I am no more capable of the opposite decision than is the alcoholic.[17]

But the contrast between the pub drinker and the alcoholic is a red herring, for the determinist's claim is that *both* the ordinary pub drinker and the alcoholic are determined in their behaviour, but in different ways. Glover must show that the deterministic account of the pub drinker *per se* is inadequate but he fails to do so. Instead, he retreats to the argument distinguishing the capacity to act, choose, or decide from any actual acts, choices or decisions done or made. But he has already conceded (and indeed his argument is supposed to meet the concession) that the question of capacity cannot be separated from the question of the exercise of the capacity to act in particular situations. His argument is no more than a reiteration of his basic position, not a defence of it from the determinist's revised attack. Thus Glover's attempt to rescue compatibilism by moving from the question of choice to that of the capacity to choose fails, for he is unable to meet the determinists

---

[15] *Ibid.*, p.77. Cf. Moore, *op.cit.*, fn.1, pp.1142-1144.
[16] *Ibid.*
[17] *Ibid.*, p.78, emphasis added.

objection that the general capacity to choose is always represented as a particular choice with regard to any given action.

As we have seen, one of the main aims of the compatibilist is to provide a rationale for certain excusing conditions in relation to some forms of behaviour without opening the Pandora's Box of determinism. This entails maintaining a notion of individual freedom even in a determined universe. The most recent attempt to defend compatibilism does so not by reference to the concept of choice, nor the concept of capacity, but through an analysis of the concept of action. Michael Moore argues that the law reflects a view of individuals as autonomous agents, and that their autonomy rests in their ability to perform basic and complex acts.[18] The performance of basic acts entails the ability to move one's body as one wills, i.e. presupposes a being 'with causal power over his own body'[19] while the idea of a complex action entails a power 'not only to move our bodies but to do so in such a way as to change external features of the world.'[20] The ability to perform basic and complex actions exists regardless of whether actions are caused or not, and is a sufficient attribute of human personality to justify the allocation of responsibility to individuals. There is a qualitative difference in the individual's position depending upon whether he has himself acted, even if the act was caused. Moore cites the argument of Hospers that the discoveries of psychoanalysis have rendered redundant the distinction between externally compelled and 'free' actions:

> Between an unconscious that willy-nilly determines your actions, and an external force which pushes you, there is little if anything to choose.[21]

For Moore, however, there is something to choose for in the latter case, the individual does not act at all, whereas in the former case he does, no matter what may ultimately have caused it. Regardless of the role of the subconscious, there is still a conscious individual act:

> a basic act is performed only when the actor knows that he is performing it. Presumably the choice to act, and the action are always determined by various factors, such as chemical balances in the brain, early environment, or character, but the fact that one acts is completely independent of there being, or not being, causes for the action.[22]

---

[18] M.S. Moore, *Law and Psychiatry* (Cambridge, 1984), p.111.
[19] *Ibid.*, p.361.
[20] *Ibid.*, p.362.
[21] Quoted in *ibid.*, p.361.
[22] *Ibid.* See also Moore, *op.cit.*, fn.1, at pp.1132-1137.

One can separate two strands in this argument. First, the quotation from Hospers indicates that Moore lays stress on the existence of a conscious act to distinguish the situation of determined unfreedom from the situation of individual autonomy. He agrees with Hospers that the 'external force which pushes' negates freedom, while denying that the unconscious does the same, because in that case a conscious act exists. The assertion of this distinction as a means of protecting individual freedom from the impact of determinism ignores, however, the fact that for the determinist, individual actions may occur, without in any way unsettling his or her view that the actions in question were caused or determined. In other words, the distinction that Moore wishes to draw is irrelevant from the determinist's point of view. We can see this if we borrow Kenny's distinction between psychological and non-psychological forms of determinism. The latter forms of determinism are akin to the 'external force which pushes', for in their view acts are directly determined by a given cause, without recourse to mediating subjective, psychological states of consciousness, etc. Psychological forms of determinism, however, regard 'action as determined by the wants and beliefs of agents, behaviour being the outward resultant of internal motivating forces operating in the mind.'[23] Thus psychological determinisms, operating with concepts of individual mental states, override the distinction which Moore attempts to make. On a psychological version of determinism, the existence of an action is irrelevant to the question of the effect of determinism on individual freedom.

The second strand of his argument concerns the claim that 'the fact that one acts is *completely independent* of there being, or not being, causes for the action'. However Moore does not show this to be so. 'The fact that one acts' may be *analytically* separable from the existence of a cause of one's action, but Moore does not show it to be 'completely independent'. It is precisely the determinist's claim that the fact of action (together with related psychological states of belief, desire, will and choice) are not independent of causal processes. Simply to assert the contrary cannot defeat the determinist's argument.

To sum up these arguments, all three identify a feature of human agency (choice, capacity to choose, ability to perform actions) which, they claim, permits them to legitimate the concept of freedom and criminal responsibility regardless of the truth of determinism. I have argued, to the contrary, that if determinism is true, then it may be conceded that all three features (or, at least, their appearance) exist, but

---

[23] Kenny, *op.cit.*, p.24.

none are adequate to ground notions of freedom and individual responsibility. If determinism is true, all three are consistent with it, and provide no independent ground for asserting individual freedom or criminal responsibility.

In effect, these modern compatibilists try to have it both ways, in a way that their late mentor Hume did not. It is instructive to examine the use to which he put his distinction between 'liberty of spontaneity' and 'liberty of indifference'. Hume argued that the delusion of 'liberty of indifference' (contracausal freedom) in part stemmed from a moral argument. Without it, it was claimed, there could be no individual responsibility, no reward and no punishment, for if all choices are determined, there can be neither responsibility nor desert. Hume's argument against this was that it was in fact 'liberty of indifference' and not 'liberty of spontaneity' which leads to a denial of responsibility and punishment. If human action is uncaused, then it is in effect chosen at random, and we have no way of knowing whether the individual was responsible for it. We can only establish responsibility if we know that the behaviour was consistent with the character and disposition of the person, i.e. if his acts were consistent with the way in which his character would cause him to behave, for otherwise 'they infix not themselves upon him, and can neither rebound to his honour, if good, nor infamy, if evil.'[24]   Likewise, punishment is only justified on the belief that what is done may have a causal effect upon future behaviour, may 'have an influence on the mind, and both produce the good and prevent the evil actions'.[25]

Thus Hume argued for 'liberty of spontaneity' like the modern philosophers, but unlike them, he did *not* argue for it on the basis that it grounded a concept of freewill, in the sense of a claim that individuals are responsible and punishable because of freely chosen acts. True, he gave to his viewpoint the name of 'liberty of spontaneity' but he used that doctrine as one of determinism rather than freedom.[26]   What the modern

---

[24] *Treatise, op.cit.*, p.411.

[25] *Ibid.*, p.410.

[26] I do not say that 'liberty of spontaneity' is a misnomer in the sense of being incompatible with any form of freedom whatsoever. I do say that it is quite incompatible with any idea of internal, subjective freedom to act or choose. Hume himself denied that any such freedom was possible. In her recent book, *State Punishment* (London, 1988), Nicola Lacey employs a Humean character conception of responsibility, but concedes in effect that this is a vulnerable basis for legal responsibility, since we are not responsible for our characters. Criminal responsibility then becomes no more than a matter of morally bad luck: *op.cit.*, p.68. Cf. M. Bayles, *op.cit*, pp.18-19. This is the true logic of the 'liberty of spontaneity' viewpoint, which the compatibilists seek to evoke. The

compatibilists wish to assert, however, is that a doctrine of determined choices can ground a justification of punishment in terms of individual freedom.   They are heirs to the Humean materialist tradition without realising its full significance.   Hume followed through the consequences of his determinism by arguing that punishment was only justified because of its ability to alter a person's character, understanding responsibility in terms of the ability to respond (responsivity) to sanctions.   His latter-day followers attempt to have it both ways: to accept determinism *and* defend a justification of punishment dependent on a conception of freewill and desert.

(2)   The Incoherence of Psychological Determinism   *(chap with not)*

This section concerns Kenny's recent attempt to rescue the idea of responsibility from the attack of the determinists by arguing that psychological determinism is an incoherent doctrine.   In a sense, it is a sidetrack from the main issue since it does not deal directly with the freewill/determinism conflict.   Nonetheless it is important to consider as an argument[27] which would otherwise undermine the conflict which I claim to exist.   We have already encountered Kenny's distinction between psychological and non-psychological determinism.   His argument is that non-psychological determinism is a coherent doctrine that is incompatible with the existence of freewill; but that psychological determinism, while incompatible with freewill, is an incoherent doctrine. It is this latter claim that will be examined here, for it is the psychological forms of determinism (be they sociological, economic or whatever) that challenge the doctrine of freewill, and it is them which Kenny attacks.

For Kenny, all forms of psychological determinism 'are incoherent because they misconstrue the nature of the mental phenomena to which they explicitly or tacitly appeal in their formulations.'[28]   His argument is twofold.   First, for the psychological determinist:

wants and beliefs are mental states or processes which stand in causal connection with bodily movements.   For this to be the case, the mental events must be capable

---

compatibilists' problem is that they seek to answer a 'Kantian' question (cf. footnote 5 above) in a Humean way.   See also below, text at fns. 51-55.

[27] For general defences of the possibility of determinism against earlier attacks, see Honderich, *op.cit.*, pp.106-113; Glover, *op.cit.*, ch.2.

[28] *Op.cit.*, p.24.

of separate identification from the physical events: they must be, as it were, separate items in the agent's biography.[29]

For the psychological determinist, wants must determine actions in such a way that the acts I perform must be the product of antecedent and discrete mental events of wanting. But, argues Kenny, there are many situations in which one's wants are not mental events distinguishable from the actions which manifest them.   For example, in writing this chapter, I may spend some time deliberating over a sentence, before deciding what I want to write. On the other hand, I may not. That is, there may be no antecedent and discrete event of 'wanting to write' separable from the act of actually writing.   Actions and explanatory wants are therefore not 'the separately identifiable item of the agent's biography which they must be if the relation between them is to be a causal one'.[30]

The validity of this criticism is questionable for two reasons. First it involves one rather crude presentation of the way in which wants determine actions. Why should wants be discrete, separable from, and antecedent to actions? Even if I do not think as I write, even if my writing assumes the speed and appearance of reflex action, it is not (hopefully!) gibberish. I nonetheless think what I write, and if asked why I wrote what I did, I would say that I wanted to write it, even though my want was not separable from my action. Of course wants cannot always be readily identified as separable, but that does not mean that they cannot be *analytically* separated for the purpose of explaining action.   Indeed, elsewhere Kenny appears to concede the point when he suggests that beliefs and wants are in some situations better seen as states accompanying events than as discrete events in themselves, without such a view calling into question their causal efficacy.[31]

Second, Kenny's criticism attacks the determinist argument at the wrong place. The question is not whether wants determine actions, for the exponent of the freewill argument could quite happily accept that that was the case. What separates the determinist from the voluntarist is

---

[29] *Ibid.*, p.27.

[30] *Ibid.*, p.28.

[31] A.Kenny, *Will, Freedom and Power* (Oxford, 1975), p.120. Kenny there counters his own admission with the assertion that 'There is no need to look for some mysterious causal link between the volition and the action...' and goes on to argue that 'if there were a causal link between the want and the action, the action would cease to be voluntary'. Neither comment, nor the general drift of the passage, furthers his argument.

not this question, but the prior question of whether wants are themselves determined.

Kenny's second criticism is more to the point, although, I shall argue, equally invalid:

Wants explain actions by being - in conjunction with an appropriate set of beliefs - the agent's reason for acting. It is the reasons for action which, according to the psychological determinist, provide the causes for action.[32]

But the operation of reasons is different from the operation of causes. Reasons do not determine behaviour in the way that causes determine effects. Prior to any act of the will is a reason for acting, but reasons are not causes, are analytically different from them, therefore psychological determinism has misunderstood the nature of the process of action. It is necessary to quote Kenny's argument at length:

Reasons explain actions that have been performed in the same way as practical reasoning leads to decisions about actions that are to be performed. Practical reasoning - reasoning about what to do - differs from theoretical deduction in an important way: to use a convenient technical term borrowed by philosophers from lawyers, practical reasoning is defeasible. That is to say, a conclusion which may be a reasonable one from a given set of premises may cease to be a reasonable one when further premises are added. (This is because the premises of practical reasoning set out the goals to be achieved and the possibilities of achieving them: a decision which is reasonable in the light of a narrow set of goals may be inadequate in the light of a larger set.) Because rules of practical inference are defeasible, whereas causal laws are not, reasons cannot be regarded as causes.[33]

This distinction, however, is a false one. Any cause (C) must be followed by an effect (E) not if C is to be the cause of E, but if C is to be the necessary and sufficient cause of E on any given occasion. In the explanation of any event in the natural world, it is always necessary to allow for the possibility of external interference by an additional cause (C1), which might intervene so that C was not followed by E without us calling into question the validity of identifying C as the cause of E in normal circumstances. Thus, the operation of causes in the natural world is as defeasible as the operation of reasons in the social world. Reason (R) may indeed not be followed by action (A) without us calling into question the validity of R as a ground for A where an additional reason (R1) intervenes, but such a model of behaviour is no different from that existing in the natural world. Therefore the distinction breaks down.

---

[32] *Freewill and Responsibility*, p.28.
[33] *Ibid.*, p.29. To the contrary, see R. Bhaskar, *The Possibility of Naturalism, op.cit.*, ch.2.

Against this, again elsewhere, Kenny argues that where there is causal interference (the operation of C1), it is still possible to give in advance an account of the action of the causal agent (C) if not interfered with. But, with reasons, this is not so. One cannot predict in advance the necessary effect of reason (R) where R1 intervenes:

Suppose that an agent, deliberating, holds in his hands a substance that he believes is poisonous. What tendency to action does this belief have, considered in isolation from the other factors which may be thought to combine with it in a mental parallelogram of forces? The answer is surely: none whatever. Of course, in combination with other factors (e.g. wants) it may lead to tendencies to act: coupled with the wish to protect his two year old son it may give rise to the tendency to put it out of the infant's reach; coupled with the wish to dispose of the brat as soon as possible, it may give rise to the tendency to put it into the infant's porridge. But neither of these tendencies can be regarded as being the result of an interference between a want and a belief.[34]

The example however is illegitimate, for a belief in the poisonous quality of a substance is not in itself a reason for action at all, in the same way as a loaded gun is not a cause of a bullet being fired. Neither has any tendency outwith the 'parallelogram of forces' which bear on it. Practical reasoning entails the conjunction of beliefs and wants. To take one of Kenny's own examples of a piece of such reasoning,[35] a belief that the 2.30 train arrives in London at 4.15 is not a reason for catching it. I must also want to be in London at or by 4.15. On the other hand, given that one knows either that I want to be in London at or by 4.15, (or that I wish to protect my infant son from the poison), it is predictable, all other things being equal, that I will catch the 2.30 (or put the poison out of my son's reach). Kenny's argument fails to drive the necessary wedge between reasons and causes.

These then are Kenny's arguments for claiming the incoherence of psychological determinism. But he does not establish his case, and so psychological determinism remains a viable doctrine. But as we have seen, it is a doctrine which is incompatible with the legal conception of action as the product of a free will upon which the idea of criminal responsibility rests.

---

[34] *Will, Freedom and Power, op.cit.*, p.116.
[35] *Ibid.*, pp.91-93.

3. FREEWILL, DETERMINISM AND CRIMINAL JUSTICE

It has been the fundamental premise of this book that the two central
contradictions identified within the philosophy of punishment are
generated by the nature of legal ideology and the form of law within a
capitalist society. Thus, while philosophical debates may appear high-
flown and far-removed from the mundane world of the law, there is
nonetheless an intimate connection between the two. If this premise is
sound, it should accordingly be possible to identify the contradiction
between freewill and determinism not just within those ideologies which
seek to justify retributive punishment philosophically, but also - in a
more 'practical' form - within the workings of the law itself. In this
section, I wish to argue that it is indeed possible to do this, both by
looking at the nature of the excusing conditions admitted by the law and
at the way in which judges approach questions of mitigation of
punishment.

(1)   Excusing Conditions

No extensive discussion of all the excusing conditions admitted within
the criminal law will be attempted here. I wish only to concentrate on
certain principal legal excuses mentioned by Hart, and within them to
focus upon certain anomalies with the defence of duress.

As we have seen, the strategy of the compatibilist defender of freewill
is to argue that provided that there is either a choice, or a capacity to
choose, or an action, it matters not whether the choice or the action is
determined. The individual concerned has nonetheless made the choice
or undertaken the action regardless of whether the choice or action is
determined. In other words, the compatibilist focuses upon individual
agency without looking, as it were, *behind* the agency to see whether or
not it was caused.

The majority of the law's excusing conditions adopt a similar focus
upon human agency to the exclusion of questions as to the conditions
which caused the agency. The law does this in order to declare that
where agency exists, there is a free responsible act. Where it does not

exist, there is no such act and the accused is excused. In other words, the law adopts in practice the compromise between freewill and determinism, known as compatibilism. However, it has been argued above that philosophical attempts to compromise in this way have failed, and so it will be open to doubt as to whether legal discourse can overcome the freewill/determinism contradiction by a similar strategy.

If we take as a representative sample of excusing conditions the five mentioned by Hart[36] (mistake, accident, provocation, insanity and duress), it can be shown that the first four of these focus, like the compatibilist, upon the presence or absence of human agency without having regard to the question of the causes behind it. With mistake and accident, this is clear in that the actor simply forms no intention to commit the criminal act, so that there is no conscious human agency.

The same is true, though less obviously, in relation to provocation and insanity. Both excuses, it is true, involve a causal factor in the shape of a precipitating condition (the provocation, 'disease of the mind'), but in both, the important point is that the condition does not cause the criminal act, but rather causes *a defect in individual agency* of which the criminal act is a consequence. In provocation, the provocative behaviour leads to 'a sudden and temporary loss of self control'[37] for the accused is 'so subject to passion as to make him or her for the moment not master of his mind'.[38] It is this lack of mental mastery rather than the provocative behaviour which leads to mitigation.[39] In insanity, similarly, classically, there must be a 'defect of reason', so that the accused knows not 'the nature and quality of the act he was doing'.[40] Again, it is this lack of mental mastery rather than the existence of mental disease *per se* which permits the excuse.[41]

If we turn to duress, however, we see that the rationale of this defence must differ from the others. In cases of mistake, accident, provocation and insanity, there is either no intention, or no rational intention, to commit a crime. In duress, however, there is neither an absence of

---

[36] *Op.cit.*, p.31.
[37] Devlin, J. in *Duffy* [1969] 1 All E.R. at 932.
[38] *Ibid.*
[39] Hence the proviso that there must be no 'cooling off period' between the provocation and the crime: G.Williams, *Textbook of Criminal Law* (London, 1978), p.481.
[40] *Daniel McNaghten's Case* 10 Cl. and Fin., p.200.
[41] This is not the case under a test such as *Durham* 214 F.2d (D.C. Cir.1954) where the legal discourse has been invaded by psychiatry, but here the criticism that is made is precisely that the legal criterion relating to the mental element in agency, *mens rea*, has been abandoned. See Moore, *op.cit.*, ch.6.

intention, nor an absence of reason. As regards intention, it is accepted that although the actions undertaken may occur 'in a moment of crisis', 'what is done will be done most unwillingly but yet intentionally'.[42] Nor is the absence of a rational will a premise of the defence. Indeed, it is precisely the ability to understand the nature of the threats made that makes the duress efficacious, and brings the defence into operation.

The significance of the duress defence is that it does not excuse because of the absence of individual agency as do the other principal excusing conditions. The individual acting under duress has, to quote Lord Simon in *Lynch*, the 'potentiality in the conscious human mind to direct conscious action - specifically, the power of choice in regard to action.'[43] The choice may be an excruciatingly difficult one, but it remains a choice open to an individual capable of rational intention and action. What, then, is the rationale for excusing persons acting under duress?

It is generally accepted that duress turns upon the admission of the *motive* of the accused in committing the act as an exculpating factor.[44] Reason and intention are both present, but they are tied to the internal motivating fear of the individual, which is itself a response to the external determining features of the duress situation. Reason and intention, then, are situated within the subjective character of the individual *and* the objective character of his social context. It is the nature of this combination of causal circumstances that forces the individual to break the law, for the threat is 'effective, at the time of the act in constraining him to perform it'.[45] Reason and intention are therefore seen as conditioned, or determined, by the conjunction of individual and social characteristics, and it is the efficacy of this determination that excuses the behaviour.

Thus what distinguishes duress from provocation or insanity is not that the possibility of behaviour being determined is recognised in the one but not in the others, but that in duress, the possibility of determinism is coupled with the existence of reason and intention. In provocation and insanity, determinism by external causes (provocation, or mental disease) is also admitted, but only to the extent that reason or

---

[42] Lord Morris in *Lynch* [1975] A.C. at 670. Cf. G. Williams, *Textbook of Criminal Law, op.cit.*, p.578; Wasik, 'Duress and Criminal Responsibility' [1977] *Crim. L.R.* 453-4. Note however, Dennis's qualification of this point in his 'Duress, Murder and Criminal Responsibility' (1980) *Law Quarterly Review* 208, at pp.224-228.

[43] See footnote 3, above.

[44] Lord Simon in *Lynch* at p.690; Wasik, *op.cit.*, pp.456-7; Smith, *op.cit.*, p.105.

[45] Lord Simon in *Lynch*, at 686.

intention are thereby excluded. It is this distinguishing feature of duress, that it recognises behavioural determinism alongside the existence of traditional notions of intention and reason, that has made it difficult for lawyers to rationalise. As one commentator puts it, 'attempts to cram the defence into legal pigeonholes have failed in the past'.[46]

What is the significance of this development in the judicial attitude to criminal behaviour? If the law allows duress as an excuse for criminal conduct, on the basis that rational, intentional behaviour is determined, why stop there? The determinist may quite legitimately argue that there is no distinction in principle between a gun pointed at the head, and an intolerable socio-economic background. To be sure, there are questions of immediacy and degree to be answered, but if determinism is admitted in principle as an excusing ground, then drawing the line between one determining factor and another can only be based on contingent or expedient considerations. The law may well wish to take 'account of the standards of honest and reasonable men', but if it does, then it ought to do so consistently.[47] But, then, where would it draw the line on ground of principle between different determining conditions? It cannot, as Lord Simon recognised in *Lynch*:

A threat to property may, in certain circumstances be as potent in overbearing the actor's wish not to perform the prohibited act as a threat of physical harm. For example, the threat may be to burn down his house unless the householder merely keeps watch against interruption while a crime is committed. Or a fugitive from justice may say, 'I have it in my power to make your son bankrupt. You can avoid that merely by driving me to the airport.' Would not many ordinary people yield to such threats, and act contrary to their wish not to perform an action prohibited by law?[48]

This passage couches the examples of threatening situations in individual psychological terms rather than in those of social environment, but it is clear that society itself through bad social conditions is quite capable of providing a threatening environment in which a crime can become a rational thing to do.[49] Duress, in other

---

[46] Wasik, *op.cit.*, p.456.
[47] The quoted words are those of Lord Morris in *Lynch* at p.670; the concern for consistency is shared by the minority judges in that case.
[48] *Lynch* at p.686.
[49] 'Fear of violence does not differ in kind from fear of economic ills, fear of displeasing others, or any other determinant of choice', says Williams, but 'A line must be drawn somewhere, for there are always reasons that impel men to break the criminal law': *Criminal Law: the General Part* (London, 1961) pp.751,758. He does not say how the line should be drawn. Cf. L. Vandervort, 'Social Justice in the Modern Regulatory State: Duress, Necessity and the Consensual Model in

words, opens up the Pandora's Box of determinism for criminal justice by revealing that there is more to the question of individual freedom than the compatibilist defences would suggest.[50]   It reveals that for lawyers themselves - at least in one situation - there is a need to go beyond the mere existence of individual agency to see the causes which precipitate particular actions.   But a door of this kind, once opened, is very hard to close on grounds of principle when one comes to consider the effect of a bad social environment upon criminality.

For example, Fletcher's defence of criminal responsibility, while based upon the concept of character rather than that of freewill,[51] confronts the issue of the relationship between individual responsibility and the broader social context within which individual agency occurs. Criminal desert and responsibility depend upon a finding that a criminal act is consistent with the accused's character.[52]   But is not character a product of social upbringing?   Fletcher argues that it is critical that we recognise a distinction between bad social background and personal character.   If we do not do so, we might excuse on the ground of prolonged social deprivation and 'the theory of excuses would begin to absorb the entire criminal law'.[53]   Yet Fletcher's argument cannot sustain

---

Law' (1987) *Law and Philosophy* 6, 205, at 220: 'It must be recognised that choices made by individuals are often influenced and sometimes 'dictated' by socio-economic factors that are themselves the *product* of collective societal *decisions*'. See also a recent effective analysis of the 'crack' problem in the U.S. in these terms by M. Davis and S. Ruddick: 'Los Angeles: Civil Liberties Between the Hammer and the Rock' (1988) *New Left Review* 170, 37.

[50] Moore (*op.cit.* at fn 18, pp.362-364, at fn.1, pp.1129-1132) argues that compulsion is not the same as causation.   I would agree to this extent: that while not all causations are compulsions, all compulsions *are* causations.   That is, compulsion is (only) one type of causation.   The problem for the legitimation of the law is to explain why it should distinguish one sort of causation from another.

[51] G. Fletcher, *Rethinking Criminal Law* (Boston, 1978), p.800.   The character conception is used as an alternative to the standard freewill conception as a means of grounding individual responsibility, i.e. it is used in a 'Kantian' rather than Humean way.

[52] Fletcher concedes however that the criminal law in fact makes no real investigation of character, limiting its investigation to the wrongful act before the court.   The principle of legality, he claims, safeguards the accused's privacy, and therefore arrests enquiries into circumstances beyond the act itself.   This is odd: the law refuses to do justice to the individual in the sense of resolving desert and responsibility out of respect for the individual's privacy.   But there is surely a greater lack of respect for the individual in the failure to punish justly than in the invasion of his or her privacy.

[53] *Ibid.*, p.801.   Moore (*op.cit.*, pp.87-88) has a parallel problem in separating out the effects of compulsion situations on criminality, which the law recognises,

this distinction for he concedes that it 'goes without saying' that the individual's character *is* shaped by his or her total life experience, which presumably may include social deprivation. Fletcher ultimately resorts to a wholly unsatisfactory functionalist argument that the criminal law 'should express the way we live' and that '[o]ur culture is built on the assumption that...we are accountable for what we do'.[54] However, we need to know not what 'our culture' does, but whether it is justified in doing it, and Fletcher provides no answer.[55] Individual responsibility and social context remain stubbornly unsynthesised in his account.

(2) Mitigating Punishment

Here, I consider a piece of reasoning which is commonplace in criminal courts. In his Report into the Brixton Riots,[56] Lord Scarman details in cause and effect terms the reasons for the 1981 risings by London's inner-city youth. The causes are both general and specific, and their conjunction provides the explanation for the occurrence of riot. On the general level, the causes include unemployment, discrimination, housing, environmental conditions, etc: 'Where deprivation and frustration exist on the scale to be found among the young black people of Brixton, the probability of disorder must...be strong'.[57] Given such a

---

from the effects of a bad character, which it does not. He argues that the ability to be a practical reasoner, rather than judgements as to the nature of character, lie at the heart of criminal responsibility, and that what justifies the duress defence is that threats represent an impediment to practical reasoning. But then he must explain why the individual's character, which could equally be thought of as an impediment to reasoned action, is not regarded as such by the law. His solution is to distinguish the two by the convenient but unconvincing device of a 'stipulative' argument that character does not constrain practical reasoning, while compulsion does. Yet Moore is committed to a realist conception of moral responsibility (*op.cit.*, fn.1, pp.1122-1123). He repeats the move in the later work by distinguishing between two meanings of 'character' without telling us why we should opt for the one that is compatible with his analysis rather than the one that is not (see p.1130, at fn.108). For further discussion of Moore, see my 'Practical Reasoning and Criminal Responsibility' in R. Clarke and D. Cornish, *The Reasoning Criminal* (New York, 1986), pp.220-225.

54 *Ibid.*, pp.801-2.
55 Moore adopts a similarly complacent reductionist defence in *op.cit.*, fn.1, pp.1144-1148. See also M. Kelman, *A Guide To Critical Legal Studies* (Cambridge, Mass., 1987), p.318. Cf. fn.26, above.
56 *The Brixton Disorders 10-12 April 1981* (Cmnd.8427).
57 *Op.cit.*, p.16.

general predisposition, all that is required is a spark to set the tinder ablaze:

Deeper causes undoubtedly existed, and must be probed: but the immediate cause of Saturday's events was a spontaneous combustion set off by the spark of one single incident.[58]

Riot is explained in terms of a complex of necessary and sufficient causes. Yet Lord Scarman at one point puts off his determinism and puts on his legal robe:

The social conditions in Brixton...do not provide an excuse for disorder. They cannot justify attacks on the police in the streets, arson, or riot. All those who in the course of the disorders in Brixton and elsewhere engaged in violence against the police were guilty of grave criminal offences, which society, if it is to survive, cannot condone. Sympathy for, and understanding of, the plight of young black people...are no reason for releasing [them] from the responsibilities for public order which they share with the rest of us....[59]

Scarman's drift is ambiguous. In part this appears to be simply a utilitarian argument concerning what society must do if it is to survive. But equally, in part, it appears to be a retributive argument concerning the guilt and responsibility of young blacks for their actions. If this is so, however, in shifting from an account of the causes of disorder to a discussion of the individuals' responsibility for that disorder, he has jumped from a discourse premised upon determinism to one premised upon individual responsibility and freewill. But he cannot have it both ways, for *either* the acts of young black people are free in a contracausal sense *or* they are causally determined, they cannot be both and no compatibilist compromise is, as has been argued above, available.

My reason for examining Lord Scarman's remarks is that something like his reasoning occurs day in day out in the criminal courts through the two stages of conviction and sentencing. For conviction, the individual is regarded as a free, juridical individual, unhindered by his or her personal or social conditions. In relation to the sentence, however, considerations of background are admitted as a means of mitigating punishment, and these normally take the form of analysis of the accused's circumstances and consideration of his or her motives. It is

---

[58] *Ibid.*, p.37. This comment rests uneasily with Lord Scarman's distinction elsewhere between 'causes' and 'conditions' (p.16). When he writes of social features being 'conditions' which predispose to rioting, and not causes in themselves, I take him to mean that those social conditions he identifies are necessary, but *not sufficient*, causes of disorder.

[59] *Ibid.*, p.14.

indeed noteworthy that the criminal law has from its modern beginnings sought to marginalise the relevance of motive to culpability. Motive, either as a claim of desperate need or of moral right, would have allowed the common people to claim hunger as a defence or justification for what the ruling classes saw purely as a question of individual property right.[60] The admission of motive into legal doctrine would have permitted a bridge to be built by poor defendants between their intentional actions and the context in which they occurred. The early criminal lawyers were adamant that this should not be allowed to happen.[61]   There therefore grew up a division between what Lord Devlin has called[62] the 'function of justice' (the attribution of criminal responsibility) which follows the logic of individual freedom on the basis of the legal categories of *mens rea* and the various excuses, and the 'function of mercy' (the admission of mitigatory circumstances) which follows a more deterministic logic of causatory circumstance.   But on the analysis presented here, mitigation of sentence is a fudge, for it diminishes punishment and responsibility on the basis of a philosophical logic which denies the possibility of punishment and responsibility, that is, the logic of determinism.[63] The dichotomies of legal doctrine and the philosophy of punishment feed into and off one another, but at the end of the day, the philosophy and the law reveal only a set of parallel unresolved contradictions.

---

[60] D. Hay, 'Property, Authority and the Criminal Law', in Hay et al, *Albion's Fatal Tree*, p.44.

[61] See Hale, *Pleas of the Crown*, 1, 54; and especially the *Seventh Report of the Criminal Law Commissioners* (1843), p.29.

[62] P.Devlin, *Samples of Law Making* (Oxford, 1962) p.73.

[63] This argument has been well made in relation to the mitigatory plea of diminished responsibility by R. Sparks in 'Diminished Responsibility in Theory and Practice' 27 *Modern Law Review* (1964), p.9. To the response, that may seem commonsensical, that freewill and determinism may be a matter of degree rather than 'all or nothing' (N.Walker, *Crime and Insanity in England and Wales, Vol.1* (Edinburgh, 1968) p.162), Moore correctly answers that believing in freedom or determinism is like becoming pregnant rather than going bald (*op.cit.*, pp.355-356, see also op.cit., fn.1, pp.1114-1118). One either believes in causal conjunctions as the basis for human behaviour or one does not: 'There is no sense to the idea of a little bit of either causation or of freedom. It makes sense to say that we are determined or that we are free, but to speak of being partly determined or partly free makes as much sense as speaking of being partly pregnant.'

4. CONCLUSION

In this chapter, I have considered the two interrelated problems of reconciling freewill and determinism and defending a concept of criminal responsibility in the criminal law. The former is a problem of philosophical theory, the latter one of more narrowly legal theory, yet they are interconnected because both start from a concept of abstract individual autonomy and both seek to reconcile such a concept with the idea of a determining context of individual action, either in the shape of philosophical determinism or the context of a link between social environment and criminality. Both problems, of legitimating individual freewill in philosophy and individual responsibility in criminal law, embody the antithesis identified in Chapter I between abstract juridical individualism and concrete (natural or social) individuality.[64] The reason for these persisting and parallel problems in philosophical and legal thought is that both theories (obviously in the latter case) are juridically based ideologies. It is their common intellectual structure at the most fundamental level that explains why legal theorists such as Fletcher and Hart search for the resolution of problems of legal theory in general philosophical discourse, but only ever succeed in replicating the same problems at a deeper level. They simply move from one kind of juridical ideology to another.

At the level of philosophical theory, the debate around compatibilism parallels the search for a reconciliation of individual right and social utility explored in the last chapter. The decay of idealism meant that abstract individualism could no longer provide a core legitimation for the philosophy of punishment. The free individual had to take second place in relation to the general social functions of the state, and, at the same time, became prey to a series of ideologies which abandoned the idea of abstract metaphysical freedom in favour of seeing the individual as a determined creature in need of reform according to behavioural techniques. The different theories of the criminologists began to jostle with, and steal the limelight from, the philosophy of punishment.[65] The

---

[64] Above, pp.8-9.
[65] See L. Radzinowicz, *Ideology and Crime* (London, 1966), N. Kittrie, *The Right to be Different* (London, 1971), D. Garland, *Punishment and Welfare* (*op.cit.*), J. Donzelot, *The Policing of Families* (London, 1980).

latter, as we have seen, became a much narrower and more technical discourse as a result. Juridical ideology, which had been at the centre of the philosophical theory of the state in the eighteenth and early nineteenth centuries, now became a subject increasingly only of interest to those actually involved in one way or another in teaching or theorising about law, with a correspondingly much restricted intellectual and political scope.

Thus it was that so much ink could be spilled on the subject of reconciling individual justice and social utility, and, in parallel, in attempting to prove that freewill and determinism were compatible. If the ideal conception of individual freedom was a dead letter, the Anglo-American philosophy of punishment had little choice but to fall back upon the Humean and utilitarian reduction of human life to natural, material processes. But while the Humean individual may be *responsive to* punishment, he is not thereby *responsible for* his (crime and hence) punishment, as the compatibilists would have it. The search for components of human agency, be it choice, capacity to choose or the ability to perform basic and complex actions that can stand over against determinism as the basis for human liberty, and the desire to deny the coherence of determinism are all attempts from within the Humean tradition to deny its logic, just as the 'mixed', 'weak' retributivist theories of punishment are all attempts from within the utilitarian theory to deny its logic. Both sorts of argument are equally doomed to failure. The combination of overweening state power and a predominant ideology of philosophical materialism in truth left those wishing to defend the individual within legal discourse with precious few good cards to play. From the end of the eighteenth to the middle of the twentieth century, social developments pushed juridical thought from the positive poles of its two antitheses (abstract individualism and individual right) towards its negative poles (concrete individuality and social power). In the process, juridical ideology was quite thoroughly emasculated.

Yet the process of legitimation must go on just as, and just because, legal practice itself must go on. Now stripped of the historical high ideals which it lent to the bourgeois revolutions of the eighteenth century, legal theory continues to seek to explain, to rationalise and to justify what lawyers do. Just as the compatibilists seek to identify facets of human agency which they can sever from the pervading context of determinism, so do the lawyers and legal theorists seek to isolate certain aspects of human conduct from the social context in which it occurs. They focus on individual intention to the exclusion of motive, and on the act rather than the context; they divide up the processes of conviction and mitigation, and admit some excuses but not others. When pressed, it transpires that there is little good reason for this other than it is what the law in fact does.[66]

The doctrines of excuse rely upon a philosophically inadequate compatibilist, soft determinist compromise in which certain individual mental states are considered as relevant to excuse, but broad social and individual conditions are not (lest, in Fletcher's words, 'the theory of excuses [sh]ould begin to absorb the entire criminal law').[67] The significance of the duress defence is that, precisely because of its exceptional nature, it indicates how the law in general draws false distinctions between individual and context.   C.A. Campbell once distinguished (in a rather elitist fashion) between two attitudes to questions of individual responsibility.[68]   On the one hand, he described what he regarded as the view of the rather ignorant, ordinary unreflective person, unconcerned with philosophical, scientific or religious theory, who would hold that any individual who is not actively constrained and is able to follow his desires unimpeded is to be held responsible for his actions.   On the other hand, the more reflective and knowledgeable person is aware that even if actions are unconstrained, they may not be free since they result from forces which determine action regardless of the absence of external impediments.   Such a person would stipulate that choices must genuinely be open to the individual as well as being unconstrained so that he could have chosen otherwise than he did.   Law is in the position of the first of these two persons, that of the ordinary, unreflective individual, for it looks for external constraints or a lack of mental capacity without looking behind these features of human agency to the causes of human behaviour in social and individual circumstance.

But it must be pointed out that the law's unreflective nature is not a failure of understanding alone.   Rather it is a product of the fundamental nature of both the legal form and the law's function.   Law is inherently concerned with *individual* responsibility and individual blame, and therefore it must focus on *individual* agency to the exclusion of its conditions of existence: law must *decontextualise* action if it is to attribute responsibility to individuals.   If it looks behind agency to its social conditions of existence, as did Lord Scarman in his analysis of urban riot, then it becomes impossible and irrelevant to blame individuals.   Social and political circumstance become the relevant level for the attribution of 'responsibility'.   Similarly, the ideal function of law

---

[66] See Fletcher, quoted above at fn.54.

[67] Again, Fletcher's words, quoted above at fn.53.

[68] In *Mind* (1951); discussed in P. Edwards, 'Hard and Soft Determinism' in Hook, *op.cit.*, pp.122-123.

is to control individuals understood as rational actors, through their (2) conviction, punishment and deterrence. If individuals were not seen in this abstract manner, but rather were placed in their social context, this function would become futile. Justice would entail not the conviction and deterrence of responsible individuals but the reform of anti-social and criminogenic conditions.[69] Hart writes that justice requires that the law 'adjusts the competing claims of human beings [by] treat[ing] all alike as persons by attaching special significance to human voluntary action'.[70] There is at the same time more and less truth in this claim than Hart realises. The law does indeed treat 'all alike as persons', for it is only by abstracting from the real differences between people in terms of their needs, biographies, social conditions, and so on, that human beings can be treated alike; and the law does indeed attach a 'special significance to human voluntary action' - the capacity to be at fault for one's actions through their decontextualisation. Law is concerned with a dehumanised form of individualism which ignores the context of individual action. Because of this, its claim to promote individual justice is shallow.[71] When criminal lawyers laud the element of justice in their practice, they should be aware of how narrow and circumscribed their recognition of it must be, so long as they remain lawyers.

(?) Lobpreisen

---

[69] I have developed this argument slightly further in terms of a distinction between 'situated' and 'abstract' (juridical) rationality, drawing upon Bhaskar's *The Possibility of Naturalism*, (*op.cit.*), ch.2 in my 'Freewill, Determinism and Criminal Justice' (1983) *Legal Studies*, 69-73 and 'Practical Reasoning and Criminal Responsibility: a Jurisprudential Approach' in D. Cornish and R. Clarke, *op.cit.*, at fn.50. The latter analysis implicitly agrees with Moore (*Law and Psychiatry, op.cit.*) that the analysis of practical rationality offers a better way of understanding criminal conduct but rejects his abstract conception of practical reasoning, which ends up replicating some of the same contradictions as the compatibilists on issues such as duress (see above, fn.53). This is because Moore, like the compatibilists, wants to legitimate the operation of legal forms of criminal justice, and therefore divorces the ability to be a practical reasoner from the social context within which practical reasoning occurs.

[70] *Op.cit.*, p.22.

[71] 'Thus the commitment of the legal form to individuality is ultimately illusory because the individuality it recognises and presupposes is in fact an alienated form of individuality - individualism.' I. Balbus, 'Commodity Form and Legal Form' in C. Reasons and R. Rich, *The Sociology of Law: A Conflict Perspective* (Toronto, 1978), p.80.

CHAPTER VIII

JURIDICAL INDIVIDUALISM, STATE POWER AND
LEGAL REASONING

1. INTRODUCTION

The last chapter concluded by taking the discussion of legal ideology
and the first antithesis of law back from the philosophy of law and
punishment to the practice of law itself through an analysis of legal
doctrine and the excusing conditions. In this chapter, I pursue the same
strategy in relation to the law's second antithesis by means of an analysis
of recent leading English cases concerning questions of criminal
responsibility and punishment. It will be my argument that the second
antithesis, between individual right and state power, whose philosophical
development is charted in Chapters V and VI, is also instantiated within
legal doctrine itself.
    The argument has two main purposes. First, I take up the analysis at ⑦
the end of Chapter VI. There, I argued that it was philosophically
impossible to defend individual right by reference to the practice of the
criminal justice system if one had already established utilitarianism as an /
hegemonic principle. Here, my contention will be that it would in any
case be misconceived to regard criminal justice, a law-based system, as a
necessary bulwark for individual right against the general interest since
it is itself, as one branch of law, a site for the conflict between individual
right and social (state) power. Here, as in questions of freewill and
criminal responsibility, there is an overlap of, and parallel between, the
legal and philosophical contradictions. Leading cases on criminal
responsibility reveal this to be the case. Second, using this analysis, I Ⓛ
will argue that the existence of the contradiction between individual right
and state power within criminal law discourse undermines and

contradicts its logic and consistency. In this area, legal reasoning must be seen as an irrational and contradictory phenomenon.

In the remainder of this introduction, I establish, using the work of D.N. MacCormick,[1] criteria for describing legal discourse as rational, criteria which are then used in the following section as the basis for an analysis and critique of three recent leading English cases relating to criminal responsibility. Then, in a third section, having concluded that the rationality of all three cases is seriously deficient, I consider why this should be so, taking up the analysis presented in Chapter I and pursued throughout the work. In a concluding section, I consider the significance of the analysis for the further development of jurisprudence, and, in particular, the relationship between traditional philosophical approaches and more recent sociological and critical approaches to the subject.

For MacCormick, legal reasoning is an essentially rational activity. It is one kind of 'attempt to impose a rational pattern on our actings',[2] guided by norms of 'impartiality and objectivity'.[3] MacCormick concedes that judges are only human, and therefore influenced by the social standards and perceptions of their place and role in society, but argues that such influences play a limited role in decision-making, because decisions are governed by norms of practical reasoning. In legal argumentation,

the essential notion is that of giving (what are understood and presented as) good justifying reasons for claims, defences or decisions. The process which is worth studying is the process of argumentation as a process of justification.[4]

MacCormick contrasts this process of argumentation, which concerns what makes sense within a legal system, with what might make sense within the world at large. Legal reasoning attends to both objectives,

---

[1] D.N. MacCormick, *Legal Reasoning and Legal Theory* (Oxford,1978). This chapter does not represent an extended analysis and critique of the modern positivist debate on legal reasoning and legal theory. It is an attempt to use an exemplary work in that tradition to expose the contradictory nature of legal reasoning about criminal responsibility in practice. I draw conclusions about the value of rationalist approaches to legal reasoning, but I concede that in the absence of an analysis of that tradition as a whole, which is beyond the scope of this work, such conclusions must be tentative. In ongoing work, I am developing the arguments of this and the previous chapter more fully. See, e.g., Norrie, 'Oblique Intention and Legal Politics' [1989] *Crim. LR*. 793. Compare M. Kelman, 'Interpretive Construction in the Substantive Criminal Law' (1981) *Stanford Law Review* 591.

[2] *Op.cit.*, p.6.

[3] *Ibid.*, p.17.

[4] *Ibid.*, p.15.

but its allegiance to the world at large must be constrained by requirements of rational decision-making.   These requirements may be expressed generally and particularly.   Generally, legal reasoning should be seen to be disinterested in approach, and based upon a weighing up of the relevant arguments and a fair and full assessment of the issues to be taken into account.   This is a general requirement of any process of practical reasoning, without which it could not be said to be seeking to attain impartiality or objectivity.

More particularly, legal reasoning occurs within the framework of an already existing and binding set of legal rules.   The legal system as a 'consistent and coherent body of norms'[5] constrains judges, whatever their political preferences, to 'do justice according to law, not to legislate for what seems to them an ideally just form of society.'[6]   This is the crucial point, for it is the notion of justice 'according to law' which checks judicial bias or subjective preference.   To be sure, rules of law may frequently not be clear, or may be bent to suit desired interpretations, so that 'according to law' may not be as stringent a requirement as it at first seems.   Nonetheless, it represents a significant residual control on judges' decision-making capacities:

'Thou shalt not controvert established and binding rules of law' is a commandment which applies to both [statute and case law], and which imposes genuine and important limits to judicial freedom of action even after we have made all appropriate qualifications to allow for the possibility of restrictive interpretation and explaining and distinguishing.[7]

This stricture upon the scope of judicial reasoning necessitates a distinction between two uses of the term 'logic'.   On the one hand, there is 'technical logic' which is a requirement of rational argument and is 'applicable to propositions only in the sense that self-contradictory propositions (e.g. 'p and not p') are logically false.'[8]   On the other hand, there is 'practical logic' which entails the substantive evaluation of the *practical* practical effects (e.g. utility) of a given rule.   Such a logic is not *logic.* irrelevant to the law, particularly where existing legal rules do not cover a particular case, but it must be kept in its place and not be allowed to ride roughshod over the intrinsic logic of the rules which already exist. This must be understood.   It is common currency among modern philosophers that moral decisions often involve a trade off between

---

5   *Ibid.*, p.106.
6   *Ibid.*, p.107.
7   *Ibid.*, p.227
8   *Ibid.*, p.38.

questions of justice and utility. But in order to defend and legitimate the concept of the rule of law, legal philosophers like MacCormick stipulate that consequential (utilitarian) arguments cannot displace already existing legal rules like trump cards played at will:

> however desirable on consequentialist grounds a given ruling might be, it may not be adopted if it is contradictory of some valid and binding rule of the system... the requirement of consistency would require rejection of an otherwise attractive ruling on the ground of its irresoluble conflict with (contradiction of) established valid rules.[9]

Bearing these two requirements of practical reasoning in mind, I will now examine some leading criminal law cases of recent years to see whether they fulfil them.

2. LEGAL REASONING AND CRIMINAL RESPONSIBILITY

The cases examined have all been decided in recent years by English judges in the highest court of criminal appeal, the House of Lords.[10] They are all, therefore, leading cases in the field of criminal responsibility. I shall examine them singly, then draw some general conclusions from the analysis.

(1)   D.P.P. v Majewski[11]

In *Majewski*, the question was whether or not intention to commit a crime could be negated by intoxication. Majewski had been charged with assault occasioning actual bodily harm and assaulting a police officer. He had been convicted in spite of his defence of being too intoxicated through drink and drugs to have possessed the necessary intention. The logic of his argument was: no man is guilty of a crime of intent unless he has the required intent. A man who commits a crime in

---

9   *Ibid.*, p.106.

10   To be precise, in one case, members of the House of Lords sat as members of the Judicial Committee of the Privy Council.

11   [1976] 2 WLR 623.

a state of severe intoxication cannot form the required intent. Assault is a crime of intent, therefore evidence of sufficient intoxication negates the intent necessary for the crime with which he (Majewski) was charged.

In delivering the opening judgement, Lord Elwyn-Jones sets the tone for the debate by noting that the appeal raises issues of considerable public importance. He affirms the utilitarian argument of Lawton L.J. in the Court of Appeal:

> The facts are commonplace - indeed so commonplace that their very nature reveals how serious from a social and public standpoint the consequences would be if men could behave as the [appellant] did and then claim that they were not guilty of any offence.[12]

He then supports this argument by noting the historical dimensions of the problem of alcohol together with the recent added dangers associated with drugtaking, and stresses that intoxication as a cause of crime is a problem 'with which the courts have had to deal in their endeavour to maintain order and to keep public and private violence under control.'[13] He then proceeds to outline both the defence and the prosecution cases. The prosecution case, with which the judges ultimately agree, is that the courts have adopted a distinction between crimes of 'basic' and 'specific' intent, a distinction that is necessary but irrational:

> [I]llogical as the outcome may be said to be, the judges have evolved for the purpose of protecting the community a substantive rule of law that, in crimes of basic intent as distinct from crimes of specific intent, self-induced intoxication provides no defence and is irrelevant to offences of basic intent, such as assault.[14]

Why should this distinction be regarded as illogical? First, it is a shadowy, ill-formed distinction so that in practice it is impossible to discern other than through judicial pronouncement what crimes fall into the two categories.[15] Second, if there is a theory behind the distinction, it rests upon the speeches of Lord Simon of Glaisdale in *Morgan*[16] and *Majewski* itself. In the latter, Lord Simon approves the definition of basic intent as 'intention applied to acts apart from their purposes', while

---

12 Quoted in [1976] 2 WLR at 628.
13 [1976] 2 WLR 628.
14 *Ibid.*
15 Cf. G. Williams, *Textbook of Criminal Law* (London, 1978), pp.428-429: 'In allocating crimes to one category or the other, the courts adopt a Humpty Dumpty attitude'; see also Smith and Hogan, *Criminal Law* (London, 1983), p.193.
16 *D.P.P. v. Morgan* [1975] 2 All E.R. 347.

specific intent involves 'intention as applied to acts considered in relation to their purposes' so that 'the *mens rea* in a crime of specific intent requires proof of a purposive element.'[17] This, however, is a distinction without a real difference. It denotes no more than an empirical differentiation that is evident, for example, in the way that certain charges are framed. Thus intentionally inflicting grievous bodily harm[18] is a crime of basic intent because the *mens rea* required is simply the intention to commit an assault, whereas 'assault with intent to commit grievous bodily harm'[19] is a crime of specific intent because the *mens rea* goes 'beyond' the act of assault to include a particular purpose (doing grievous bodily harm). But this is purely contingent in that the 'additional' purpose in the latter crime could quite easily be omitted by reformulating it as part of the *actus reus*. The distinction rests on a verbal contingency. Similarly, murder is said to be a crime of specific intent, yet its *mens rea* requires no more than an intention to kill or do grievous bodily harm, i.e., no additional purposive element.[20]

The third reason for conceding the distinction's illogicality is the most significant. Even if one were to concede that one could differentiate between basic and specific intent in a coherent and logical way, one would still be forced to note that crimes of basic intent remain crimes of *intent* regardless of the appended adjective. In this context, the judges in *Majewski* found themselves in great difficulty, for the originator of the basic/specific distinction, Lord Birkenhead in *Beard*,[21] had himself acknowledged that proving intent in crimes of specific intent 'is, on ultimate analysis, only in accordance with the ordinary law applicable to crime, for, speaking generally..., a person cannot be convicted of a crime unless the mens was rea.'[22] Accordingly, if specific intent requires proof simply as one branch of intent in general, there is no basis for a distinction whereby crimes of basic intent do not require proof of intention while crimes of specific intent do. The distinction is irrelevant, as another judge, Lord Salmon, makes clear:

Intention, whether special or basic..., is still intention. If voluntary intoxication by drink or drugs can, as it admittedly can, negative the special or specific intention necessary for the commission of crimes such as murder or theft, how can you justify

---

[17] [1976] 2 WLR 637-8.
[18] *Offences Against the Person Act 1861*, s.20.
[19] *Offences Against the Person Act 1861*, s.18.
[20] Smith and Hogan, *op.cit.*, p.193. Cf. Williams (*op.cit.*),pp. 429-430.
[21] *D.P.P. v. Beard* [1920] AC 479.

in strict logic the view that it cannot negative a basic intention, e.g. the intention to commit offences such as assault and unlawful wounding? The answer is that in strict logic this view cannot be justified. But this is the view that has been adopted by the common law of England, which is founded on common sense and experience rather than strict logic.[23]

Lord Salmon's distinction between 'commonsense and experience' and X 'strict logic' alerts us to what the judges are doing here. Far from adhering to the requirements of what MacCormick calls 'technical logic', they are quite openly prepared to plump for arguments of a directly utilitarian nature - regardless of the logical consequence. The following comment of Lord Simon of Glaisdale in *Majewski* pithily confirms this:

It is all right to say 'Let justice be done though the heavens fall'. But you ask us to say 'Let logic be done even though public order be threatened', which is something very different.[24]

(2)   R. v Caldwell[25]

In considering *Caldwell*, we turn to a question of statutory interpretation. Section 1(1) of the *Criminal Damage Act 1971* states that 'A person who without lawful excuse destroys or damages any property [intentionally or recklessly] shall be guilty of an offence.' The question that had to be decided by the House of Lords in this case concerned the meaning to be

---

[22] [1920] AC 504, quoted by Lord Elwyn-Jones in [1976] 2 WLR 632. Cf. Williams (*op.cit.*), p.430: '[the judges] distinguish between offences on grounds of policy, while pretending to derive the distinction from definitions.'

[23] [1976] 2 WLR 640.

[24] A comment made during submissions and quoted in agreement by Lord Edmund-Davies at [1976] 2 WLR 651. It has been argued by Dashwood ('Logic and the Lords in *Majewski*' [1977] *Crim.LR* 532, 591) that the charge of illogicality is 'less formidable' than the criticisms levelled at the case suggest. The claim is a loose one (is the charge 'a little formidable'?) but in essence his argument is that 'a more specific rule can be recognised as an exception to a more general rule with which it appears to conflict; while the aim of providing the criminal law with a coherent structure based upon general principles... must on occasion yield place to other aspects of legal policy', (p.596). But an exception to a rule is only permissible if the 'more specific rule' can be legitimately identified and defined. The House of Lords were unable to do this. And *Majewski* not only meant a derogation from general *principles*, it also entailed an unjustified derogation from an established *rule*.

[25] [1981] 1 All E.R. 961.

attached to the term 'reckless' and in particular whether there had to be an element of subjective awareness of risk on the part of the accused concerning the act that he had perpetrated.

Prior to *Caldwell*, the law, as established in the case of *Cunningham*,[26] and in line with what had been taken to be English law since the time of Kenny, had been that 'in any statutory definition of a crime', 'recklessness' occurs where 'the accused has foreseen that the particular kind of harm might be done and yet has gone on to take the risk of it.'[27] This stipulation of an element of advertence in relation to the risk to be taken is denied by Lord Diplock for the majority in *Caldwell*. 'Recklessness' may now be advertent or inadvertent, it occurs where an individual

either has not given any thought to the possibility of there being any such risk or has recognised that there was some risk involved and has nonetheless gone on to do it.[28]

Lord Diplock justifies this change in the law by arguing that while the 1971 Act replaces and revises the *Malicious Damage Act 1861* in which the term 'malicious' embraced recklessness in its subjective form alone, the distinction between advertence and inadvertence in the taking of risks is 'fine and impracticable'.[29]

It calls 'for a meticulous analysis by the jury of the thoughts that passed through the mind of the accused at or before the time he did the act'[30] and this 'weakness' in the definition is compounded by the fact that there is no difference in blameworthiness between he to whom it had occurred 'that there was a risk that someone's property might be damaged' and he who 'did not even trouble to give his mind to the question whether there was any risk'.[31]   Accordingly, Lord Diplock argues that it cannot be assumed that it would be Parliament's intention to retain the old usage. There can be

no warrant for making any such assumption in an Act whose declared purpose is to revise the then existing law as to offences of damage to property, not to perpetuate it. 'Reckless' as used in the new statutory definition of the *mens rea* of these offences is an ordinary English word. It had not by 1971 become a term of legal art

---

26 [1957] 2 Q.B. 396.
27 Quoted at [1981] 1 All E.R. 964.
28 [1981] 1 All E.R. 967.
29 [1981] 1 All E.R. 964.
30 [1981] 1 All E.R. 965.
31 [1981] 1 All E.R. 965. The terms in which Lord Diplock describes the inadvertent risk taker are loaded. To 'not even trouble to give one's mind'

with some more limited esoteric meaning than that which it bore in ordinary speech....[32]

Given that Parliament's intention could not have been to perpetuate a 'fine and impracticable' distinction, Lord Diplock adopts the 'literal' approach to the interpretation of the term 'recklessness'. How legitimate is his argument? According to MacCormick, the correct method of statutory interpretation entails the sifting of a number of possible approaches to establish the intention of Parliament. The literal approach is one of these, but is defeasible where another approach is indicated. MacCormick quotes with favour a judgement of Lord Simon which cites five 'principal avenues of approach to the ascertainment of the legislative intention'.[33] These include 'examination of the social background...in order to identify the social or juristic defect which is the likely subject of remedy' and 'A conspectus of the entire relevant body of the law for the same purpose.'[34]

How does Lord Diplock's judgement measure up to these aspects of a proper approach to statutory interpretation? As regards the juristic background to the 1971 Act, it was the product of a report of the Law Commission which clearly stated that the aim of their proposal to change the law of criminal damage was to replace the term 'malicious' with the terms 'intention' and 'recklessness' so that '*the same elements as are required at present should be retained,* but that they should be expressed with greater simplicity and clarity'.[35] The clear aim of the reform was to change the form but not the substance of the law. While it is not permissible for a judge to consider a report such as that of the Law Commission in order to establish a term's meaning, it is permissible and proper to consult such a report in order to establish the nature of the *mischief* the act is intended to remedy. Yet Lord Diplock makes no reference to the Law Commission's report while acknowledging the need to establish the intention of Parliament.

As regards the second criterion for establishing the meaning of an Act, the nature of the 'relevant body of the law', Lord Diplock effectively

---

suggests an awareness that there is something to which one ought to give one's mind.

[32] [1981] 1 All E.R. 966.

[33] *Op.cit.*, p.210.

[34] From *Ealing London Borough Council v. Race Relations Board* [1972]A.C.342 at 361, and quoted in MacCormick, *op.cit.*, pp.211-212. The other three avenues are (3) 'regard to the long title of the statute', (4) 'scrutiny of the actual words to be interpreted in the light of established canons of interpretation, and (5) 'examination of the other provisions of the statute in question'.

[35] English Law Commission Report No.29, para. 44, emphasis added.

states that there is no such body since the meaning of the term 'reckless' had not 'by 1971 become a term of legal art'. Yet the test of advertent risk-taking as the basis for 'recklessness' had been long laid down and was well entrenched in *Cunningham*. Both this and the previous point were made forcibly in a dissenting judgement by Lord Edmund Davies:

> Professor Kenny used lawyers' words in a lawyers' sense to express his distillation of an important part of the established law relating to *mens rea*, and he did so in a manner accurate not only in respect of the law as it stood in 1902 but also as it has been applied in countless cases ever since.... And it is well known that the Criminal Damage Act 1971 was in the main the work of the Law Commission, who...defined recklessness [in the traditional way].[36]

It is not only that Lord Diplock fails to observe these compelling reasons for not changing the legal definition, it is also that he fails to address the questions raised by Lord Edmund Davies. He makes no reference to the Law Commission report, and he fails to consider that the 'fine and impracticable' distinction to which he refers had been the law of the land for a number of years (and would remain it in relation to offences containing the term 'malicious' without evident impracticability in the future).[37]   It appears that Lord Diplock has turned a (presumably advertent) blind eye to the Act's genetic and juristic background. Needless to say, evasion of the legislative intention as evidenced by clearly established methods of interpretation pointing in a clearly perceptible direction is the antithesis of the rational appraisal at the heart of the MacCormickian analysis. Why should Lord Diplock (and the other judges who voted with him) have acted in this way?

The reasoning behind *Caldwell* is similar to that in *Majewski*. The concern is that juries will be sidetracked by a 'fine and impracticable' distinction calling for 'a meticulous analysis of the thoughts that passed through the mind of the accused' from the business of convicting those who are, in the judges' view, blameworthy. In this situation, it appears that the opportunity to change the law afforded by the new Act of Parliament, regardless of the clearly evinced legislative intention and the legal consequences of so doing, proved too much for the judicial majority, who accordingly sacrificed rationality to utility. The decision

---

[36] [1981] 1 All E.R. 96.
[37] *W. (A Minor) v. Dolbey* [1983] *Crim.L.R.* 681, and at the cost of potentially bewildering practical consequences in the law: see J.C. Smith and B. Hogan, *Criminal Law*, 6th ed., (London, 1988) p.67.

in *Caldwell* is a piece of utilitarian opportunism which stands opposed to a proper rational approach to statutory interpretation.[38]

(3)   Abbott v The Queen[39]

Abbott concerned the availability of the defence of duress to a charge of murder as principal in the first degree. It followed the earlier case of *Lynch*[40] which had held that the defence was available to a principal in the second degree, i.e. to an accomplice. Although English law makes a distinction between degrees of involvement in crime, this is a formal distinction and does not normally have significant legal effects.[41] Despite this and the fact that the judges in *Abbott* declared themselves bound by the *Lynch* decision, a majority in the later case denied the defence to a principal in the first degree. The case accordingly hinged upon the ability of the majority to distinguish the two cases satisfactorily, either by restricting the ratio in *Lynch* or by distinguishing the facts in the two cases. Lord Salmon, delivering the majority judgement, put forward four main reasons for not following *Lynch*.

First, he claimed that the ratio of *Lynch* was restrictively formulated by those sitting on the case. Declaring himself 'bound to accept the decision of the House of Lords in Lynch's case,' there is nonetheless nothing in it that supports its application to Abbott's circumstances. Indeed, he contends, the majority in the earlier case 'said nothing to support the contention now being made on behalf of the appellant. At best...they left the point open.'[42]   Emboldened by this initial thrust, but somewhat contradictorily, he proceeds then to claim that the weight of opinion in *Lynch* was *against* its extension to a principal in the first degree. He quotes from the judgement of Lords Morris and Wilberforce to support his view, and, adding these passages to those of the minority in *Lynch* (Lords Simon of Glaisdale and Kilbrandon) he argues that 'the majority of the House was of the opinion that duress is not a defence to a

---

[38] Hence the unveiled disgust of leading academic commentators, see J.C. Smith [1981] *Crim. LR*. 393-396, G. Williams, 'Recklessness Redefined' 40 *Camb. L.J.* (1981) 252.

[39] [1977] A.C.755.

[40] *D.P.P. v. Lynch* [1975] A.C.653.

[41] Both because it is impossible to draw any real distinction between perpetrator and accessory (G.Williams, *op.cit.* (1978) p.583) and because the law has always stated that 'the stroke of one is the stroke of all' (Smith and Hogan, *op.cit.* p.211).

[42] [1977] A.C.761

charge of murder against anyone proved to have done the actual killing.'[43]

Second, Lord Salmon argues that the application of duress to the Abbott situation runs up against the weight of the common law tradition which 'from time immemorial' has accepted 'that duress is no defence to murder, certainly not to murder by a principal in the first degree.'[44]

Third, he argues that to allow the defence to Abbott would entail 'the destruction of a fundamental doctrine of our law'[45] upon which it ought to be the prerogative of Parliament not the courts to legislate. Fourth, conjoined with this argument, is the view that the result of so changing the law 'might well have far-reaching and disastrous consequences for public safety to say nothing of its important social, ethical and maybe political implications.'[46]   Lord Salmon concludes this argument with reference to Lord Simon's words in *Lynch* that the courts might be granting a 'charter for terrorists, gang-leaders and kidnappers' and by commending the well-known view of Stephen that criminal law is itself a system of threats which are not to be withdrawn simply because opposing threats have been encountered by the accused.   How convincing are these arguments?

The first argument aims to restrict the rule in *Lynch* by limiting its *ratio*. A reading, however, of the judgement in *Lynch* makes it clear that Lord Salmon's interpretation is tendentious.   Lord Morris did doubt the applicability of the rule to an actual murderer, but he stated the matter with caution,[47] adding that he fully appreciates that 'the facts will be much less direct and straightforward than those which...I have described.'[48]   As for Lord Wilberforce, in quoting from his judgement, Lord Salmon omits the crucial passage in which his Lordship finds

---

[43] *Ibid.*, p.762.

[44] *Ibid.*, p.763.

[45] *Ibid.*, p.765.

[46] *Ibid.*

[47] [1975] A.C.671. Dennis argues that Lord Morris expressly supports the distinction. I think this is too strong, but agree with the general conclusion that Lord Salmon's assessment of *Lynch* involved 'something of a distortion': I. Dennis, 'Duress, Murder and Criminal Responsibility' 96 *Law Quarterly Review* (1980), 212. Dennis also raises, discusses and dismisses two other reasons offered for distinguishing the cases by Lord Salmon which I have omitted as peripheral to his judgement.

[48] [1975] A.C.672.

no convincing reason, on principle, why, if a defence of duress in the criminal law exists at all, it should be absolutely excluded in murder charges whatever the nature of the charge.[49]

Further, in enlisting the support of the minority judges who had opposed the admission of the defence in *Lynch*, Lord Salmon ignores the logic of their view that if the defence were allowed to a Lynch, it would be arbitrary and irrational to deny it to an Abbott.[50] Thus an attentive reading of the judgement in *Lynch* makes it clear that there is no basis for restricting its *ratio*. Four of the judges (Lords Wilberforce, Simon, Kilbrandon and Edmund-Davies) are for the extension of the defence on grounds of logic and principle, while the fifth (Lord Morris) leaves the question open.

The second and third reasons given by Lord Salmon may be dealt with together. As regards the weight of authority 'from time immemorial' and the 'prerogative of Parliament', the answer to both points is the same: these may have been relevant arguments prior to *Lynch*, but cannot be after it. *Lynch* is itself the most recent and weighty of authorities and Lord Salmon has already recognised himself to be bound by it. The rule of precedent does not allow the citation of earlier less persuasive authority in order to bypass recent binding case law. If *Lynch* is binding in principle, then Lord Salmon must find genuine reasons to distinguish it. The same is true as regards the argument about parliamentary prerogative. In *Lynch*, the courts had already taken it upon themselves to develop the law of duress in accordance with what the majority saw as normal common law principles, rejecting the argument, clearly expressed by Lord Kilbrandon, that their decision was tantamount to significant judicial legislation. Given *Lynch*, *Abbott* could certainly follow in its wake.[51]

As for argument four, the utilitarian argument, little need be said of this other than that it too had been canvassed in *Lynch* (by Lord Simon of Glaisdale) and rejected by the majority. Thus, examining these arguments, we see that the first entails misreading the words (or the logic) of the judges in the earlier case, while the second, third and fourth all involve an attempt to avoid the substance of *Lynch* while paying lip service to its binding character. *Abbott* is an evasion of the logic and implication of *Lynch*.

---

[49] [1975] A.C.681. While omitting this passage, Lord Salmon nonetheless quotes from the immediately preceding paragraph.

[50] [1975] A.C. 692, 702.

[51] Cf. Dennis, *op.cit.*, 214-5, 217-8.

What could have saved the majority in *Abbott* from this conclusion would have been an attempt not to sidestep a binding precedent, but some attempt at a rational distinction between a principal in the first and second degree.   In other words, given the (acknowledged) binding character of *Lynch*, Abbott's case could perhaps have been distinguished on some argued-for principle.   Yet here we find the most surprising omission on the majority's part: Lord Salmon makes no attempt to distinguish the two cases in this way.   He relies wholly on the selective misreading of *Lynch* together with the other arguments mentioned above.

Accordingly one must agree with the minority in *Abbott* that as regards the most important issue - the issue of principle - whether or not 'any acceptable distinction can invariably be drawn between a principle in the first degree to murder and one in the second degree',[52] the majority judgement does not even address the point.

Why then should the majority have decided in *Abbott* to side-step *Lynch*, and to do so 'without advancing cogent grounds'?[53] It appears from the polemical character of his comments that uppermost in Lord Salmon's mind was his consideration of the disutilitarian consequences of allowing the defence.   He regards it as 'incredible' that the courts should permit 'the added dangers to which in this modern world the public would be exposed, if the change in the law proposed on behalf of the appellant were effected.'[54]   Here his argument becomes similar to that adopted in *Majewski*, in that, once again, 'technical logic' must be sacrificed to 'practical logic' and this, it is submitted, is the rationale behind the decision:

We are not living in a dream world in which the mounting wave of violence and terrorism can be contained by strict logic and intellectual niceties alone.[55]

---

[52] [1977] A.C.768.
[53] [1977] A.C.772.
[54] [1977] A.C.764.
[55] [1977] A.C. 764.   The untenability of the *Lynch / Abbott* distinction was conceded in the more recent case of *R v Howe* [1987] 1 All ER 771.   The House of Lords recognised there that it was necessary either to move forwards and concede the defence to a principal in the first degree or backwards and exclude it entirely for a person charged with murder.   They chose the latter.   In so doing, they have not removed the anomalies resultant upon their irrationality, only replaced them with fresh ones.   The judges in *Howe* recognised this but ducked their *legal* responsibility by suggesting that the solution to injustice and anomaly would be the use of administrative discretion by the Home Secretary or Parole Board (*loc.cit.*, 780, 790).   The resort to discretion is a standard legal ploy for

(4) Analysis

MacCormick acknowledges that his interpretation of legal reasoning as a rational process entails the proferring of 'eminently falsifiable hypotheses'.[56]   Analysis of the admittedly limited sample of cases presented in this section does reveal that judges are prepared to override the logic of valid legal rules and binding precedent in cases which could not reasonably be described as hard.   For MacCormick, problems of relevancy, interpretation or classification must be raised so as to clear the way for consequentialist arguments.[57]   In *Majewski, Caldwell* and *Abbott*, no such problems existed; even allowing for the often deceptive nature of the easy/hard distinction,[58] these were not hard cases in which the rules had run out.   Even making 'all appropriate qualifications to allow for the possibility of restrictive interpretation and explaining and distinguishing',[59] it appears that in these cases a significant number of judges was prepared illegitimately (according to the rationalistic analyses) to sacrifice legal rationality to social utility.

In the process, their judgements lose their logical bite and assume the colour of practical rationalisations for the desired ends.[60]   In the great majority of individual judgements (thirteen out of seventeen) the judges are prepared to accede to this process.   Only in the minority judgements (four) do judges stand up on behalf of reason and against rationalisation. Thus, the highest judges in the land have either been prepared to declare openly their defiance of logic (Lords Salmon and Elwyn-Jones in *Majewski*, Lord Salmon in *Abbott*) or to turn conveniently blind eyes to

---

evading contradictions that the law cannot handle, as the contrast between the processes of conviction and sentencing, discussed in Chapter VII shows.

[56] *Ibid.*, p.13.
[57] *Ibid.*, p.198.
[58] Cf. MacCormick, *op.cit.*, ch.8.
[59] *Ibid.*, p.227.
[60] Cf. G.Williams, *Textbook of Criminal Law* (2nd ed.) (1983, London) p.16 who states that the judges are capable in criminal law cases of 'what is popularly called 'special pleading' - that is, rationalisation accompanied by misdirection and legerdemain. The legal pros and cons are not fairly stated... The court selects the arguments and authorities leading to the conclusion it desires, and minimises or ignores the weight of authority or force of arguments going the other way.' Yet the main textbook writers continue to present legal doctrine as if this was not a regular feature of deciding cases, but peripheral to an idealised conception of the law as a rational and principled whole.

rules of statutory interpretation or precedent where necessary (Lord Diplock in *Caldwell*, Lord Salmon in *Abbott*). Accordingly, it is fair to argue that there are counter-instances to falsify MacCormick's hypothesis that law is a rational process. Against this, it is open to MacCormick to argue that these examples are too few in number to represent a genuine challenge to his thesis, and that they may be dismissed simply as 'bad' decisions. This is indeed an anticipatory defence in his book.[61]   Against it, however, three points may be made. First, the argument contains a danger of tautology: to argue that counter examples of judicial illogic are 'bad' because they are irrational begs the initial question as to the nature of judicial reasoning. Second, on the question of numbers, it must be left to the reader to judge the significance of the small number of examples I have been able to discuss in the space available. I am aware that I have not been able to follow through all the ramifications of even these three cases,[62] or introduce other examples.   Readers may be able to supply their own examples either from criminal law or from other areas of law where the potential for conflict between the legal rules and (what judges regard as) social or political utility is high.[63]   For my part, I would claim that given the status of the cases, the relatively large number of judicial opinion that they contain, together with the fact that as decisions of the highest courts, they represent only the 'tip of the iceberg' of legal arguments that have already been canvassed at lower levels of the process, they represent a *prima facie* case against a rationalistic approach to legal reasoning.

Third, in stating the last point, my argument is *not* that judicial reasoning is always explicable in terms of the judicial evaluation of consequences, or, at least, a crude form of that argument. It is always open to judges to argue from the logic of a case, as the minority judgements in *Caldwell* and *Abbott* make clear, and there are very good

---

[61] *Ibid.*, p.13.

[62] For example, it has not been possible to consider attempts by some of the judges in *Majewski* to further rationalise their position through arguing that intoxication is itself a form of recklessness (Lords Elwyn-Jones, Edmund-Davies), or a form of *mens rea* (Lord Simon), or another form of unspecifiedly culpable activity (Lord Salmon).   None of the arguments is very plausible; indeed Lord Edmund-Davies concedes that his approach 'would probably [be] condemn[ed] ... as savouring of 'judge-made fiction'.' ([1976] 2 WLR 654).

[63] Cf. Williams, *op.cit.*, fn.60: 'Ordinary lawyerly reasoning, as generally employed in *civil* cases, may be rejected in favour of fallacious and shallow grounds.' See also R.Ferguson in (1979) *British Journal of Law and Society* 6, 272, at p.274.

examples within criminal law of this occurring. In *Morgan*,[64] it was held that since rape entailed the intention to have non-consensual intercourse, it would be logically contradictory to hold that it could be committed where the accused believed unreasonably that his victim was consenting. The judges stuck to the logic of the law. Indeed, in *Morgan*, the judges not only refused to admit illogic into the law, they self-consciously pinned, their colours to the mast of reason.[65]

My argument therefore is not that judges can not or do not argue rationally, but rather that their commitment to rational logic is conditional and defeasible rather than categorical. While rational argument is for judges an end in itself, it is not unqualifiedly so: sufficiently strongly desired social or political goals may defeat it. If this is so, it is necessary to ask why judicial reasoning cannot be seen *pace* MacCormick simply as one specialised branch of practical reasoning. In terms of the general argument of this book, it is necessary to consider what is the connection between the case analysis presented here and the antithesis between individual right and state power, which, I claim, the cases reflect.

3. SPEAKING THE LANGUAGE OF LAW

The two questions just posed are interconnected in that an answer to the first can be arrived at through an answer to the second: that is, the clash between utility and rationality in the criminal law cases analysed stems

---

[64] *D.P.P. v Morgan* [1975] 2 All E.R. 347.

[65] Thus Lord Hailsham, at 360: 'I cannot myself reconcile it with my conscience to sanction as part of the English law what I regard as logical impossibility, and, if there were any authority which, if accepted would compel me to do so, I would feel constrained to declare that it was not to be followed.' But it cannot be said to be a matter of individual judicial psychology. It was also Lord Hailsham who stated in *Howe* that 'Consistency and logic, though inherently desirable, are not always prime characteristics of a penal code based like the common law on custom and precedent' [1987] 1 All E.R. 780. Similarly, Lord Edmund-Davies, on the minority side of the rational angels in *Caldwell* and *Abbott*, voted with the majority in *Majewski*, explicitly discounting the overriding requirement of logic in law: [1976] 2 All E.R.167. The facility with which the judges jump from one kind of argument to the other indicates the centrality of both sorts of argument to legal decision-making.

from the clash between state power and individual right argued for as the second antithesis of law in modern society.

It has been argued that the essential legal form in a society based upon commodity exchange is that of the abstract and equal rights-bearing individual. Law, through this form, represents the interests of equal individuals, investing them with rights which it itself protects as an arbitrator between individual conflicts. Reflecting a conception of social order in which no individual is to be held above any other individual, law speaks a 'language of equality'[66] which includes not only all individuals but also the state itself which is regarded from this point of view as 'one among many'.

However, for the law to speak in a particular voice without that voice being heard and attended to would clearly be of little value to those whom it seeks to protect. Accordingly, it is necessary for the law's 'language of equality' to be conjoined with a form of political organisation (the state) which possesses sufficient power and universality to have its commands enforced generally throughout society. Thus, law, as a source of individual right, requires at the same time the existence of a general form of social organisation, authority and power in order to make the protection of individual right possible. In order that the 'language of equality' may be heard and obeyed it must be tied to its opposite: a general and omnipotent power source which, while presenting itself as representing the general social interest, in fact embodies particular social-political interests and points of view.

The effect of this antithesis between individual right and social power is that while the individual must look to the state to enunciate the 'language of equality', whether it in fact does so is conditional upon its (the state's) own perception in a given case of the value of so doing. Since the ideology of the modern democratic state presupposes the existence of law as the embodiment of individual right, and since, accordingly, legal doctrine is rationally framed to accommodate such right, there are incentives of both a legitimative and logical kind why the law should continue to embody the 'language of equality'. But, and this is the important point, there is no power beyond the power of the state to guarantee that it will articulate its decisions in such a language.

Thus, the connection between rationality and individual right stems from the nature of law. To the extent that law embodies individual right, its rationality will be a rationality *of* individual right. But, to the extent that individual right is overriden by the dictates of state power, to that

---

[66] The idea of a 'language of equality' is taken from an unpublished doctoral thesis of that title by T.S. Midgely: *The Language of Equality* (1978) Edinburgh.

extent will the law's rationality, as the expression of individual right, also come under threat.

In relation to criminal law, the existence of a language of equal rights is embodied in the rules which protect the individual from unlawful state intervention or punishment. Often these rules are quite inadequately formulated so that it is fair to ask whether or not the judges have any intention to articulate a 'language of equality' between the state and the individual.[67] But in one area - that of criminal responsibility - such a language is sufficiently well entrenched in notions of *mens rea* (intention and recklessness) and of excusing conditions (duress, intoxication, etc.) that departures from the defence of individual right in favour of social utility must also be departures from the logic of the law itself. Thus, in *Majewski*, the desire to convict intoxicated persons overrides the defence of intoxication but only by means of a negation of the logic of *mens rea*; in *Caldwell*, the desire to convict persons regarded by judges as reckless overrides and evades the express intentions of Parliament and the known legal precedents; and in *Abbott*, the perceived need not to provide a 'charter for terrorists' leads the defendant to the scaffold by means of a sidestep of the existing legal authority. The fact is that judges in the criminal law see themselves not just as the creators of rational legal doctrine but also, as one of their number has put it, 'as at least as much concerned as the executive with the preservation of law and order'.[68] The problem is that here, as elsewhere, 'law' and 'law and order' are by no means necessarily identical virtues, and judicial reasoning is perforce torn between them.

In Chapter I, it was argued that law was founded on a tension between individual right and state power. That tension is expressed very practically in the cases examined here in the form of judicial illogic and irrationality. Judges are forced to choose between individual right and social utility. To the extent that the 'language of equality' is entrenched within the rules relating to criminal responsibility, judges are forced to choose between the conflicting values of 'technical' and 'practical' logic. That choice is not, *pace* MacCormick, foreclosed by the requirements of practical reason. Where the judges choose the latter over the former, legal reasoning becomes a cover for the formulation of policy objectives that go beyond the logical constraints of the law. In the process, judicial logic slides from rationality into rationalisation. This may be, in MacCormick's terms, 'bad reasoning', but it remains nonetheless legal

---

[67] See D. McBarnet, *Conviction* (London, 1981).

[68] Lord Devlin, quoted in J. Griffith, *The Politics of the Judiciary* (London, 1977), Fontana, p.191.

reasoning, in the broader (non rationalist) sense that it is something the judges regularly do. The rationalist analysis picks up one side of the antithesis between individual right and social power, labouring the former to the exclusion of the latter. It therefore idealises the language of the law as a pure logic of juridical individualism and ignores the contradictory tendencies within the legal form.

4. CONCLUSION

The analysis presented in this chapter, as with the analysis of the second half of the last chapter, uses the standpoint of a sociological approach to analyse and explain the development of legal doctrine. It treats legal doctrine as ideology and not simply philosophically, as one form of practical reasoning. The contrast between the two approaches can be thrown into relief if it is placed in the context of the debate within jurisprudence as to the relative merits of sociological approaches and more traditional analytical approaches to the subject.

It has frequently, but not invariably, been argued by those who espouse a sociological viewpoint that traditional analytical jurisprudence is no more than a preliminary to the work of a true legal science governed by principles of social theory. Thus Cotterrell agrees that 'inquiries into the nature of legal forms and concepts' are valid, but contends that they are not 'fully adequate to serve the needs of legal science'. They should rather be seen 'as incomplete parts of a wider theoretical enterprise', as 'an aspect or component of social theory, concerned to structure inquiries about the nature of law as an empirical social phenomenon.'[69]

This amounts to a restructuring of legal science in which the traditional jurisprudential approaches are subsumed within a broader sociological approach. Such a restructuring most crucially entails that we no longer attempt to see law as rational and systematic, but rather as a contradictory agglomeration of different elements and tendencies. It

---

[69] R. Cotterrell, 'English Conceptions of the Role of Theory in Legal Analysis', *Modern Law Review* (1983) 46, p.681, at pp.697-698.

in no way displaces the central concern of legal theory with analysis of doctrine and with conceptual analysis... But these elements cannot be considered only in so far as they are rational or systematic: many of them, in modern legal systems, are contradictory, only vaguely or partially elaborated in doctrine, and can be explained in their rise, modification and decline only in relation to complex historical conditions.... [Social theory] holds out the prospect of contributing to explanation of the transformations of legal doctrine in a way that transcends mere rationalisation.[70]

Cotterrell's point is that analytical jurisprudence, in attempting to portray law as a rational edifice and enterprise of necessity ends up rationalising what is in essence an irrational and contradictory set of institutions, concepts and practices.   Sociological analyses can put such rationalisations in their place by developing 'a broader understanding of the law in modern conditions.'[71]

To the rather crude attack of some sociologists who consider analytical jurisprudence to be a complete waste of time, MacCormick rightly responds that a sociology of law must itself be committed to the conceptual analysis necessary in order to define its terms, for it 'necessarily presupposes some criterion not only as to what a legal system is, but as to what is a law.'[72]   This is clearly right: a prerequisite for any sociological analysis is a definition of terms, a conception of what it is that is to be analysed.   In the same article, however, MacCormick stresses the limitations of traditional legal analysis without a complementary sociological awareness:

Is conceptual analysis worthwhile? Is it worth trying to analyse the use within law of concepts such as 'contract'? If one is interested for any purpose in the legal system, the answer must be 'yes'. A concept which features so prominently in so many legal systems deserves study and understanding in its primary context, namely that of legal systems.... But if we look at 'the law' only, there is a risk that we will make two errors. First, we may assume that the use of the term 'contract' must be the same for all systems and all times, and second, at the same time our analysis will tend to be based on excessive attention to a particular system at a particular time. Technically speaking, we will interpret a particular *conception* of contractual relations as though it were identical with the (logically) universal *concept* of contract.[73]

Particular laws 'belong to particular times, places and circumstances' and the explanation of legal concepts is 'at least in part to be sought within

---

[70] *Ibid.*, pp.698-699.
[71] *Ibid.*
[72] 'Challenging Sociological Definitions', *British Journal of Law and Society* (1976) 3, p.88.
[73] *Ibid.*, p.93.

sociology and economic history.'[74]   This argument perhaps admits of
two different interpretations.   First, it may suggest that while the two
approaches are complementary, conceptual analysis *by itself* remains a
valid task for legal science.   It may need to be supplemented by
sociological awareness, but study and understanding of concepts in their
primary context, the law, is important within its own terms. The second
interpretation is that conceptual analysis is only possible as a
preliminary to sociological analysis, or, put differently, that the findings
of conceptual analysis are always, and only, a first step to the more
fundamental enquiries of social theory. The first interpretation suggests
a 'separate but equal' approach, whereas the second suggests an 'under-
labourer' conception of analytical jurisprudence and a 'master-discipline'
conception of sociological analysis.
    If we compare these two approaches in terms of the analysis of legal
reasoning presented in this chapter, MacCormick's account follows the
first approach, while my own account follows the second.   What is
indicated by the study of *Majewski, Caldwell* and *Abbott* is that while the
presentation of law within its own terms as a rational edifice is a
necessary preliminary to an exploration of the way law works, that
exploration ultimately leads to the rejection of the law's mode of self-
presentation, and as a result relies upon further theoretical development
external to law in the field of social theory.[75]   Legal irrationalism
requires explanation as much as legal rationalism, and it is necessary to
go outwith law to the social forms of law and state in order to elucidate
this problem. To remain within the traditional rationalistic analysis is to
ignore the fundamental, social and historical contradictions at the heart
of the law.

---

[74] *Ibid.*, p.94.
[75] Kelman's American critical legal studies analysis of criminal law is strong on
    drawing out contradictions and rationalisations within the law, but lacks a social
    theory of legal form that can properly explain their structure. He ends up with a
    crude and badly differentiated class reductionist stance: see *op.cit.* at fn.1.,
    pp.670-671.

CHAPTER IX

THE LIMITS OF LEGAL IDEOLOGY

1. THE PHILOSOPHICAL-HISTORICAL DEVELOPMENT OF THE LIBERAL IDEAL OF CRIMINAL PUNISHMENT

In this book, I have sought to understand the liberal theory of punishment in a way that is radically different from other approaches to the subject. First, I have attempted to show that the modern development of the philosophy of punishment should be understood as a contradictory rather than rational phenomenon. The standard philosophical method of intellectual synthesis and resolution of conflict is inadequate to a theoretical discourse whose premises are fundamentally in opposition with each other. There is a tension between the social phenomena of criminality and punishment on the one hand and their representation within the philosophy of punishment on the other that ensures that any attempt to rationalise that philosophy will end up as rationalisation, that is, as an attempt to resolve the irresoluble, to paper over the intellectual cracks.

Second, I have sought to show that there is a logic *behind* the contradictions of an historical kind, and that a definite intellectual development can be traced within the philosophy of punishment as writers within the tradition both grapple with the intellectual problems bequeathed to them by their predecessors and mediate their treatment of those problems in accordance with the urgent historical and political developments of their time. There is both an internal and external element to the analysis. From the inside, I examine the discursive techniques and forms available to the philosophers; from the outside, I show how these techniques and forms are historical data of an emergent and developing kind, and are part of a social reality that is itself emergent and developmental - within particular, historical limits. The crucial interconnection between the internal, philosophical and external, historical elements of the work is provided by the concept of the ideology of juridical individualism outlined in chapter I.   That ideology is a historical 'discovery' in the epoch of capitalist society in which the market and market relations play a central role.   The world of free and equal juridical individuals, of the abstraction of 'man' as a universal subject - a sort of ideal homunculus - becomes the core ideological concept in the liberal theory of criminal punishment at the same time as, in Foucault's words, 'the abstract juridical forms of contract and exchange'[1] begin to assume a dominance in social and economic life.   It is the antitheses within that ideological form, outlined in chapter I and charted throughout the book, which give the liberal theory of criminal punishment its contradictory 'logic' and which act, in conjunction with the development of historical events, as the driving tension behind the trajectory of the theory, and which the theory is never able to overcome.

Third, I have sought to show that the current impasse of the philosophy of punishment is a product of this inability of the discourse to transcend its limits, with the result that it is doomed forever (within the current historical period) to go 'round in circles'.   I want to now summarise the development of the philosophy of punishment that has led to this situation in which we find ourselves 'at sea as to first principles'.[2] My starting point was Hobbes's attempt to establish political (and punitive) authority on the back of a materialist view of people and society.   He retained the aim of a moral justification of state power, but his materialism could provide no basis for a normative legitimisation of the sovereign and his actions.   Hence the 'play' on the concept of 'natural law' *and* the central role that he gave to the moral-juridical moment of individual consent in the social contract.   From his point of view, Habermas has stressed the significance of the former element in the Hobbesian philosophy but missed the latter.[3]   MacPherson, on the other hand, focussed on the material individuality (the egoism) of Hobbesian man, and identified this crucial element as a specifically bourgeois historical discovery by Hobbes; but he missed the essential schizophrenia of *Leviathan* in which the dark, brutal egoist becomes, on fairs and holy days, an ideal juridical individual - a bright alter ego, whose presence is in no way presaged in the materialist analysis.[4]

---

[1]   See ch.I, fn.18.
[2]   See Maine's comment, ch.I, fn.1.
[3]   See ch.II, text at fns. 34-36.
[4]   *Ibid.*, fn. 69

It is the Hobbesian dualism that gives us a starting-point into the analysis of the modern classical philosophy of punishment. *Homo juridicus*, first cousin to economic man, emerges onto the stage of philosophical history fully-fledged as the founding principle of modern state sovereignty and authority. It is his rightful consent that establishes the basic notion of *do ut des*, of the transference of a liberty amongst equal individuals which allows for the legitimate constraint of the sovereign. From the other side of Hobbes's philosophy, the creation of punishment is only too necessary: men's natural wilfulness from this standpoint needs a strict control through sovereign punishment. But the compatibility between the ideal theory of consent and the prosaic reality of constraint is superficial. Given his nature, what man would or could consent to his punishment; given the moral-juridical capacity, how could such an individual *need* punishment? There is a contradiction between the surface *form* of the theory and its content as a *bellum omnium contra omnes*, between the presentation of social consensus and underlying social conflict. That conflict is understood in an individualist fashion (though remember Hobbes's reflections on the 'common people'⁵) but, following MacPherson, it is a conflict that is nonetheless to be understood historically, resulting from and reflecting the birth of a specifically bourgeois society founded upon competition for resources and power.

Moving to the classical statements of the modern theory of punishment in Kant and Hegel, we find that the essential components that Hobbes had set in motion, and in tension, in his philosophy are combined and recombined in highly sophisticated ways in order to attempt to resolve the contradiction between the ideal (the moral) and the real (the actual, the material). In Kant, the attempt is made to achieve a radical separation of moral form and natural content, but the hermetic sealing off of the rational and normative from the real and the practical is only achieved at the price of rendering the former incompetent either to pass judgement on the latter⁶ or to mediate relations within that sphere.⁷ Thus it is that an ideal theory of punishment can have nothing to say about the justice of punishment amongst mere mortals, nor establish sound measures for that most prosaic of social facts, punishment. Furthermore, with Kant, the gap between form and content now becomes recognisable as a *social* gap, for Kant acknowledges (around the edges

---

⁵ *Ibid.*, text at fn. 63.
⁶ A. MacIntyre, *A Short History of Ethics* (London, 1967), pp.197-198; R.P. Wolff, *The Autonomy of Reason* (New York, 1973), ch.2.; G. Lukacs, *op.cit.*, pp.110-149.
⁷ See ch.III, section 3.

of his materialist understanding of human nature) the social quality of wrong-doing in a world where false incentives to action are everywhere.[8] The gap now becomes one between juridical appearance or representation (rational individualism) and social reality (a world of incentives to individual criminality).

Hegel did most to stop the more distasteful elements of social reality from impinging upon the world of rational individuals comprehended in his philosophy. With great ingenuity, he did it in a way that appeared to incorporate reality within the rational (and vice versa). The cunning of the Hegelian method lay in its ability to lay hold upon those elements of material reality which corresponded to the ideal, while shunning those elements which contradicted it. Thus punishment and criminal justice, prosaic institutions, become emanations of the Idea on its speculative path through history and society, but are only presented in so far as they conform to the requirements of the Idea. If the rational is real *and* the real is rational, then all thoughts of social irrationality - for example of crime as a fixed and necessary social phenomenon - must and can be cast aside in the wake of reason's triumph.[9] But it turned out that history was more cunning than Hegel and the philosopher was forced to acknowledge the turbulent and inequitable nature of 'rational', bourgeois (civil) society, and thence to recognise the class basis of criminality among the poor and the rebellious. Content rebelled against the ideal form that sought to speak through it like a ventriloquist's dummy, and Hegel was anxious enough about the fate of civil society to recognise it. But the question then arose, what role was the state to play in a world where rational atomised individuals turned out to be aggressive, needy occupants of inequitable class positions? The concept of the state, in the realm of crime and punishment, had not been premised upon social, structural recalcitrance on the part of members of civil society. Hegel did not hesitate to say that if individuals did not behave as individuals should, then nor could states be expected to. The juridical form of the *Rechtsstaat also* turned out to be an appearance hiding a deeper reality as Hegel justified the death penalty for petty theft. The State became (what it always was behind the juridical form) a mechanism of social control on behalf of one class over another.[10] Class conflict is the 'worm in the bud' of the ideal penal theory of Hegel.

With Kant and Hegel, the elements within the modern classical theory of punishment receive their most sophisticated expression. Already,

---

[8] *Ibid.*, text at fns. 69, 70.

[9] See ch.IV, section 3*(1)*.

[10] *Ibid.*, section 4.

however, we can see the temptation for these elements to tear the theories apart.   Kant agonises over the question of social justice and Hegel subverts his own theory on the subject of the death penalty. These were theories of the bourgeois Enlightenment; that is, they were theories that expressed a *political* as well as a philosophical idealism.[11] At this stage in historical development the philosophers could still maintain a basic conviction in the value of their central terms.   Later on, however, thinkers in the tradition had to recognise that the fabric of an ideal juridical individualism could not be made to stretch any further to cover the emerging crises of social development within capitalism.[12] The effects of poverty and pauperism, of idleness and drunkenness, of exploitation and vice upon the criminalty of the body politic could not be ignored or represented as a matter of pure individual choice.   The English Hegelians, writing in late Victorian England, did not initially discard this notion, but they sought to hedge it around by reconceiving the state not as a *Rechtsstaat* but as a social, interventionist state, designed to cure defects in minds that could not be relied upon to follow rational tenets.   In this situation, the classical theory began to fall apart. Because society and social order were no longer understood to rest upon individual consent or reason, juridical individualist ideology could no longer be the true basis for the political legitimation of social institutions.   Simultaneously, the state could no longer be seen as an ideal counterpart to a society of free individuals, as a juridical *primus inter pares*.   More emphasis had to be placed upon the role of the state as an institution that 'knows better' and that intervenes in order to make people better citizens.[13]

In this move, the classical relationship between form and content breaks down at the level both of the individual and of the state.   With regard to the former, individuals are no longer portrayed as free, equal and rational.   They are *socially* formed and, where poor, potentially inadequate.   The juridical form of the responsible rational individual begins to dissolve into the social context of individual life.[14]   Similarly, the state is no longer the guarantor of individual right, administered equally.   It must move amongst and against the lower classes ensuring their proper participation in social arrangements.   Behind the rhetoric of welfare, the aim is reconstruction of the poor and the inadequate,

---

[11] See J. Ree, M. Ayers, A. Westoby, *Philosophy and its Past* (Hassocks, 1978), ch. 3, especially pp.89-90.

[12] See ch.V, text at fns. 5-8.

[13] *Ibid.*, text at fns. 9 and 10.

[14] *Ibid.*, section 2(2)(1).

regardless of their actual will in the matter.[15]   The state's form of neutrality dissolves as it intervenes in class relations.   For T. H. Green, the historical developments in Victorian England necessitated a re-theorisation of Hegelianism which emphasised the whole over its parts, the state over its citizens.   But this tendency, to 'reify the universal as against the individual', was nonetheless still 'counteracted by [an] adherence to the progressive tendencies of Western rationalism'[16] with the result that the theory was not only contradictory but also profoundly unstable in its elements.[17]   Lesser philosophers within the same tradition sought to resolve the contradictions by removing one pole of the central antithesis and by moving entirely in the direction of statist, collective authority against the individual.   Green had opened up this avenue, but he had baulked at progressing too far down it.   Philosophers like Bradley and Bosanquet marched ahead, confident that they were armed with an idea 'whose time had come'.   The state would deal with crime directly and ruthlessly as the whole crushed its recalcitrant parts.[18]   Thus it was that in the final phase of its development, the retributive philosophy became transformed into the opposite of what it had been. From being an expression of individual autonomy and defence of individual right, it became a principle of authoritarian state interventionism without regard to or respect for the individual.   But this doctrine still retained the name 'retributivism', leading to its utter discredit in an intellectual culture where fascism remained an eccentric and borderline conviction.

It is crucial to note that the downfall of retributivism at the beginning of the twentieth century was an essentially organic and dialectical playing out of the contradictions within the philosophy in the context of the developing historical realities of capitalist society.   It was the increasing tension between the ideal juridical foundations of the theory and the underlying social developments, between its form and content that led to its downfall as the concepts of the rational individual and the *Rechtsstaat* were both discarded to meet the same requirement: a more 'effective' form of social control.   From the late nineteenth century, the interventionist ideology of 'welfarism' and social eudaemonism grew to replace the old juridical ideologies of individual responsibility and the rule of law[19] (or at least to knock them sideways as they - temporarily, as

---

15 *Ibid.*, text at fns. 44-46.
16 H. Marcuse, *op.cit.*, pp.391-2.
17 See ch.V, section 2*(3)*.
18 *Ibid.*, section 3.
19 See ch.VI, text at fns. 74-76.

it turned out - took centre stage).   As a result, and in the context of the
'organic' self-destruction of retributivism, it was hardly surprising that it
should be a utilitarian theory emphasising social intervention for the
general good as part of a commitment to social amelioration in a
welfare-liberal polity that should emerge as the predominant justification
of punishment.   Retributivism had shot its bolt; utilitarianism, it
transpired, was the idea whose time had really come.

It was in this way that the intellectual framework for the familiar
twentieth century debates was set.   The legacy of retributivism's decline
was a discursive terrain in which the elements of juridical individualism
had been displaced from centre stage but had to be constantly re-asserted
within a polity that remained ideologically liberal.   Utilitarianism started
off from the position of the need to promote the social good, but then
had to incorporate into its analysis a juridical element in support of
individual right so as to defend itself against the charge of
authoritarianism.[20]   Similarly, utilitarianism was predominantly based
upon the materialist analysis of individual conduct which had emerged
with the Enlightenment and which tended to reduce individual
subjectivity and responsibility to the effects of psychological and
physiological processes.[21]   This then had to be offset by arguments
which could rescue the concept of responsibility from the reductionist
context.[22]   In both situations, however, the assertion of the twin juridical
values of individual right and responsibility was fundamentally
weakened by the hegemonic position of the overarching utilitarian,
materialist theory.   Juridical individualism had to be inserted into an
intellectually hostile environment.   Individual rights against social
intervention had to be defended within the discourse of social
intervention, and individual responsibility and freedom had to be
asserted within a discourse of determinism.   Having ceased to be a
fundamental principle of social and political theory, as it had been within
the modern classical approach, juridical individualism, like an old
aristocrat fallen upon hard times, had to scratch a living as best it could
with second rate materials.   Juridical individualism had become a
secondary, technical element within an over-arching materialist
utilitarian theoretical context and could not regain the glorious primacy it
had enjoyed in the period of revolutionary political enlightenment.
Criminality had passed into the worlds of social science and social

---

[20] See generally, ch.VI.
[21] Of course not every form of utilitarianism corresponds to this description.   It is
the predominant Benthamite form that is referred to here.
[22] See generally, ch.VII.

policy; juridical punishment had become an intellectually outmoded idea,[23] hanging on by little more than the theoretical skin of its teeth. The theories based upon the form of juridical individualism persisted, and the ideas continued to 'go round in circles', but the circles became in the twentieth century ever-diminishing in size and intellectual scope.

2. THE RETURN TO KANT

It is in the context of the historical decline of retributive philosophy that we can understand the ambivalence and ambiguity present in the writings of those who have recently returned to Kant (or, at least, a modernised version) through the so-called justice model.   This philosophical move which developed in the 1970s and early 1980s emerged as a response to increasing dissatisfaction with the utilitarian and rehabilitative consensus that had existed in the criminal and penal process.   It was becoming clear that greater injustices could be perpetrated under an ideology of welfare than under the juridical ideology of punishment that welfare had supplanted.   The move to a justice model, premised on Kantian principles, entailed a desire to limit the ability of the state to intervene in the lives of individuals.   In Von Hirsch's words, it involved 'a crucial shift in perspective from a commitment to do good to a commitment to do as little mischief as possible.'[24]

But why this return to retributive principles of 'guilt' and 'just deserts'?   Had these concepts not been discredited many years earlier in the critiques of both philosophers and criminologists?   How could these ideas, apparently so definitively consigned to the scrapheap, emerge as the bright and shining hope for penal reform?   The key to answering this question lies in recognition of the thoroughly contradictory nature of this return to Kantian principle.   For example, the criminologist, Stanley

---

[23] I emphasise 'intellectually' because it is clear that juridical ideology will continue to play a fundamental role in Western societies regardless of its intellectual justifiability.   Ideas can and do retain their currency long after their deficiencies have been exposed where they continue to reflect the principles embodied in dominant social relations. While the moral narrative constructed around law has become threadbare, the need to legitimate it remains.

[24] A. Von Hirsch, *Doing Justice, op.cit.*

Cohen could describe the 'justice model' as 'the most promising possible' option for criminology to espouse, yet in the next breath, counsel extreme caution as to the dangers of such an approach. The 'justice model' is in fact extremely *unjust* because it denies what criminology has known for a century, that individual criminal acts are always inherently social phenomena. The 'justice model' makes us 'forget that by the time many offenders get to this wonderful justice system the damage has already been done.' It is obvious, says Cohen, 'to anyone who has spent five minutes in a court or prison that it would be blatantly *unjust* to return - even as an intermediate tactic - to an undiluted classicism.'[25]

Again, we are back in the contradiction between the *form* of criminal justice and the *content* of social relations and criminal conduct. As early proponents of the 'justice model' put it, the attempt to establish 'a just system of criminal justice in an unjust society is a contradiction in terms. Criminal justice is inextricably interwoven with, and largely derivative from, a broader social justice.'[26]

In considering this debate one has very much the sense of a clutching at philosophical straws in the face of a recalcitrant reality. Lucien Seve's description of 'a science [which] goes round in circles' is very much to the point. Consider Cohen's bewildered summing up of the development of criminology in the late seventies:

Once upon a time it was radical to attack law; then it became 'radical' to attack psychiatry. As we now rush back to the bewildered embrace of lawyers, who always thought we were against them, we should remind ourselves just what a tyranny the literal rule of law could turn out to be.[27]

Amongst the philosophers, Murphy has come closest to confronting the contradiction between criminal and social justice, between a model of punishment based upon an abstract juridical conception of agency and

---

[25] S. Cohen, 'Guilt, Justice and Tolerance: Some Old Concepts for a New Criminology' in D. Downes and P. Rock, *Deviant Interpretations* (Oxford, 1979), pp.35-41.

[26] American Friends Service Committee, *Struggle for Justice* (New York, 1971) p.6. A. Ashworth, 'Criminal Justice and Deserved Sentences' [1989] *Criminal Law Review* 340, at 354 argues that this criticism is misplaced because the law is not an instrument of social reform, rather a 'public quantification of ... blameworthiness.' Social reform is the business of government policy, not law. This argument misses the point that punishment is aimed at giving '*just* deserts'. The judgement of *blameworthiness* can only artificially be narrowed to avoid the social context of actions.

[27] *Op. cit.*, p.41.

the concrete determinations of conduct within social life.[28] He concedes that 'modern societies largely lack the moral right to punish'[29] and seeks to resolve the issue by hitching his Kantian theory of punishment to a Marxian analysis of social injustice. If we consider that 'institutions of punishment are necessary and desirable' and we are to have the moral right to inflict it, we must first have 'reconstructed society in such a way that criminals genuinely do correspond to the only model that will render punishment permissible.'[30] The paradox of this position is, as Murphy notes, that if crime is a general product of social conditions, then such a restructuring of society would entail that 'crime itself and the need to punish would radically decrease if not disappear entirely.'[31] Here, Murphy is only repeating a logic that we have already seen in Kant himself.[32] If we lived in a world that had been radically restructured, why *would* we consider institutions of punishment to be 'necessary and desirable'?[33] On the other hand, without such a restructuring punishment is unjustified.

Thus the return to the justice model is a highly contradictory affair. Written from the point of view of a modern awareness of the social roots of criminality,[34] it is impossible for proponents not to exhibit an extreme ambivalence about their project. However, it is wrong to examine the 'justice model' only in its negative aspect. From one point of view, the justice model leads not to justice but to injustice. From another point of view, however, it is a means of seeking to impose limits upon the power of the state, and this is the aspect that proponents of the model have most emphasised. A system of strict punishments may be unjust, and therefore oppressive, when viewed in the context of broader social relations. It may be (relatively) liberative when viewed as a check upon

---

[28] See above, ch.3, text at fn.63.

[29] Murphy, *Retribution Justice and Therapy*, *op.cit*, p.95.

[30] *Ibid.*, p.110.

[31] *Ibid.*

[32] Above, ch.III, text at fn.70.

[33] It is surely not insignificant that Murphy, who is most aware among the Kantians of the contradictions within the theory (see ch.III, text at fns.7, 82), is also closest to giving it up. The contradictions within Kantianism tear the theory apart, making its thoughtful espousal a troublesome business.

[34] This is not true of all modern retributivists. E. Van den Haag for example rejects the relevance of social environment to blameworthiness. He does so in a manner that can fairly be described as merely assertive and unreflective. See, for example, his 'Refuting Reiman and Nathanson' (1985) *Philosophy and Public Affairs* 165, 168. While using the language of retributivism, there is a strong unchecked utilitarian foundation to his position as in his acceptance of torture (p. 171) if it can be proved to have an additional deterrent effect.

state power. It is necessary to understand both the positive and negative aspects of the justice model.

The key to these two aspects lies in the important duality within the ideology of juridical individualism, outlined in chapter I. There, it was argued that there were two contradictions at the heart of legal ideology concerning the nature of the individual and the nature of the state. The first contradiction exists between the abstract individualism of the law and the concrete individuality of human beings in different social contexts, with different needs, experiences and personalities. In this context, the liberty of the abstract juridical individual appears shallow and insignificant when contrasted with the real human needs of actual human beings in particular social contexts. It is obscurantist in its ability to hide the underlying social relations which provide the actual springs of human conduct behind the 'front' of the abstract responsible individual. From the point of view of a politics of human liberation, abstract juridical individualism, with its shallow concepts of freedom and equality, is a barrier to the achievement of real human freedom and equality, both of which require the transformation of social relations, not a spurious respect for an abstract model of the individual. This much is implicit in the self-critique of the 'justice modellers', that we have considered above. Marx expressed much the same point of view when he described the formal rights of bourgeois society as providing a 'narrow horizon' beyond which a communist society would have to go.[35]

With regard to the second contradiction, however, between individual right and social power, things look quite different. Here, the juridical form entails an assertion of the rights of the individual against the interests of the state, so that from the point of view of a politics of human liberation, juridical individualism is an important positive element in this antithesis. In this context, we can see that bourgeois right's 'narrow horizon' remains valid and worth defending. Better a narrow horizon than no horizon at all. The strengths and weaknesses of the 'justice model' are embedded within this complex duality of juridical ideology. It is the two-sided nature of such ideology that accounts for the ambivalence of those who support the 'justice model', and it is because of the complexity of the legal form that any politics which dismisses legal ideology wholesale will throw out a very important baby with some admittedly rather murky bathwater.[36] A considered politics must take both aspects of juridical ideology into account.

---

[35] 'Critique of the Gotha Programme' in K. Marx and F. Engels, *Selected Works in One Volume*, (London, 1968), p.320.

[36] It must be stressed that this is not a return to a defence of the autonomy of legal forms. Forms like the justice model themselves emerge out of the context of

3. THE IDEAL AND THE ACTUAL

We are left with a nuanced analysis of juridical individualism which recognises from one side the obscurantist and, in the Marxist term, fetishised character[37] of the legal form; from the other side, the liberative and safeguarding role of individual right is also acknowledged. For this reason, no proper analysis of the legal form can either defend it wholesale or repudiate it wholesale. In the postscript to his historical analysis of the development of the bourgeois criminal law, E.P. Thompson argues that the 'rule of law' is a juridical-political concept that transcends class divisions and has a quality that elevates it beyond the purely historical.[38] Yet his own analysis shows that his paean to the law is overdone, for two reasons. First, the rule of law was introduced primarily as a means of oppression of the peasantry and developing working class. The bourgeoisie sought an efficient system of law which would clearly establish very tight bonds of legality and punish illegal behaviour resolutely.[39] Often, what was regarded as illegal was what had previously been accepted by all social classes as lawful conduct and as a matter of customary right.[40] The introduction of the rule of law from the point of view of the poor and the powerless was not regarded as a good, it was a fetter and a means of protecting the property of the rich. To have fixed rules prohibiting a peasant from doing what he had

---

political struggle (see, e.g., D. Fogel, 'We Are The Living Proof': The Justice Model of Corrections (Cincinatti, 1975)), and derive their particular content accordingly. What was the product of a left-liberal political movement in the 1970s for the reduction of punishment became in the different political climate of the 1980s an argument for stricter punishment. Legal forms are not substitutes for political action, they are forms of mediation of political struggle, possessing a particular and historical specificity.

[37] K. Marx, Capital, vol.1 (London, 1954), pp.76-88; E. Pashukanis, op.cit.,pp.109-117.

[38] E.P. Thompson, Whigs and Hunters (Harmondsworth, 1977), p.268.

[39] D. Hay, 'Property, Authority and the Criminal Law' in D. Hay et al., Albion's Fatal Tree (Harmondsworth, 1977); M. Foucault, Discipline and Punish (Harmondsworth, 1979), pp.82-103. This was even more starkly the case where Western legal forms were imposed in colonial contexts: J. Fisch, Cheap Lives and Dear Limbs (Wiesbaden, 1983).

[40] Thompson, op.cit., pp.240-241; Foucault, ibid.

previously done without hinderance was no advance from the peasant's viewpoint.

Second, the rule of law was not regarded from the ruling classes' point of view as anything to be taken too seriously when it came to the rights of the working class. When it came to developing the law, criminal law was the last area in which adherance to rational legal principle occurred or was to be expected.[41] To be sure, where it was a matter of the rights of the middle classes and landowners to private property, the lawyers spoke loud and clear,[42] but when it came to the rights of those who confronted private property as a limit upon their actual freedom and social equality, things were different.[43] As Foucault expresses it in his analysis of the penal reform movement on the continent of Europe, the arguments for the rule of law and the rights of the subject, while universal in their form, had two quite distinct targets. One was against the 'super-power' of the absolute sovereign, who needed to be controlled in the interests of the bourgeoisie. The other was against the 'infra-power' of the masses who also needed to be controlled in the interests of the bourgeoisie.[44] The difference was that in the former case, the rule of law was designed to protect the bourgeoisie from autocratic rule; in the latter case, it was designed to control the illegality of the masses. This difference in function and in content necessarily led to a difference in form, in emphasis upon the quality of legal rights to be bestowed upon the different sectors of the population. The rule of (the criminal) law was introduced as a means of more effectively controlling the illegality of the common people with the judges paying little more than lip service to the rational controls that this placed on state power.

On the other hand, there is something in what Thompson says. As time wore on, the logic of the rule of law became interwoven into the character of judicial discourse so that the judges were (and are) forced to take it seriously. This does not mean that they will always follow the dictates of its logic, as the examples in chapter VIII make clear. To the extent that they do not do so, however, they are forced to cover up their actions, for the rule of law has become a part of the publicly declared legitimating ideology of the Western polity. Thus it is that the rule of law, which in the realm of criminal law began as a means of more effective social control and exploitation, came to possess an emergent,

---

[41] Thompson, *ibid.*, pp.208-211, 251-254.

[42] C. Hill, *Intellectual Origins of the English Revolution* (Oxford, 1965), p.257; D. Little, *Religion, Order and the Law* (New York, 1969), p.174.

[43] D. Hay, *op. cit.*; C. Hill, *Reformation to Industrial Revolution* (London, 1967), pp. 113-114; Thompson, *op.cit.*

[44] *Op. cit.*, p.87

potential quality as a safeguard of the rights of all classes, including those who were exploited. Such a safeguard is never either guaranteed in itself or necessarily adequate in its terms. It must be fought for, defended and extended all the time. Nonetheless, it is an emergent and potential quality of the rule of law, of the juridical discourse of individual right.

At the same time, however, it must be reasserted that this positive aspect of the rule of law remains tied to the negative aspect: that the rule of (the criminal) law is primarily a mechanism for protecting the property of those who possess it from those who do not, and, more generally, of maintaining a level of social control over those whose position in society makes them victims at the same time as they victimise others.[45] In this context, the ideal Kantian form of criminal justice is in contradiction with the actuality of crime and criminality. Capitalist society gave birth at one and the same time to relations of social exploitation and to an ideal juridical form. They were part and parcel of the same social and economic moment in history: the birth and growth of capitalism as a market society. Hence it is that theories based upon the ideology of juridical individualism are constantly shadowed by the darker and more brutal social existence of struggle and oppression. The two go together as a hand fits in a glove.

It is the nature of crime as a product of social conflict and malaise that lurks behind the idealism of the Kantian theory of punishment, and which makes any ultimate justification of punishment in Kantian terms impossible. Analysis of the historical development of the philosophy of punishment makes it clear that the radical disjuncture between the ideal and the actual is no passing feature. It is a constant and fixed quality which necessarily undermines a principled justification of punishment in an unprincipled society. Because of this, any attempt to moralise punishment in capitalist society along the lines of individual desert is doomed to failure.[46] Juridical form and content remain in contradiction,

---

45 On the modern class distribution of processed criminality, see, e.g., J. Braithwaite, *Inequality, Crime and Public Policy* (London, 1979); R. Quinney, *Class, State and Crime* (New York, 1980); S. Box, *Power, Crime and Mystification* (London, 1983), and *Recession, Crime and Punishment* (London, 1987). See also the quotation from the 1967 U.S. President's Commission on Law Enforcement in Murphy, *op. cit.* (1979), pp.113-114, and M. Davis and S. Ruddick, *op. cit.*, ch.7, fn. 49. For a graphic literary depiction of the social reality of criminality, see Tom Wolfe, *The Bonfire of the Vanities* (London, 1988), pp.121-122.

46 In his *Trials and Punishments* (Cambridge,1986), pp.298-299, Duff accepts that punishment on neo-Kantian lines cannot be justified in our present system, and concludes unhappily that it is necessary to revert to a utilitarian deterrent

so that any attempts at rationalisation and legitimation can only succeed on the basis of an occlusion of the fundamental, historical relationship between the Western individualist ideology of punishment and the underlying social character of criminality and state power.

---

rationale for punishment, despite his rejection of the adequacy of such a theory for the justification of punishment. This involves a pragmatic acceptance of punishment loosened off from the question of its justifiability. But if criminal punishment occurs in the context of social relations which are criminogenic, then it is not only that individual punishment is unjustified, it is also in itself unjust (c.f. Duff, *op.cit.*, p.230). Thus any pragmatic acceptance of punishment must recognise that it entails at the same time an acceptance of positive injustice. In her *State Punishment* (London, 1988), pp195-198, Lacey considers the same question and concludes similarly that there may be 'indirect non-ideal' reasons for punishment. She also suggests the notion of a 'second-best' (or third, fourth ...nth-best) justification of punishment depending on the degree of injustice in the society in question. This leads to considerable further problems. What are the boundaries of the different levels of justification? How do we know when the justifications run out? In a second best society, is half of any punishment justified? Are the punishments of some but not other criminals justified, depending on the degree of their deprivation? Is 'moral luck' a relevant counter-consideration (see above fn.26, ch.7)?

BIBLIOGRAPHY

Acton, H. *The Philosophy of Punishment* (1969) London, MacMillan.

American Friends Service Committee, *Struggle for Justice* (1971) New York, Hill and Wang.

Ashworth, A. 'Reason, Logic and Criminal Liability' *Law Quarterly Review* (1975) 102.

Auerbach, P., Desai, M., Shamsavari, A. 'The Transition from Actually Existing Capitalism' (1988) *New Left Review*, 170, 61-78.

Aune, B. *Kant's Theory of Morals* (1979) Princeton, University Press.

Baier, K. 'Is Punishment Retributive?' in H. Acton, *The Philosophy of Punishment (op.cit.)*

Balbus, I. 'Commodity Form and Legal Form' in C. Reasons and R. Rich, *The Sociology of Law: A Conflict Perspective* (1978) Toronto Butterworth.

Bayles, M. 'Character, Purpose and Criminal Responsibility', *Law and Philosophy* (1982) 1, 5.

Beccaria, C. *Of Crimes and Punishments* (1964) Oxford, O.U.P.

Beck, L. *A Commentary on Kant's Critique of Practical Reason* (1960) Chicago, University Press.

Benn, S. 'An Approach to the Problems of Punishment' in H. Morris, *Freedom and Responsibility* (1961) Stanford, University Press.

Benton, T. *The Rise and Fall of Structural Marxism* (1984) London, MacMillan.

Bentham, J. *The Theory of Legislation* (1975) New York, Oceana.

Bentham, J. *An Introduction to the Principles of Morals and Legislation* in J. Bowring, *Collected Works* (1962) New York, Russell.

Bhaskar, R. *A Realist Theory of Science* (1975) Leeds, Leeds Books.

Bhaskar, R. *The Possibility of Naturalism* (1979) Brighton, Harvester.

Bosanquet, B. *Some Suggestions in Ethics* (1919) London, MacMillan.

Bosanquet, B. *The Philosophical Theory of the State* (1965) London, MacMillan.

Bottomley, A.K. 'The 'Justice Model' in America and Britain' in Bottoms, A.E. and Preston, R.H. *The Coming Penal Crisis (op.cit.)*.

Bottomley, A.K. *Criminology in Focus* (1979) Oxford, Martin Robertson.

Bottoms, A.E. and Preston, R. *The Coming Penal Crisis* (1980) Edinburgh, Scottish Academic Press.

Box, S. *Power, Crime and Mystification* (1983) London, Tavistock.

Box, S. *Recession, Crime and Punishment* (1987) London, MacMillan.

Bradley, F. 'Some Remarks on Punishment', *International Journal of Ethics* (1893-94) 4, 269.

Bradley, F. 'The Vulgar Notion of Responsibility' in *Ethical Studies (op.cit.)*.

Bradley, F. *Ethical Studies* (1927) Oxford, Clarendon.

Bradley, F. *Collected Essays vol.1* (1935) Oxford, Clarendon.
Braithwaite, J. *Inequality, Crime and Public Policy* (1979) London, R.K.P.
Cain M. and Hunt, A. *Marx and Engels on Law* (1979) London, Academic Press.
Cattaneo, M. 'Hobbes's Theory of Punishment' in K. Brown, *Hobbes Studies* (1965) Oxford, Blackwell.
Cohen, S. 'Guilt, Justice and Tolerance: Some Old Concepts for a New Criminology' in D. Downes and P. Rock, *Deviant Interpretations* (1979) Oxford, Martin Robertson.
Coole, D. *Women in Political Theory* (1988) Sussex, Wheatsheaf.
Cooper, D. 'Hegel's Theory of Punishment' in Z. Pelczynski, *Hegel's Political Philosophy* (1971) Cambridge, C.U.P.
Cotterrell, R. 'English Conceptions of the Role of Theory in Legal Analysis', *Modern Law Review* (1983) 46, 681.
Cotterrell, R. 'The Sociological Concept of Law', *Journal of Law and Society* (1983) 10, 241.
Dashwood, A. 'Logic and the Lords in *Majewski*' [1977] *Criminal Law Review*, 532, 591.
Davis, M. 'Harm and Retribution' (1986) *Philosophy and Public Affairs*, 236.
Davis, M. and Ruddick, S. 'Los Angeles: Civil Liberties Between the Hammer and the Rock' (1988) *New Left Review* 170, 37.
Day, J.P. 'Retributive Punishment', *Mind* (1978) LXXXVII, 498.
Dennis, I. 'Duress, Murder and Criminal Responsibility' *Law Quarterly Review* (1980) 208.
Devlin, P. *Samples of Law Making* (1962) Oxford, O.U.P.
Donzelot, J. *The Policing of Families* (1980) London, Hutchinson.
Duff, A. *Trials and Punishments* (1986) Cambridge, C.U.P.
Durkheim, E. 'Two Laws of Penal Evolution' (1973) *Economy and Society*, 307.
Edwards, P. 'Hard and Soft Determinism' in S. Hook, *Determinism and Freedom in the Age of Modern Science* (*op.cit.*).
Engels, F. 'Ludwig Feuerbach and the End of Classical German Philosophy' in K. Marx and F. Engels, *Selected Works in One Volume* (*op.cit.*).
Ewing, A. 'Punishment as a Moral Agency' *Mind* (1927) XXXVI, 292.
Ewing, A. *The Morality of Punishment* (1929) London, Kegan Paul.
Ferguson, R. Review of *Legal Reasoning and Legal Theory* (MacCormick) *British Journal of Law and Society* (1979) 6, 272.
Ferri, E. *The Positive School of Criminology* (1901) Chicago, Kerr.
Fine, B. *Democracy and the Rule of Law* (1984) London, Pluto.
Fisch, J. *Cheap Lives and Dear Limbs* (1983) Wiesbaden, Franz Steiner.
Fletcher, G. *Rethinking Criminal Law* (1978) Boston, Little Brown.
Fletcher, G. 'Law and Morality : a Kantian Perspective' (1987) *Columbia Law Review* 87, 533.
Fletcher, G. 'Why Kant' (1987) *Columbia Law Review* 87, 421.

Flew, A. 'The Justification of Punishment' in H. Acton, *The Philosophy of Punishment* (*op.cit.*).

Fogel, D. *'We Are the Living Proof': The Justice Model of Corrections* (1975) Cincinnati, Anderson.

Foucault, M. *Discipline and Punish* (1977) Harmondsworth, Peregrine.

Garland, D. *Punishment and Welfare* (1985) Aldershot, Gower.

Garland, D. 'Foucault's 'Discipline and Punish' : an Exposition and Critique' (1987) *American Bar Foundation Research Journal*, 847.

Gauthier, D. *The Logic of Leviathan* (1969) Oxford, Clarendon.

Glover, J. *Responsibility* (1970) London, R.K.P.

Goldman, A. 'The Paradox of Punishment' (1979) *Philosophy and Public Affairs*, 42.

Green, T. H. *Lectures on the Principles of Political Obligation* (1901) London, Longmans and Green.

Griffith, J. *The Politics of the Judiciary* (1977) London, Fontana.

Gross, H. *A Theory of Criminal Justice* (1979) New York, O.U.P.

Habermas, J. *Theory and Practice* (1974) London, Heinemann.

Hale, M. *Pleas of the Crown* (1736).

Halevy, E. *The Growth of Philosophic Radicalism* (1972) London, Faber.

Hampton, J. 'The Moral Education of the Criminal' (1984) *Philosophy and Public Affairs*, 208.

Hampton, J. *Hobbes and the Social Contract Tradition* (1986) Cambridge, C.U.P.

Hare, R. *Moral Thinking* (1981) Oxford, Clarendon.

Hart, H.L.A. *Punishment and Responsibility* (1968) Oxford, Clarendon.

Hay, D., Linebaugh, P., Rule, J., Thompson, E., Winslow, C. *Albion's Fatal Tree* (1977) Harmondsworth, Peregrine.

Hegel, G. *The Philosophy of Right* (1952) Oxford, O.U.P.

Hegel, G. *The Philosophy of Nature* (1970) Oxford, Clarendon.

Hill, C. *Intellectual Origins of the English Revolution* (1965) Oxford, O.U.P.

Hill, C. *Reformation to Industrial Revolution* (1967) London, Weidenfeld and Nicholson.

Hirst, P. *On Law and Ideology* (1979) London, MacMillan.

Hobbes, T. *Leviathan* (ed. C. MacPherson)(1968) Harmondsworth, Penguin.

Honderich, T. *Punishment: The Supposed Justifications* (1976) Harmondsworth, Peregrine.

Hook, S. *Determinism and Freedom in the Age of Modern Science* (1961) New York, Collier.

Hume, D. *A Treatise of Human Nature* (1888) Oxford, Clarendon.

Hume, D. 'Of the Original Contract' in *Essays Literary, Moral and Political* (1898) London, Longman.

Ignatieff, M. *A Just Measure of Pain* (1978) London, MacMillan.

Inwood, M. *Hegel* (1983) London, R.K.P.

Jameson, F. *Marxism and Form* (1971) Princeton, Princeton University Press.

Johnson, P. 'Bradley and the Nature of Punishment' in A. Manser and Stock, *The Philosophy of F.H. Bradley* (1984) Oxford, Clarendon.

Kamenka, E. and Tay, A. 'Beyond Bourgeois Individualism: the Contemporary Crisis in Law and Legal Ideology' in Kamenka, E. and Neale, R. *Feudalism, Capitalism and Beyond* (1975) London, Edward Arnold.

Kant, I. *The Philosophy of Law* (1887) Edinburgh, Green.

Kant, I. *The Moral Law* (1948) London, Hutchinson.

Kant, I. *The Metaphysical Elements of Justice* (1965) Indianapolis, Bobbs-Merrill.

Kant, I. *Werke, vol.6*, Konigliche Preussische Akademie.

Keat, R. and Urry, J. *Social Theory as Science* (1975) London, R.K.P.

Kelman, M. 'Interpretive Construction in the Substantive Criminal Law' (1981) *Stanford Law Review*, 591.

Kelman, M. *A Guide to Critical Legal Studies* (1987) Cambridge, Mass., Harvard U.P.

Kenny, A. *Will, Freedom and Power* (1975) Oxford, Blackwell.

Kenny, A. *Freewill and Responsibility* (1978) London, R.K.P.

Kittrie, N. *The Right to be Different* (1971) London, John Hopkins.

Korner, S. *Kant* (1955) Harmondsworth, Penguin.

Lacey, N. *State Punishment* (1988) London, Routledge.

Levine, A. 'Rawls' Kantianism', *Social Theory and Practice* (1974) 3, 47.

Little, D. *Religion, Order and the Law* (1969) New York, Harper and Row.

Lukacs, G. *History and Class Consciousness* (1968) London, Merlin.

Mabbott, J. 'Professor Flew on Punishment' in H. Acton, *The Philosophy of Punishment* (*op.cit.*).

Mabbott, J. 'Punishment' in H. Acton, *The Philosophy of Punishment* (*op.cit.*).

MacCormick, D.N. 'Challenging Sociological Definitions', *British Journal of Law and Society* (1976) 3, 88.

MacCormick, D.N. *Legal Reasoning and Legal Theory* (1978) Oxford, Clarendon.

MacIntyre, A. *A Short History of Ethics* (1967) London, R.K.P.

Mackie, J. *Hume's Political Theory* (1980) London, R.K.P.

MacPherson, C.B. *The Political Theory of Possessive Individualism* (1962) Oxford, O.U.P.

Marcuse, H. *Reason and Revolution* (1941) London, R.K.P.

Marx, K. *Capital, vol.1* (1954) London, Lawrence and Wishart.

Marx, K. and Engels, F. *Selected Works in One Volume* (1961) London, Lawrence and Wishart.

Marx, K. 'Critique of the Gotha Programme' in K. Marx and F. Engels, *Selected Works in One Volume* (*op.cit.*).

Marx, K. 'The Eighteenth Brumaire of Louis Bonaparte' in K. Marx and F. Engels, *Selected Works in One Volume* (*op.cit.*).
Marx, K. and Engels, F. *The German Ideology* (1970) London, Lawrence and Wishart.
Marx, K. *Grundrisse* (1973) Harmondsworth, Pelican.
Marx, K. *Early Writings* (1975) Harmondsworth, Pelican.
Marx, K. 'Critique of Hegel's Doctrine of the State' in K. Marx, *Early Writings* (1975) Harmondsworth, Penguin.
McBarnet, D. *Conviction* (1981) London, MacMillan.
McLellan, D. *The Young Hegelians and Karl Marx* (1969) London, MacMillan.
McTaggart, J. *Studies in Hegelian Cosmology* (1901) Cambridge, C.U.P.
Melossi, D. and Pavarini, M. *The Prison and the Factory* (1981) London MacMillan.
Midgely, T. S. *The Language of Equality* (1978) Edinburgh University, Ph.D. thesis.
Moore, M. *Law and Psychiatry* (1984) Cambridge, C.U.P.
Moore, M. 'Causation and the Excuses' (1985) *California Law Review* 73, 1091.
Morris, A. and McIsaac, M. *Juvenile Justice?* (1978) London, Heinemann.
Mundle, C. 'Punishment and Desert' in H. Acton, *The Philosophy of Punishment* (*op.cit.*).
Murphy, J. *Retribution, Justice and Therapy* (1979) Dordrecht, Reidel.
Murphy, J. 'Does Kant Have a Theory of Punishment?' (1987) *Columbia Law Review* 87, 509.
Neumann, F. *The Democratic and the Authoritarian State* (1964) New York, Free Press.
Neumann, F. *The Rule of Law* (1986) Leamington Spa, Berg.
Neumann, F. and Kircheimer, O. *Social Democracy and the Rule of Law* (1987) London, Allen and Unwin.
Norrie, A. 'Marxism and the Critique of Criminal Justice' *Contemporary Crises* (1982) 6, 59.
Norrie, A. 'Freewill, Determinism and Criminal Justice' (1983) *Legal Studies*, 69.
Norrie, A. 'Thomas Hobbes and the Philosophy of Punishment' (1984) *Law and Philosophy* 3, 299-320.
Norrie, A. 'Practical Reasoning and Criminal Responsibility' in R. Clarke and D. Cornish, *The Reasoning Criminal* (1986) New York, Springer Verlag.
Norrie, A. 'Justice and Punishment in Adam Smith' (1989) *Ratio Iuris,* 227.
Norrie, A. 'Oblique Intention and Legal Politics' [1989] *Criminal Law Review*, 793.
Norrie, A. Review Essay of Lacey, *State Punishment* (1990) *International Journal of the Sociology of Law* 18, 112.

Norrie, A. 'Locating the Socialist *Rechtsstaat*: Underdevelopment and Criminal Justice in the Soviet Union' (1990) *International Journal of the Sociology of Law* 18, 343-359.

Outhwaite, W. *New Philosophies of Social Science* (1987) London, MacMillan.

Packer, H. *The Limits of the Criminal Sanction* (1968) Stanford, University Press.

Parker, H. 'Boys Will Be Men: Brief Adolescence in a Down-Town Neighbourhood' in G. Mungham and G. Pearson, *Working Class Youth Culture* (1976) London, R.K.P.

Pashukanis, E. *The General Theory of Law and Marxism* (1978) London, Ink Links.

Pashukanis, E. *Selected Writings* (ed. P. Beirne and R. Sharlet) (1980) London, Academic Press.

Paton, H. *The Categorical Imperative* (1953) London, Hutchinson.

Plamenatz, J. *The English Utilitarians* (1958) Oxford, Blackwell.

Plant, R. *Hegel* (1973) London, Allen and Unwin.

Poggi, G. *The Development of the Modern State* (1978) London, Hutchinson.

Quinney, R. *Class, State and Crime* (1980) New York, Longman.

Quinton, A. 'On Punishment' in H. Acton, *The Philosophy of Punishment (op.cit.).*

Radzinowicz, L. and Turner J. *The Modern Approach to Criminal Law* (1945) London, MacMillan.

Radzinowicz, L. *Ideology and Crime* (1966) London, Heinemann.

Raphael, D. *Hobbes* (1977) London, Allen and Unwin.

Rashdall, H. Note, *International Journal of Ethics* (1894-95) 5, 243.

Rashdall, H. *The Theory of Good and Evil vol.1* (1907) Oxford, Clarendon.

Rawls, J. 'Two Concepts of Rules' in H. Acton, *The Philosophy of Punishment (op.cit.).*

Ree, J., Ayers, M. Westoby, A. *Philosophy and its Past* (1978) Hassocks, Harvester.

Reyburn, H. *The Ethical Theory of Hegel* (1921) Oxford, Clarendon.

Richter, M. *The Politics of Conscience* (1964) London, Weidenfeld and Nicholson.

Ross, W.D. *The Right and the Good* (1930) Oxford, O.U.P.

Rusche, G. and Kircheimer, O. *Punishment and Social Structure* (1939) New York, Columbia U.P.

Sayer, D. *Marx's Method* (1979) Brighton, Harvester.

Seve, L. *Marxism and the Theory of Human Personality* (1975) London, Lawrence and Wishart.

Smart, J. and Williams, B. *Utilitarianism, For and Against* (1973) Cambridge, C.U.P.

Smith, A. 'On Actus Reus and Mens Rea' in P. Glazebrook, *Reshaping the Criminal Law* (1978) London, Stevens.

Smith, A. *Lectures on Jurisprudence* (1978) Oxford, Clarendon.
Smith, J. and Hogan, B. *Criminal Law* (1983) London, Butterworths.
Smith, J. Note, *Criminal Law Review* (1981) 393.
Sparks, R. ' 'Diminished Responsibility' in Theory and Practice', *Modern Law Review* (1964) 27, 9.
Sprigge, T. 'A Utilitarian Reply to Dr. McCloskey' *Inquiry* (1965) 8, 264.
Stedman Jones, G. *Outcast London* (1971) Oxford, O.U.P.
Stick, J. 'Charting the Development of Critical Legal Studies' (1988) *Columbia Law Review* 88, 407.
Stillman, P. 'Hegel's Idea of Punishment', *Journal of the History of Philosophy* (1976) 14, 169.
Strauss, L. *Natural Right and History* (1953) Chicago, U. Chi.P.
Strauss, L. 'The Spirit of Hobbes's Political Philosophy' in K. Brown, *Hobbes Studies* (1965) Oxford, Blackwell.
Sumner, C. *Reading Ideologies* (1979) London, Academic Press.
Taylor, C. *Hegel* (1975) Cambridge, C.U.P.
Taylor, C. *Hegel and Modern Society* (1979) Cambridge, C.U.P.
Taylor, I., Walton, P. and Young, J. *The New Criminology* (1973) London, R.K.P.
Taylor, I., Walton, P. and Young, J. *Critical Criminology* (1975), London, R.K.P.
Thompson, E. *Whigs and Hunters* (1977) Harmondsworth, Peregrine.
Unger, R. *Law in Modern Society* (1976) New York, Free Press.
Van den Haag, E. 'Refuting Reiman and Nathanson' (1985) *Philosophy and Public Affairs*, 165.
Vandervort, L. 'Social Justice in the Modern Regulatory State: Duress, Necessity and the Consensual Model in Law' (1987) *Law and Philosophy* 6, 205.
Von Hirsch, A. *Doing Justice: The Choice of Punishment* (1976) New York, Hill and Wang.
Von Hirsch, A. *Past or Future Crimes* (1986) Manchester, M.U.P.
Walker, N. *Crime and Insanity in England and Wales, vol.1* (1968) Edinburgh, E.U.P.
Walker, R. *Kant* (1978) London, R.K.P.
Wasik, M. 'Duress and Criminal Responsibility', *Criminal Law Review* (1977) 453.
Watkins, J. *Hobbes's System of Ideas* (1973) London, Hutchinson.
Watson, G. *Free Will* (1982) Oxford, O.U.P.
Williams, G. *Criminal Law: the General Part* (1961) London, Stevens.
Williams, G. *Textbook of Criminal Law* (1978) London, Stevens.
Williams, G. 'Recklessness Redefined', *Cambridge Law Journal* (1981) 252.
Williams, G. *Textbook of Criminal Law* (2nd ed.) (1983) London, Stevens.
Williams, H. *Kant's Political Philosophy* (1983) Oxford, Blackwell.
Woffinden, B. *Miscarriages of Justice* (1989) Sevenoaks, Coronet.
Wolfe, R. P. *The Autonomy of Reason* (1973) New York, Harper.

Wolfe, T. *Bonfire of the Vanities* (1988) London, Picador.
Wootton, B. *Crime and the Criminal Law* (1963) London, Stevens.
Zweig, A. *Kant, Philosophical Correspondence 1759-99* (1967) Chicago, U. Chi. P.

REPORTS

Criminal Law Commissioners (1843) *Seventh Report*
English Law Commission Report No. 29.
Scarman, Lord. *The Brixton Disorders 10-12 April 1981* (1981), Cmnd.8427.

CASES

Abbott v R. [1977] AC 755
Daniel McNaghten's Case 10 Cl. and Fin., 200
D.P.P. v Beard [1920] AC 479
D.P.P. v Majewski [1976] 2 WLR 623
D.P.P. v Morgan [1975] 2 All ER 347
Duffy [1969] 1 All ER 92
Durham v U.S. 214 F.2d. (D.C. Cir.1954)
Ealing London Borough Council v Race Relations Board [1972] AC 342
Lynch v D.P.P. [1975] AC 653
R. v Caldwell [1981] 1 All ER 961
R. v Cunningham [1957] 2 QB 396
R. v Graham [1982] 1 All ER 801
R. v Howe [1987] 1 All ER 771
W. (A Minor) v Dolbey [1983] Crim LR 681

Materialism, in Marx 8; in Hobbes 16, 25, 32, 33, 35, 36, 61, 143, 190; in Kant 61-62, 192; in the utilitarian tradition 102, 114, 143, 150, 163, 195
McTaggart, J. 118-123, 135
Mens rea 161, 172, 174, 176, 185
Metaphysical 12, 13, 42, 45, 50-52, 54, 59-61, 63, 68, 136, 162
Midgely, T.S. 184n
Mill, John Stuart 115
Mistake, Defence of 141, 155
Mitigation of punishment 13, 56, 97, 140, 154, 155, 159-161, 163
Moore, G.E. 115
Moore, M. 115, 140n, 147, 148, 158n, 159n, 161n, 165n
Moral good in punishment 101, 117; Moral guilt 97, 111, 117; Moral improvement 116, 122; Moral liberation 91; Moral reform 122; Moral intuition, as basis for retributivism 117; Moral organism, society as 107; Moral surgery, punishment as 107
Morality 72, 73, 92, 115, 121
Morris, Lord 177-179
Motive 23, 57, 78, 156, 160, 161, 163
Mundle, C. 136n
Murder 31, 55, 56, 60, 67, 69, 172, 177-180; principal in the second degree to 177, 180
Murphy, J. 41, 42, 55, 57n, 61n, 62n, 148n, 197, 198
Mystificatory, Ideology as 8, 9, 12

Natural law 8, 25-27, 30, 36, 190; Natural laws 26, 27, 62; and the methodology of natural science 25
Nazi Germany 131
Necessity 25-28, 40, 47, 48, 55-60, 62, 71-73, 83, 100, 101, 108, 130, 143, 187
Neumann, F. xv, 5, 7

Offences Against the Person Act 1861 172

Pandora's Box of determinism 147, 158
Pashukanis, E. xv, 5, 7, 11, 113, 135; Theory of legal ideology 7; Autonomous wills, legal relations based upon 113, 135
Paton, H. 46n, 47n
Philosophy of punishment *see* Punishment, Philosophy of
Philosophy of right (Kant) 43; *Philosophy of Right* (Hegel) 5, 69, 70-72, 79, 81, 84-86, 88, 89;
Plamenatz, J. 66n
Plato 57, 79n, 88n
Police 83, 160, 171
Political economy 7; Economic man 191
'Popular justice' xvii
Poverty 83, 84, 87, 90, 193
Practical reasoning 152, 153, 168-170, 183, 186; and Practical logic 169, 180; compared with Technical logic 169
Property 53, 69, 73, 74, 82, 157, 161, 173, 174, 200-202
Proportionality 2, 72, 81, 84, 85, 90, 98, 117, 123-125, 128
Provocation, Defence of 141, 155, 156
Public law 11, 43, 52, 113
Punishment 1-7, 11-25, 27, 30-34, 36, 37, 39-45, 50-63, 65-69, 71-73, 75-78, 80-82, 84-90, 93-111, 131, 132, 134, 137, 139, 140, 142, 149, 150, 154, 159-163, 165, 167, 185, 189-192, 195-198, 202, 203; of the innocent 1, 32, 33, 100, 124, 126, 127, 130, 133
Punishment, Philosophy of xiv, 1-6, 12, 15, 16, 20, 23, 31, 33, 36, 37, 41, 65, 77, 89, 90, 103, 119, 128, 129, 191, 192, 198, 202; and education 115, 118, 123-125; and welfare of the community (Bradley) 106; as deterrent 94, 115, 120, 124; as Preventive 31, 93-95, 98, 106; as reformatory 93, 94, 106, 119; Definitional Stop argument 126, 127; General Justifying Aim of punishment 129, 134; Impasse in the 2-4, 12, 190; Medical

Law and Philosophy Library

Managing Editors:
Alan Mabe, *Florida State University, Tallahassee, Florida*
Michael D. Bayles†, *Florida State University, Tallahassee, Florida*
Aulis Aarnio, *University of Helsinki, Finland*

Publications:

1. E. Bulygin, J.-L. Gardies and I. Niiniluoto (eds.): *Man, Law and Modern Forms of Life*. With an Introduction by M. D. Bayles. 1985   ISBN 90-277-1869-5

2. W. Sadurski: *Giving Desert Its Due*. Social Justice and Legal Theory. 1985
                                                                                ISBN 90-277-1941-1

3. N. MacCormick and O. Weinberger: *An Institutional Theory of Law*. New Approaches to Legal Positivism. 1986   ISBN 90-277-2079-7

4. A. Aarnio: *The Rational as Reasonable*. A Treatise on Legal Justification. 1987
                                                                                ISBN 90-277-2276-5

5. M. D. Bayles: *Principles of Law*. A Normative Analysis. 1987
                                                    ISBN Hb: 90-277-2412-1; Pb: 90-277-2413-X

6. A. Soeteman: *Logic in Law*. Remarks on Logic and Rationality in Normative Reasoning, Especially in Law. 1989   ISBN 0-7923-0042-4

7. C. T. Sistare: *Responsibility and Criminal Liability*. 1989   ISBN 0-7923-0396-2

8. A. Peczenik: *On Law and Reason*. 1989   ISBN 0-7923-0444-6

9. W. Sadurski: *Moral Pluralism and Legal Neutrality*. 1990   ISBN 0-7923-0565-5

10. M. D. Bayles: *Procedural Justice*. Allocating to Individuals. 1990 ISBN 0-7923-0567-1

11. P. Nerhot (ed.): *Law, Interpretation and Reality*. Essays in Epistemology, Hermeneutics and Jurisprudence. 1990   ISBN 0-7923-0593-0

12. A.W. Norrie: *Law, Ideology and Punishment*. Retrieval and Critique of the Liberal Ideal of Criminal Justice. 1991   ISBN 0-7923-1013-6

KLUWER ACADEMIC PUBLISHERS – DORDRECHT / BOSTON / LONDON